100

BOOKS BY ERIC BOGOSIAN
AVAILABLE FROM TCG

The Essential Bogosian
(Includes *Talk Radio, Drinking in America, funHouse, Men Inside*)

Humpty Dumpty and Other Plays
(Also includes *Griller, Red Angel, Non-Profit Benefit*)

Notes from Underground
(Also includes *Scenes from the New World*)

100
(*monologues*)

Pounding Nails in the Floor with My Forehead

Sex, Drugs, Rock & Roll

Sex Plays
(Includes *1 + 1, Skunkweed*)

subUrbia

Talk Radio

Wake Up and Smell the Coffee

100

(MONOLOGUES)

ERIC BOGOSIAN

THEATRE COMMUNICATIONS GROUP
NEW YORK
2014

100 (monologues) is published by Theatre Communications Group, Inc.,
520 Eighth Avenue, 24th Floor, New York, NY 10018-4156

The publication of *100 (monologues)*, by Eric Bogosian, through TCG's Book Program, is made possible in part by the New York State Council on the Arts with the support of Governor Andrew Cuomo and the New York State Legislature.

Special thanks to Ruth and Stephen Hendel for their generous support of this publication.

TCG books are exclusively distributed to the book trade by Consortium Book Sales and Distribution.

LIBRARY OF CONGRESS CATALOGING-IN-PUBLICATION DATA
Bogosian, Eric.
[Plays. Selections]
100 : (monologues) / Eric Bogosian.
pages cm
ISBN 978-1-55936-464-5 (pbk.)—ISBN 978-1-55936-773-8 (ebook)
1. Monologues, American. I. Title. II. Title: One hundred.
PS3552.O46A6   2013b
812'.54—dc23   2013039060

Book design and composition by Lisa Govan
Cover design by Mark Melnick
Cover photographs © Paula Court

First Edition, April 2014

For Jo Bonney—my director, my muse, my love

ACKNOWLEDGMENTS

The monologues in this volume span a period of thirty years, and I owe many thanks. First of all to a core group of colleagues and friends who have graced me with their support again and again. I also want to thank those who were only passing through but made a major impact on the work.

Jo Bonney and I have worked together from the first day we met in the summer of 1980. With particular regard to the monologues in this book, Jo's dramaturgy and direction were key. Thanks are not enough. This volume is hers as much as mine.

Fred Zollo has stood by me through thick and thin, producing, directing (*Talk Radio* at The Public), arguing, cajoling. He has been the voice in my ear since we were teenagers. Thanks, Fred. And thanks to my two great mentors in the theater: Joseph Papp and Wynn Handman, who produced the first solos at their theaters.

After a show in the Village thirty years ago, George Lane took me aside and explained to me that I was a writer as well as an actor and that he was going to represent me. Thanks, George, it's been fun.

Thanks to Ronald Taft, who has been much more than a trusted advisor, but my ally and good friend.

Thanks to Philip Rinaldi, who has brought dignity and excellence and friendship to a tough game.

These solos started out as entertainment for a small community of visual artists who supported the early work with their laughter and applause. Special thanks to Paula Court (whose photos grace the cover of this volume), Cindy Sherman, Robert Longo, Michael Zwack, Tom Bowes and Roselee Goldberg.

Friendship and work is an exciting combination. Special thanks to Carin Goldberg, Robert Falls, Emily Gerson Saines, Michael Morris, Michael Rauch, Ira Sachs, Pat Sosnow, Nick Paleologus, Van Lagestein and Bob Riley for their deep and articulate support and friendship.

A special thanks to my great friend Tim Carr, who always knew what it could be.

There would be no *Talk Radio* without Tad Savinar. Thank you, Tad. There would be no stage version of the play without Joseph Papp and Gail Merrifield. And with Ed Pressman and Oliver Stone, the world got to know about it. Thanks to all.

Thanks to Amanda Moran and Nikole Beckwith who guaranteed that first impressions would always be good ones. Special thanks to Mark Russell.

This volume is a compilation of almost thirty years of publishing my solos and plays. Publication began under the wise guidance of David Rosenthal. For the last twenty years, Terry Nemeth and Kathy Sova at TCG have published my theater work with enthusiasm and loving care. Thanks, guys.

It's impossible to put up dozens of productions without involving hundreds of wonderful people. I can't name everyone here, but I would like to give special thanks to: Kevin Adams, Jackie Apple, John Arnone, Peter Askin, Dominick Balletta, André Bishop, Robert Brustein, Michael Carlisle, Barbara Carroll, Robert Cole, Michael Dorf, Jerry Frankel, Roy Gabay, Frank Gero, Rebecca Green, Wynn Handman, Jeanne Hedstrom, Ruth and Steve Hendel, John Howard, Bernie Jacobs, Steve Jones, Rob Klug, Will Knapp, Jan Kroese, Hal Luftig, Mary MacArthur,

ACKNOWLEDGMENTS

Joan Marcus, Jan Nebozenko, Jeffrey Richards, Kathy Russo, Kim Ryan, Liev Schreiber, Elliott Sharp, Walt Taylor, Jonathan Trumper, Brian Wallis and Martha Wilson.

Finally, thanks to my folks, Edwina and Henry, who encouraged and loved me in every enterprise.

CONTENTS

Introduction
By the Author   xvii

FROM "MEN INSIDE" (1981)

1   Freakshow   3
2   Superman!   5
3   Nice Shoes   7
4   Party!   10
5   Held Down   12
6   Rodeo   14
7   Christmas Tree   16
8   Looking Out for Number One   19

FROM "VOICES OF AMERICA" (1982)

9   New Action Army   22
10 Sale, Sale, Sale!   24

CONTENTS

11 Li'l Doggie Dog Food   26
12 Real Italian   28
13 Fat Fighter   29

FROM "MEN IN DARK TIMES" (1982)

14 The Leader   30

FROM "ADVOCATE" (1982)

15 The Throat   33
16 Alone Together   35

FROM "FUNHOUSE" (1983)

17 In the Dark   37
18 Insurance   39
19 Inside   41
20 The Specialist   42
21 Starving Children   44
22 Calamari   47
23 Honey, I'm Home!   51
24 The Pacer   53
25 Shining Star   56

FROM "DRINKING IN AMERICA" (1986)

26 Journal   59
27 American Dreamer   62
28 Ceramic Tile   65
29 Commercial   69
30 Melting Pot   71

31 Our Gang 74

32 No Problems 81

33 Godhead 84

34 The Law 86

35 Fried-Egg Deal 90

FROM "TALK RADIO" (1987)

36 It's Not How Much You Make,
It's How Much You Take Home 92

37 Denise 94

38 I'm Here. I'm Here Every Night 96

FROM "SEX, DRUGS, ROCK & ROLL" (1991)

39 Grace of God 98

40 Benefit 100

41 Dirt 106

42 The Stud 110

43 Stag 113

44 Bottleman 120

45 Candy 124

46 Rock Law 126

47 X-Blow 133

48 Live 137

49 Dog Chameleon 140

50 Artist 145

FROM "NOTES FROM UNDERGROUND" (1993)

51 April 14 150

52 May 18 152

CONTENTS

FROM "POUNDING NAILS IN THE FLOOR WITH MY FOREHEAD" (1994)

53 America — 155

54 Molecules — 158

55 Intro — 162

56 Inner Baby — 166

57 The Glass — 170

58 Red — 175

59 The Fan — 181

60 Rash — 184

61 The Recovering Male — 190

62 Medicine — 193

63 The Messenger — 196

64 Blow Me — 198

FROM "31 EJACULATIONS" (1996)

65 Number 19 — 203

FROM "WAKE UP AND SMELL THE COFFEE" (2001)

66 The Promise — 205

67 Intro — 206

68 Voice in the Wilderness — 211

69 Faith — 213

70 Arabs — 217

71 The Offer — 220

72 The Airport — 222

73 Gold Card — 224

74 Upgrade — 228

75 Harmonious — 230

76 Breakthrough — 232

77 The Audition — 235

78	The Ladder	237
79	In the Air	242
80	Captain	245
81	The Crash	247
82	The Meeting	249
83	Sheep	252
84	The Highway	256

FROM "THIS IS NOW!" (2005)

85	This Is Now	260
86	Smoking	263
87	Cheese	267

"ORPHANS" (1980–2000)

88	Confession	269
89	The Quiet Man	271
90	Beat Poem	273
91	Food	276
92	Little Dog	278
93	Art	280
94	The Dream	282
95	Reach Out	284
96	No Crime	287
97	Victim	291
98	Gated	295
99	Wood	298
100	Poem	301

Building Character: My Method for Creating the Solos *An Essay by the Author*	303
A History: Productions, Recordings and Publications	317

INTRODUCTION

I did not set out to write monologues. The very word "mono-logue" sounds boring and I never wanted to make boring the-ater. I wanted theater rocked by mad performance and streams of words that rose up into geysers of meaning that went beyond what they seemed to say. I didn't want to *tell* you, I wanted to *ask* you.

Before the monologue shows, I wrote more than a dozen pieces, most of which are now lost (except for the photos taken by my good friend Paula Court). Some were experiments. For example, I wrote a play and had it translated into Spanish. I don't speak Spanish. I found an all-Latino cast and directed them in the play without ever really knowing what they were saying. This play, *Sheer Heaven*, was performed a dozen or so times before Anglo audiences. It was like watching a foreign film without the subtitles.

I wrote a play made of unrelated vignettes. Glenn Branca supplied some music. I hired another large cast. Scenes about hookers were jammed up against sweet scenes of grampas and grandchildren. This piece, *The New World*, was an attempt to make "pictures" the way my friends, Robert Longo, Cindy Sher-man, Jack Goldstein and Michael Zwack were making pictures with their visual art. It was an exciting piece. Then the theater got burglarized and I lost all the equipment I had borrowed from friends. I lost a ton of hard-earned money.

And so on. I wrote and wrote. And sometimes I wrote monologues because I was interested in them as chunks of words, piles of words. I sometimes performed in my plays, and I usually played someone who was very angry. I created an act called *The Ricky Paul Show* that was crafted to start riots in the theater or clubs where it was performed. People threw bottles. Fights broke out. It was fun.

And then I wrote a solo called *Men Inside*, a series of monologues designed to explore all the characters living within me: an inventory of characters. This piece became very popular. For the first time, my work was embraced by the (small) crowds that showed up downtown.

Eventually, Joe Papp heard about my solo work, and I visited his offices on Lafayette Street. He asked me to perform a bit for him. My hope was that he would produce my larger plays. Instead, he produced *Men Inside* in 1982. The following year, he produced *funHouse*. When we were writing the press release, he asked me who my director was and I told him that Jo helped me with the pieces. Joe Papp proclaimed Jo Bonney the director, and in that way her career in the theater began. Fred Zollo and Frank Gero moved *funHouse* to Off-Broadway, and with that transfer I entered a different, more commercial world: I was no longer only performing to a downtown art-house crowd.

In 1984 I needed to take a break to sort out some personal issues. I cleaned up my act and I began to write again. In 1985 I spent the year writing yet another set of monologues that would become *Drinking in America*. Wynn Handman directed that piece and produced it at his American Place Theater. *Drinking in America* became a bona fide hit, and it led to my returning to Joe Papp and The Public Theater with *Talk Radio*, as well as three more solos over the next fourteen years.

I did not set out to write monologues, but the more involved with the form I got, the more interesting it became to me. I liked the energy and excitement of speaking directly to an audience. I liked arranging the portraits of characters to create a larger whole. I liked the difficulty of writing and performing such complex stuff. Performing and writing these monologues took me to the limit of my abilities.

The monologues were funny, and that implied that I was funny. I was often mistaken for some kind of comedian and compared to Lenny Bruce. But if I related to Lenny Bruce, I also related to David Mamet. The object was not to make people laugh, but to engage them as fully as possible. I was interested in taboo and how people think, how a handful of words could delineate a universe.

The result, after thirty years of work, has been a giant slag heap of monologues. The vast majority of the monologues included in this book are from my solo shows, but I've also included monologues from *Talk Radio* and *Notes from Underground*, and from shows that had very limited runs, such as *Advocate* and *This is Now!*, or monologues that did not make it to the final performance: *Orphans*.

Except for the show Wynn directed, Jo Bonney directed me in every one. Jo was essential to understanding what should be kept and what should be cut. She urged me toward greater detail and exploration and, on more than one occasion, greater sleaze. In all these ways, she is co-author of this body of work.

The monologue is a form that is a great challenge to write and perform. It asks the writer and the performer to rise above the usual effort and give it all you've got. When I performed these shows, I had one simple motto (an old Hell's Angels' saying): "When in doubt, knock 'em out."

Enjoy.

Eric Bogosian
New York
April 2014

100

FROM "MEN INSIDE"

(1981)

1

FREAKSHOW

Ladies and gentlemen! Step right up and see the freaks. The freakshow is about to begin . . .

Twenty-five cents, two bits, one-fourth of a dollar . . .

Right behind this curtain, ladies and gentlemen, step right up, come as close as you like, examine them to your heart's content . . .

See the Fat Lady, the fattest woman in the world! Weigh her on our scales and be amazed! She's huge, a veritable Leviathan!

See the Snake Boy with scale-like skin, there's nothing like him, the Eighth Wonder of the World!

The Deaf, Dumb and Blind Man, watch him stumble, watch him fall! Fun for the whole family.

The He-She! Is it a man? Is it a woman? Only you can decide!

See the Pimply Dwarf commit acts unspeakable! Watch him dance with a poodle!

Once in a hundred years, a Negro and a Chinaman mate and we have the Offspring, right behind this curtain, ladies and gentlemen, a medical impossibility.

Yes! Yes! And for the same price, tonight only, see Doctor Cyclops, the one-eyed man. He'll give you the cold stare!

And his friend, the Legless Wonder. He's got wheels instead of legs, wheels instead of legs. A one-man roller derby.

And finally, for the first time in captivity, not an imitation, not a duplication, but the real thing. A genuine, homosexual Siamese Twin.

Step right up, ladies and gentlemen, step right up. The freak-show's about to begin!

2

SUPERMAN!

Little boy leaps off a table, pretending to fly.

(To the Superman *theme song)* SUPERMAN! Duh-duh-duh duh-duh-duh-duh-duh-duh-duh!

Pssssshhhhhhh!!!!!

Hi Dad! I was just practicing my Superman, Dad!

Am I doin' it right, Dad? Am I doin' it right? Hey Dad, guess what I did today? I ran as fast as I could and I threw a rock at a bird and I killed it!

Pretty good, huh Dad?

Hey Dad, when I grow up I'm gonna be just like you, huh Dad? I'm gonna be tall and strong and never make any mistakes and drink beer and shave and drive a car and get a check. I'm gonna be just like you, huh Dad?

Dad, can I ask you a question?

When I grow up I'm not gonna be poor, am I Dad?

Am I?

I'm not gonna be a poor old bum on the street. All smelly and living in a box, am I Dad? I'm gonna be rich like you, huh Dad?

And . . . Dad? I'm . . . I'm not gonna be a alcoholic, am I Dad? Like Mr. Johnson down the street, never cuts the lawn. I'm not gonna be an alcoholic with a big red nose and throwing up.

And I'm not gonna be a junkie either, am I Dad? Like on *Kojak*. And not have a life worth living and OD all the time. I'm not gonna OD, huh Dad, huh?

Dad? Joey says I'm gonna be a homo! I'm not gonna be a homo, am I Dad? *Homo!* We're not homos, are we Dad?

Dad? NO WAY I CAN BE A NIGGER, HUH DAD, HUH? 'Cause you're not a nigger and Mom's not a nigger, huh? Huh? HUH? We're American, huh Dad?

Dad? I got one more question. When I grow up . . . I'm . . . I'm not . . . gonna . . . gonna go . . . I'm . . . *(Begins stuttering and falls to the floor in a fit)*

3

NICE SHOES

Very friendly, but with growing menace:

Hey . . . hey . . . you . . . you with the glasses. Come here. Come
here for a second, I wanna ask you a question . . . No come here.
I never seen you around the neighborhood before and I just want
ta meet ya . . . What's ya name? . . . Mike? Michael . . . Mike. How
ya doin' there, "Mike"? I'm Sonny, this here's Joey and this is
Richie. He's a big guy, huh?

. . . Hey . . . hey . . . hold on for a second, Mike, don't walk
away from me when I'm talking to you . . . Uh . . . I just saw
you walkin' around here and uh, I never seen youse before and
you're wearing all these nice clothes—Joey! Lookit dis guy's
clothes . . . nice clothes . . . I like the clothes . . . These are the
kind a clothes you wanna be wearin', Joey . . . Bet you got these
clothes up Bloomingdale's didnja?

And the shoes! Nice shoes! I like those shoes, huh? Richie,
check out Mike's shoes . . . I like those shoes, Mike . . . Hey! You
know what we call shoes like dose? "C-Shoes," "C-Shoes." . . .
You wanna know why? . . . 'Cause dey cost a C-note . . . hundred
bucks, get it?

(Laughing, he turns to Joey) Pretty funny . . . C-shoes, huh? . . . *(Whips around, noticing Mike getting away)*

Hey-hey-hey-hey-hey . . . Mike, don't walk away from me when I'm talkin' to you here now! That's very impolite, you know? You're being impolite to me . . . and you're embarrassing me in front of my friends . . . You're insulting me in front of my friends . . . and when somebody insults me I get angry . . . I get angry and I hurt people . . . heh heh.

RICHIE, SHUT UP! SHUT YA FUCKIN' MOUTH!

Don't listen to him, he's full a shit. I won't let him lay a hand on you . . . This fight is between you and me . . .

Look, it's OK . . . it's OK . . . all youse gotta do is apologize to me and everything'll be cool, all right? Just get down on your knees and apologize and—

RICHIE! STAY OUT OF IT! . . . PUT IT BACK . . . Put the blade back in ya pocket . . .

Now Mike, look what you started, everybody's gettin' excited around here. Richie's gettin' angry, next thing Joey's gonna get angry . . . Just get down on ya knees and apologize and then Richie won't think I'm an asshole . . .

(Condescendingly) That's great . . . Just for a second . . . just stay down there for a second . . . YA NOT A HOMO, ARE YA MIKE? Hey Joey, this guy down on his knees ya think maybe he's a homo? Haha . . . And do me a favor while you're down there. Just slip your shoes off for a minute, will ya? Joey! Get the shoes! . . . You comfortable there, Mike? You're sure ya not a faggot, are you? You better not be, walking around this neighborhood. We'll castrate ya!

Here Mike, get up. You don't want to stay down there all day. Let me brush you off. Hey Mike, we're just fucking with ya head. You can take a joke, can't you? Sure you can! I wanna tell you something: Mike, you're a good shit. Any time you need anything in this neighborhood, you just come see me, Sonny, and I'll take care of you, OK? You need fireworks, weed, anything like that, you come see me, OK? OK! *(Shaking hands with him)* Well, it was nice talking to you, but we gotta get going, I'll see ya later . . .

Hmmmm? What? What shoes? *(Turning back to Joey)* These shoes? These are *my* shoes, Mike. These are my C-Shoes. I just bought these shoes up in Bloomingdale's. Joey? Richie?

(Looks down at Mike's feet) Oh, you don't got no shoes! Hey Joey, lookit dis guy's got no shoes! Richie, look! . . . Hey, how come you got no shoes? . . . All those nice clothes and no shoes! How'd dat happen? You're gonna get cold with no shoes! Ain't he gonna get cold?

(Laughing right into Mike's face) Oh! I think we got a crybaby here! I think he's gonna start crying. *(Suddenly Sonny stops laughing, gets a very cold look in his eyes)* Hey Richie, did you hear that? What was that word he just said?

(Lunging for Mike, grabbing him and talking slowly) Hey Mike, we don't like swearing around here. Huh? Fuckface? Scumbag? *(Fast, dangerous, pulling him up off the ground, so that we can see Sonny's eyes just over his fists)* Hey, hey. You come walking around this neighborhood, embarrassing me around my friends, swearing at me in front of my friends, hey let me tell you something, Mr. Nice Shoes, Mr. Faggot: You worried about not having no shoes? You're lucky you still got feet! *(Pause; he throws Mike to the ground)* Get the fuck out of here! *(Beat)* Asshole! . . . Come on. *(Laughing as he walks away with Richie and Joey)* . . . Joey, lemme see my shoes . . .

4

PARTY!

Yo! I'm standin' on a street corner, I'm lookin' good, I'm feelin' good. I'm thinkin' about sidewalks and saxophones! I'm thinkin' it's a beautiful summer's night. I got on my brand-new clothes. I got me a bottle of wine. I wanna go out tonight! I wanna go out and par-tee! I got on my bran'-new shoes, *(Indicates shoes)* got on my bran'-new pants, *(Indicates pants)* got on my bran'-new shirt. *(Models shirt to audience)* Check that shirt out . . . Qiana, baby . . . Same as silk, same as silk! Got on my bran'-new "doo" aftershave. *(Does a jump and claps his hands)* Um! I'm too good to waste! I wanna go out tonight and party! I wanna go dancin'! I wanna go rollerskatin'! I say, Lord above, I am all dressed up tonight, Lord, I am looking good, and I am feeling good. Look at me! Look at me! *You* can't even believe how good I look!

Lord, I need me a little girl. Where's my little girl, Lord? Where's my little girl? Where's my . . . *(He sees the girl of his dreams down the sidewalk)* . . . There she is jus' a walkin' down the street! There she is jus' a struttin' down the street! She got on them high-heeled shoes, swishy skirt, see-through blouse, lipstick, perfume . . . *(Inhales the scent of the girl as she passes him)* . . . Hey, baby, hold on jus' a minute, where you goin' to? What's your name?

You're lookin' good, and I'm lookin' good, whatchoo say we go get some Chinese food, go bowlin'?

Hey, baby, don't pass me by, I'm the superfly, I'll make you fly . . . Yo! Sister! I wanna ask you a question: You know what time it is? *(Shouting at her retreating figure)* Yo, sister! Yo, sister! Yo, BITCH, get yo ass back here, I'm talkin' to you! Hey! Come on, baby, whaddya say, we'll have a good time? *(Beat)* Yeah, I know your type, twenty bucks, right? *(Turns away)* Who the hell she think she is? *(Turns back to her, shouting)* Who the hell you think you are? Miss America or something? You got no right walkin' around lookin' like that! Enticin' men . . . Slut! Whore! Prostitute! . . . Ruined my whole evening!

5

HELD DOWN

A man turns quickly, while seated.

Forget it! Just forget it, OK? No, I don't want a neck rub, Cheryl. No, I don't want a back rub either. No, I don't want that rubbed either. I don't want anything rubbed right now, keep your rubbing to yourself. Leave me alone. Don't touch me. I know I know I know . . . I'm sorry, OK? Is that what you want me to say? I'm sorry . . .

(Beat.)

Listen, Cheryl, we've got to get something straight between us, OK? . . . Every night can't be like last Wednesday night, all right? I have a lot of things on my mind, I've been working hard lately, I'm tired and that party tonight didn't help things . . . I know, I know, I know it's not important, I know you don't care . . . I don't care, nobody cares, all right?

    It's just sex. What do we need sex for? We're just having a sexual relationship. What do we need sex for? Let's just play Trivial Pursuit for an hour or so . . . I know I'm being childish . . .

I know . . . You're right, it happens to every guy once in a while. Every guy once in a while can't . . . It's normal, it's natural . . . It happens to every guy . . . Every guy once in a while, it's normal, it's natural, it happens to every guy . . . SHIT! It doesn't happen to every guy, it happens to me. It happens to me. It's ME, it's ME, it's ME, it's me . . . and it's you, Cheryl . . . No, no lemme talk . . .

At the party tonight you spent the whole night hanging out with Robert in the kitchen. I saw you. Giving him those eyes, those "guess what I'm thinking about" eyes. All right, you're attracted to Robert. I understand. He just got that promotion, he's got a lot of money now, a lot of prestige, power, cocaine. What else could a girl want? Money, power, prestige, cocaine. I know what turns you on, Cheryl, I know because it's what turned you on about me in the first place. And I'm glad Robert got that promotion. Good. It couldn't have happened to . . . I'm glad he got that promotion. Fine. Good. Yes, Robert got that promotion. He got it because he's a back-stabbing, ass-licking slime . . .

OK? OK? I could have gotten that promotion. I could have gotten it. But see, I have a little problem. I have too much *integrity*, see? I've got too many principles. My problem is that I go into work every day and I sit at my desk and like a sucker I try to do the best job I can. I sit at my desk eight hours a day, knock myself out and everybody sits at their desks and they watch me work. Because they know they're not as good as I am so they're afraid of me, so they watch me. They conspire against me because they're inferior. I am surrounded by a conspiracy of mediocrity just trying to hold me down, hold me down, HOLD ME DOWN, HOLD ME DOWN . . .

(Looks at his lap, stops shouting) You know what your problem is, Cheryl? You're insatiable. You're never satisfied. You can't get enough. No guy is good enough for you. He has to be a success in the daytime, he has to be a success at night. He has to be a superman and a superstud. You don't need a man, you need a machine. No wait, I know what you need, you need a real insensitive, male-chauvinist-pig cowboy. That's what you need. With the spurs . . . Yeah, a real cowboy . . .

6

RODEO

Very fast-paced, jittery, jumping around the stage. High-pitched "cowboy voice":

Whooooeeeee! Boy you shoulda been there, we took that sucker down! It was good, it was real good! *(Moves his hands as if he's steering a car)* RRRRRMMMMM!!! Ninety-five miles an hour—BOOM! I hit that Winnebago, guy never knew what hit 'er! Just pushed 'im right off the side of the road.

I'm lookin' in my rearview mirror and I see that guy—he's jumped out of his car, jumpin' up and down, pissed off! I couldn't resist: I bang a U-ey, come back beside him and get out. Guy says to me, *(In deep Texas accent)* "Come here boy, I wanna talk to you!" I said, "I wanna talk to you, too!" *(Takes a look right, then left)* BING! BANG! Guy never knew what hit him! Left enough rubber on that road to make a new set of tires!

I tell you, when it gets goin' that fast and hard I get high! Musta been doin' two, three hundred per . . . Billy was pullin' 'em so fast he broke a knuckle . . . You know that Billy when he starts pullin' those beers, pullin' those beers . . . jus' sittin' in the backseat like a hog in a corncrib, suckin' down that brew, half naked, covered with sweat and stink . . .

The beer cans rollin' aroun' on the floor and I musta been doing a hundred and fifty mph! . . . All of a sudden, I see this girl walkin' down the street, right? I couldn't resist . . . I hit the brakes and start followin' her in the car, real slow like. Real Playboy-bunny type of girl, you know? I'm followin' real slow, givin' her my "evil eye" and she's jus' a walkin' down the sidewalk like she don't notice! . . .

All of a sudden, Billy pops out the back window: "Hey baby, hey baby, come 'ere, I wanna kiss your face!" She says, "Kiss my ass!" So Billy, you know what Billy says? You know what he says??? "I can't tell the difference!" I can't tell the difference! Pretty good, huh? That Billy's some kind of comedian, huh? Some kind of comedian. "I can't tell the difference!" WHOOOOEEEE!

(With no warning, he violently starts miming shooting a rifle three times in three different directions) BOOM! BOOM! BOOM! Wished I had a machine gun, coulda killed me even more deer . . . Killed me three deer, had to leave two behind! Didn't have room on the car for 'em! I jus' took this one big bloody buck, took him and strapped him onto the front of the car, tied him right onto the bumpers. So I'm goin' down the highway, musta been doin' three, four hundred miles per hour . . . Billy's passed out in the backseat, and the blood starts comin' right up onto the windshield! I had to use my windshield wipers jus' so I could see! *(Laughs)*

I come into this gas station—car's all covered with blood, right?—come into this gas station and the boy says to me: "You boys look like you been busy!" Billy hangs his head out the window like some kind of old dog, he says: "Sure have!" And pukes all over the guy's shoes! Whoooooeeeee!!! We know how to have a good time!

7

CHRISTMAS TREE

Middle-aged man, slumped in a chair.

Vinnie, Vinnie, Vinnie, Vinnie . . . When you gonna get married, huh? When you gonna settle down . . . You come in here every Monday morning with that bum friend of yours . . . what's-his-name the alcoholic there, what's-his . . . Tommy . . . Tommy the alcoholic! You come in here every Monday morning, you been banging this chick, you been banging that chick . . . you been drinking, you been wasting ya paycheck . . .

Hey, hey, Vinnie, ya twenty-eight years old, you're a bum . . . You understand me? Uh? You're a bum and that friend a yours, Tommy, he's a bum too . . . and my kid Tony, he's a bum too. You're all bums. Bunch a bums. No sense a responsibility, nothin'. My kid Tony, seventeen and a half years old. He's got whatever he wants to have. Upstairs his own bedroom, his own cable-TV, Space Invasion . . . seventeen and a half years old he's playing with toys . . .

For his birthday he wants, he wants a 'lectric guitar, so we buy him a 'lectric guitar . . . He's down in the basement till two o'clock in the morning playing the goddamn thing. Driving everybody crazy. Dog's barkin', everybody's awake.

You see my LTD out here? Who put the dent in my LTD? Who put the dent in that? Mr. Punk Rock. "You got insurance, Dad," he says to me, "you got insurance"! . . . I come home the other day from work, four-thirty in the afternoon . . . he's lying on the couch like some kind of old man. I says to him, "Tony, what are you doin' lying on the couch? Go do your chores!" He says to me, "I did my chores, Dad." I says, "What chores, what chores you do around this house? Tell me, I want to know . . ."

He says to me, "I fed the dog, Dad." I fed the dog!? I give a shit that dog starves to death! He fed the dog! What is that? He's got no responsibility!

When I was his age, Vinnie, when I was his age, every day after school I had to go down to da Big Bear market and load boxes fa a buck an hour, a buck an hour. That was my responsibility . . . My mother was sick, my brothers was no good. Every day.

And when I got outta high school I got drafted and I went to Korea. You know what Korea was? . . . A war, smart-ass . . .

I went to Korea and I served my country. That was my responsibility . . .

And when I come back, everybody I knew was getting married . . . eh! I got married, too . . . I didn't know what the hell I was doin' . . . but I'll tell you something, Vinnie, it was the best thing I ever did in my life. The best thing. And you wanna know why? I'll tell you why . . .

'Cause a Christmas. 'Cause a Christmas morning . . .

Christmas morning, ya get up nice and early in the morning, ya know, with ya wife? And ya come downstairs and ya put the presents under the tree, ya know? And ya got the tree all lit up with the little bulbs and the tinsels and the lights dere? I like dose Christmas trees, gifts underneath all nice and shiny. And you have a nice cup a coffee and you have ya bathrobe on, and ya just sittin' dere nice and quiet on da couch with the wife . . . the oil burner's on . . . And dose kids come runnin' down da stairs all happy and laughin' and da dog's barkin' and everybody's tearin' up dere presents and everybody's happy. And dose kids look up at you and dey love you. Dey love you, Vinnie . . .

And den and den dere's Christmas dinner and everybody comes over da house. Ya mother and ya brothers and ya sisters and the kids, and everybody's sitting around eatin' whatever they want to eat . . .

And I sit there at that table, Vinnie, and I look at my family and I think to myself: All this belongs to me. This is my house, this is my family, this is my food on the table, my goddamned dog on the floor . . . It's all mine, it all belongs to me, Vinnie . . .

And it makes me feel good inside, you know. It makes me warm.

That's why you gotta get married, Vinnie. You don't get married you're never gonna have a Christmas tree. Single guys, they don't got Christmas trees . . .

8

LOOKING OUT FOR NUMBER ONE

A man with a microphone addresses the audience:

I want you all to do something for me right now . . . I want you to take a look at the person sittin' next to you. Go ahead, don't be shy . . . And now I want you to answer a question for me: What do you see? Do you see a success story? Do you see a potential millionaire? And what does your neighbor see when he looks at you? What do you see when you look in the mirror in the morning? Do you see a success? S-U-C-C-E-S-S! Success, that is what we are here to talk about tonight . . .

There is only one person in this world who really matters: Yourself! It is your job, it is your daily task to do one very simple and obvious thing: Look out for number one. The world follows certain rules, certain laws . . . And the first law has been the same since Adam and Eve: Survival of the fittest! If you want the best for you and yours, you will remember that one fact . . .

Now, I go to work every day. I'm given a job and I do it, I do it the best I can . . . I go all over this great country of ours and I talk to people just like you: good, solid, white, middle-class Americans. I talk to them about success. That's my job. At the end of the week, I'm given a paycheck. That money belongs to me. I earned it, I deserve it! I don't ask for charity, I don't ask for a handout! I don't go down to some government office and ask them to pay my bills for me, no sir!! I am a member in good standing of the free-enterprise system. *(Pause)*

I used to be ashamed that I owned a big home with a swimming pool. I used to be ashamed that I owned two beautiful cars: a Mercedes and the Eldorado I saw many of you admiring as you came into the building . . . I used to be ashamed that my children went to a school free of disagreeable influences . . . that we lived in a neighborhood free of disagreeable influences . . . I felt *guilty* that we ate roast beef on Sunday afternoons! . . . Well, let me tell you something, friends . . . We do not live in the Garden of Eden. We live right here on earth! And some will suffer, while others prosper, as it is written in the Bible.

Now, if you could ask the most successful men who ever lived, "What is the secret? What is the secret of your success?" Ask Andrew Carnegie . . . ask John D. Rockefeller . . . ask Bob Hope . . . If you could ask them, what would they tell you? They would tell you that there are two kinds of people in this world: There are the haves and the have-nots. Do you want to be a have? Do you want to look at this world, from the bottom lookin' up or from the top lookin' down? 'Cause if you do, if you do, you better get out there and you better get a piece of what belongs to you . . . You want the good things in this world, you better get out there, you better hustle! 'Cause if you don't, if you don't, you will be a have-not; and if you are a have-not, you can only lose . . . If you are hungry, no one will feed you . . . If you are hurt, no one will take care of you . . . If a great storm comes from above and destroys the very home you live in . . . no one will replace it, no one will care. Unless you care. Unless you've taken care to take care of number one!

All kinds of people in this world: There are the poor, the foolish, the stupid, the crippled, the elderly . . . Nothing you can do about them . . . They've always been around, they're always gonna be around. The bleeding-heart liberals think you should take care of those who can't take care of themselves . . . the haves think you are responsible for the have-nots! You are responsible for only one person: Yourself.

You are brought into this world as a single individual, you will live your life as a single individual. You will enjoy your own joy and you will experience your own pain . . . Life is a struggle, man is an island . . . Love . . . love, my friends, love is loving yourself first. Thank you. Amen.

FROM "VOICES OF AMERICA"

(1982)

NEW ACTION ARMY

Man in uniform speaks directly to the camera, friendly, open, easy:

Hey! Can I ask you a question? Are you a confused young guy? Don't know where you're going? Can't find a job? Lonely? I *may* have the answer for you. But first let me ask you this: How'd you like to have a job where you travel all over the world? A job where you learn a skill, wear a free uniform, meet a bunch of great guys and even earn a little money?

If your answer is: "Yes!" you might be the kind of guy we're looking for for the NEW ACTION ARMY . . .

How'd you like to handle a lethal weapon? Work with explosives? Be feared and even hated by everyone you meet? Get to know real prostitutes? PLUS wear a uniform that's recognized (and respected) just about everywhere . . . while you hang out with a bunch of great guys who like to have fun, play cards and drink?

And how 'bout the *excitement*? . . . You think bungee jumping is fun? You like roller coasters? How about putting your life on the line twenty-four hours a day! That's excitement. You can't beat it. And if you *do* get injured you can be sure of one thing:

We'll be there to support you with the best medical care (and cool meds!) money can buy!

So whaddya say? The army's a lotta fun! Come on and be a part of it!

The New Action Army—Where the Action Is!

10

SALE, SALE, SALE!

Very, very fast, loud, nonstop:

Sale, sale, sale, sale, sale, sale! Come on down girls, we've got great savings, great buys 'cause it's SUMMERTIME DOLLAR-DAYS DISCOUNTS this month at ZEEBO'S Department Stores!

Ready for summer barbecues? We are, with nifty hibachis, fully automatic gas-driven barbies, electric charcoal cookers and portable turning spits. All on sale with colorful matching accessories: racks, forks, aprons, lawn chairs. Start your garden now. We've got seeds, hoses, shovels . . . all you add is the elbow grease . . . But make sure you're dressed right: we've got sunhats, sea socks and sand shoes on sale now! Watch the figure, girls: sexy squeeze girdles, and extra-sharp pointed Dardee uplift padded under-wire support bras, disposable nylon stockings, on sale now! And for Junior, matching play clothes, pail-and-shovel set, harness and tether! Don't forget Dad: we've got tools for the car, adjustable liquor cabinets and—just in this week—bowling shoes and fabulous fishing hats! Gramma wants to come along? She'll need a cane, maybe a wheelchair . . . all on sale! We've got realistic leatherette bones for Fido, electric guitars for the young rockers, and fully automatic submachine guns for Uncle!

Sale, sale, sale, sale, sale, sale! We've got barbecues galore and all the trimmings 'cause it's Summertime Dollar-Days Discounts this month at all Zeebo's Department Stores! Better hurry!

11

LI'L DOGGIE DOG FOOD

Sound effect of cattle.
   Deep Texas drawl:

HEYAAAH! HEYAAAH! Git on there, li'l doggies!

(Dog bark.)

Hi there, fella!

(Bark.)

(Chuckle) Being a working cowboy is no easy job . . . I'm roping cattle from sunup to sundown, keeping those li'l doggies in line . . . That's why I got my partner here, King. *(Bark)* . . . Heh heh . . . He works hard, too!

   At the end of the day, when I'm ready to eat a nice big steak, well you know, King is pretty hungry, too . . . *(Bark)* Heh heh . . . That's why I give him Li'l Doggie Dog Food—all meat, chunks of beef! Hell, he's around those cows all day long . . . you bet he wants to eat one! *(Bark)*

That's why he gets the real thing, the best thing: pure, one-hundred-percent, grade-A, all-American prime beef! Those Hindus won't touch it, but hell, my dog sure will!

(Bark.)

My dog's a working man . . . he deserves to eat like a man. Doesn't your dog deserve the same? Li'l Doggie All-Beef Dog Food—for the little man in the house . . . *(Bark)* Heh heh . . . HEYAAAH!!!

(Cattle sound.)

12

REAL ITALIAN

This is Mario at Mario's Real Italian Restaurant.

We got clams! We got lobsters! We got spaghetti, anchovies, lasagna, soup du jour! We got the best cooks in town, the best sauce, the best garlic bread.

And don't forget Mario's "Mama Mia" salad bar with all the radishes, carrots, shrimps, Bac-O-Bits, lettuce, cottage cheese, swiss squares, celery sticks, swedish meatballs, cucumbers, croutons, and ten different dressings you can eat!

You wanna eat? You wanna eat till you DIE? Come on down to Mario's Real Italian—Route 115 and the Old Colony Turnpike behind Bamberger's in Paramus!

We'll feed you like your mama used to! *Mangia!*

(New voice) Open for lunch and dinner. All major credit cards accepted!

13

FAT FIGHTER

Fat-fat-fat-fat-fat-fat-fat . . .

Take a look in the mirror, what do you see? A slim, shapely, sensuous woman? A woman who attracts men when she walks down the street?

Or do you see fat?

Around the neck, around the thighs, around the waist . . . What about your wrists, your ankles, your cheeks? Look carefully, fat is everywhere . . .

If you're fat, you need help. You need . . . FAT FIGHTER, the new proven formula that dissolves fat as it accumulates. Now you can eat as much as you like all day long and not gain a pound. Just take two FAT FIGHTERS before you start eating, then eat ice cream, cake, candy, butter, potato chips, spaghetti, beer, thick cream soups, pies, heavy breads, french fries, syrups, puddings, lard, milkshakes, fudge, chocolates, pancakes, waffles, pâté, oil, grease, pizza, cookies . . . and not gain a pound!

FAT FIGHTER is all you need . . . and it's guaranteed . . .

And remember, FAT FIGHTER contains no harmful ingredients, just pure one-hundred-percent dextroamphetamine sulfate.

FAT FIGHTER . . . when you're FAT FAT FAT!

FROM "MEN IN DARK TIMES"

(1982)

14

THE LEADER

A man at a podium.

It is with honor and great joy that I stand before you today. For today we mark a turning point in the history of our great nation. Today we can see very clearly the horizon of our destiny before us. As a people, we gather together to celebrate the defeat of a pernicious and dangerous threat to our individual freedom. Today we can say to ourselves: "We have been challenged and we have met that challenge." As Martin Faust remarked on a similar occasion: "A people is judged by its greatest dangers."

We have met our greatest danger and we have defeated it. We have done what has been necessary. We have utilized the forces at our disposal. We have found the criminals and they will be punished. Once again we live in a land that is devoted to the law, to order and to the rule by the people for the people.

For the criminal, the treasonous and the barbarous have no place in our society. Because a land without law is a land without boundaries. Without law we are not better than savages, without a framework to live by, everything is chaos. Without a strong leadership to guide us, we are lost. When certain "elements" of our society are allowed to run rampant, to foster their own law, then all are endangered. *(Voice rising)* Those who wish to do things their own way, those who wish to declare themselves enemies of the people, enemies of our nation, must be taught the lessons of obedience. They must learn that the strong hand of discipline will come from above. We must act from strength, not weakness.

For the time has come. The time has come for our great nation to return to the glory it once knew. The time has come for our great nation to know the fruits of its labor. To savor the honey of its goodness and fairness. The time has come to eradicate the rot that has undermined us. To show that we are a nation undivided and strong. It is time that a once great people should return to their greatness, to conquer those who would have it another way.

We are gathered here today to celebrate a victory. A victory not only of our country against its enemies, but of good against evil. It is a moral victory. It is a victory of the spirit. And to the victor must go the spoils.

For it is destiny that it be so. It is the destiny of a great people. Destiny is shaped by history and the history of all mankind is from darkness and servitude to enlightenment and freedom. It is our task—no—our *duty*, to seize the torch and carry it forward. *(Arm raised)* It is our duty to seize the power and carry it forward. It is our duty to seize history and carry it forward.

This is our duty and we will do our duty. No petty misfits can stand in the way of good men. No miserable and perverted terrorists and their terrorist leaders. No antisocial minorities who think they have the answers. No people of foreign blood who seek to contaminate our good earth and our good life.

Ours is a strong nation. Ours is a proud nation. Ours is a nation of upright men standing in God's illumination. We have the strength of the just, the will of the righteous. We are the chosen people. We must show the others the way. We must lead the others. We must rule the others.

There is only one road that can possibly be followed: Our road, the right road. Those who stand in the way of the right road, in the way of history and progress, will be pushed aside. We cannot be hampered by the lame and the impotent. They have no chance of success, no future. We must have the courage to smash all resistance. The future belongs to the righteous. The future belongs to the strong.

The time has come. *(Pounds the podium)* The time has come to give a lesson to the world. For the good of all we must display our power. We must punish the errant at whatever sacrifice. We must be prepared to lose all, so that we may gain all. We must be prepared to destroy all, so that we prevail over all. We must make the world understand what it means to reckon with absolute power.

All empty words must end and men everywhere must understand: *If necessary we will make the world shiver.* We will vanquish history. We will have the courage to do what is right. If forced, we will let loose the dogs. We will unsheath the long knives. We *must* be satisfied. We *will* be satisfied. If we cannot know satisfaction, then none will know satisfaction. The lesson will be taught and darkness will reign. Our destiny calls us. We must show the way. The bells will toll, the time has come. If light will not be victorious, let darkness reign.

FROM "ADVOCATE"

(1982)

15

THE THROAT

Spoken formally:

I am constantly amazed, almost frightened, by the sensitive complexity of the human physical plant. The human body, that is.

Consider the throat. Normally used for transmitting air, food and speech, it is the body's most vital highway. It is nothing less than the path between heart and mind. And it must be kept in perfect working order, clean of debris, lubricated, warm and nourished.

It is esthetically pleasing as well. For the neck is one of the most graceful and erotic parts of the body. The slightest touch on the throat brings feelings of titillation and pleasure.

The throat is such a sensitive thing. A small disorder can cause a sore throat—or worse—a diseased throat. Fever and pain set in and, if they persist, the throat becomes a source of intense irritation.

It becomes the sole center of conscious attention. Imagine for a moment a canker in the throat. Sore and open. Deep inside. Burning. Or many cankers, inflamed and bleeding. The throat becomes dry as the pain increases. It is impossible to swallow.

Then the discovery that the cankers are malignant. Cancer of the throat. Life-threatening. It must be removed. Perhaps the vocal cords are destroyed in the process; a hole is left. A new voice is created. The whole personality changes. Crippled . . . perhaps no voice at all. Mute.

The throat is very vulnerable. It must be protected at all costs. Imagine being punched in the throat. Or strangulation. Asphyxiation. Tighter and tighter, then blackout.

A piece of wire is all that's needed. But perhaps the worst of all is the most spectacular: the slitting of the throat with a straight razor.

One deft move, deep and quick. The wound is fatal, yet consciousness persists . . .

16

ALONE TOGETHER

A man stands deep in the corner of the stage, almost mumbling.

Hello, remember me? I'm right here where you left me. Right in that dark corner . . . I've been waiting . . .

Come on, gimme a smile. You owe me that. After all this time. All my memories . . .

Wait, nothin' to be scared of. You know me . . . harmless. Nothin' but a joke. Always was, always will be . . .

You didn't think I was gonna stay way back there forever, did you? Huh. Pushing my broom. Hauling the big roller trash cart filled with milk cartons and apple cores . . . No, not forever . . . Huh . . .

You may have forgotten me, but I remember. When you've got the time, you remember everything . . .

I even kept your picture. See? . . . Oh, you don't want to look? You don't like it? I do. I look at it all the time. Nice outfit . . . nice colors, school colors, right? I know . . .

It catches you just the way. That way you used to be. That smile. That laugh. I remember your laugh very well. Seems like you were always laughing . . . You used to laugh at me kinda, huh?

Wait a minute, you just got here . . . I wanna ask you . . . You still that way? You're not laughin' now. You seem pretty serious now . . . Why are you so serious?

We can have some fun . . . It's just you and me down here, you know . . . Funny you should come down here after all these years. But you know, I've always been here. Always . . .

Wait . . . I know . . . we can tell each other stories . . .

Well . . . about things that have happened. I bet a lot of interesting things have happened to you since then. You were always so interesting. You always had such interesting things to say . . . What? Sure, I heard you talking . . . And I remember every word. You and your friends had so much to say in those days, so young . . . so satirical . . . Huh?

I have a good memory. For stories.

Like one time, I was down here. All alone. Just about where you're standing right now, near that damp spot, and I heard this noise . . . Just a little noise. In the wall there . . . Scratchin'. Something scratchin' against metal . . . I almost stopped breathing.

Then I pulled that piece of metal back . . . Very slowly. As careful as I could. I looked in and it was dark, of course.

Up jumps this rat, right at my face . . . That was all it was. A rat. I killed it in one kick. Just a rat . . . huh.

It was so quiet down here and that rat went and bothered me with its scratchin'. Disturbed me, you know.

Like just now, it was real quiet and peaceful . . . and then, what do you know, there you were.

Just like it was yesterday . . .

FROM "FUNHOUSE"

(1983)

17

IN THE DARK

A voice begins in darkness. Slowly lights come up on a man at a table speaking into a microphone.

I wait for dark, the black comes for me. Some people are afraid when the sun goes down. But for me, for me, it's good in the deep dark. Warm and dark and close. Some people are afraid of small places, tight spots, restrictive. Not me. I'm in the right place, the good dark place. Like a baby in its womb, like a rat in its hole . . . I'm OK.

Ever see the black skid marks out on the highway? Ever wonder what happened? I don't. I think about the tires, the rubber . . . the black rubber. Burning. Melting. Pouring down in ropes, in sheets, in long black ribbons all around me. Twisting all around me. Around and around. Black and tight, close and dark. Holding me. Hiding me in the darkness . . .

Don't you love the smell of black rubber? The way it feels against the skin? Maybe not—it's an acquired taste. Some people never get used to it.

You can work your way up: black leather, then black spandex, then black rubber. Tight. Black. Rubber. Up against you. Pressing. Keeping. Holding. Resilient but firm. Every muscle, every inch is encased in pure black . . .

The arms, the legs, the chest, the groin, the head. All smooth, all black . . . completely hidden. In my black cocoon I'm where no one can find me, no one can hurt me, no one can touch me. I'm safe in the dark, I'm happy in my hiding place.

I don't have to think, I don't have to feel . . . and the best part is . . . I don't have to see . . .

18

INSURANCE

A man is seated at a desk, talking on the phone.

Hello. Suzy? Hi, Suzy. Uncle Freddy. Is Daddy home? . . . Uncle Freddy. Can you get your daddy, please? . . . Get your father, Susan! Thank you! . . .

Hello, Mr. Stearns, Fred Stanley down at Mutual Insurance! Sorry to bother you around dinnertime, but I was just going over your homeowner's policy and I was kind of shocked to see you don't have very much life insurance . . . Yes, well, five thousand dollars isn't very much, Mr. Stearns. *(Laughs)* I know you don't care what happens after you die, but what about your wife and kids, Mr. Stearns? . . .

Your wife has a job, OK . . . but let's say something should happen and your wife couldn't work? Well, let's say there was a car accident, you were left fatally injured and your wife paralyzed for life? She wouldn't be able to work then, would she, Mr. Stearns? Or, let's say you and the missus go to see a play one night in New York City. You come out of the theater, you get mugged, a gun goes off, you get a bullet in the brain, you're left in a coma for months and months and months . . . wife has to give up her job just to come see you in the hospital. What would happen then, Mr. Stearns? Have you thought about that?

Have you thought about cancer, Mr. Stearns? What about cancer? . . . I know you're having dinner right now, but this might be the most important decision you ever make in your life, and I think dinner can wait for five minutes . . .

Mr. Stearns, I've seen it time and time again: husband dies, wife's left with no pension, no life insurance, she has a mortgage to pay off . . . You know, of course, Mr. Stearns, most women in this country outlive their husbands. Hundred thousand widows in this country, Mr. Stearns, hundred thousand! . . . What? . . . No, she probably won't get remarried, Mr. Stearns, very few women do . . .

Mr. Stearns, follow me for just a second, will you? You die, you're dead, you're in the ground! Mrs. Stearns has no pension, no life insurance, she has a mortgage to pay off . . . little Suzy's in the hospital with some kind of rare bone disease. What happens then? Have you thought about that? Have you thought about it? Do you know how many widows are homeless, Mr. Stearns? Do you know how many homeless women become prostitutes, Mr. Stearns?

I'm not saying that, I'm not saying that, Mr. Stearns. I'm just saying that I know you're a loving father and husband, and you only want the best for little Suzy and . . . uh, right! Right! Edwina. Lovely name Edwina . . . and you'd hate to leave Edwina and Suzy unprotected in this terrible and frightening and—let's be honest with each other, Mr. Stearns—perverse and disturbed world we live in today . . . Why, I could show you street corners in New York where little girls no more than fifteen years old sell themselves . . . and their mothers standing right next to them . . .

Yes, oh . . . ummm, well, ha ha . . . oh, I'd say around two-hundred-and-fifty-thousand-dollars' worth would do the trick . . . Easy terms . . . easy terms, we'll work something out, don't worry . . . When can you come by? . . . Tomorrow? Tomorrow I'll be here all day. Eleven o'clock? That would be great, Mr. Stearns, I'll see you tomor—what? Oh, don't worry about the cost, we'll talk about that tomorrow . . . Look, Mr. Stearns, get back to your roast beef dinner . . . and say hi to, uh, Edwina for me. And Mr. Stearns? . . . Take care! *(Hangs up)*

19

INSIDE

A man standing with a microphone speaks in a singsong voice:

OK, gentlemen, this is it, what you've been waiting for, right through that door. Inside, inside! All your dreams come true, don't be blue, this is it, check it out! I said don't wait, don't hesitate. Run don't walk, show's about to start! See it, feel it! Live, living, real. In full color, completely open, fully revealed, "X"-posed for your eyes only! A house of dreams, your very own *Fantasy Island*. If it turns you on, we got it: black, white, red and yellow; boys and girls at your disposal; men and women behind closed doors! Until you are satisfied! Check it out! Just for you, just the way you want it. You can't do better, nobody offers more. Now, now, now, now, now! No tricks, no substitutions, it's the real thing. A mental orgy, an experience! For you, for them. Lose yourself. Immerse yourself in the delirium of total abandon. All the way, all you ever wanted, all you can take! Inside, inside, come right inside and get it. Get it hot! Get it now! Dreams, dreams, dreams, dreams, dreams . . .

20

THE SPECIALIST

A man stands and talks in a straightforward manner to the audience:

The first piece of equipment you want to make sure you have on hand is a nice big bucket . . . around so big, so deep. *(Indicates with hands)* . . . Just fill that up with water. Nice and deep. Right up to the brim. Take your subject by the back of the neck. Firm grip. Bring him over to the bucket . . . and push his head right under the water. Baptize him. Put the fear of God into him . . . Soak 'im good.

Then up . . . then back down again . . . Fifteen, twenty seconds is good. Just watch the air bubbles. Air bubbles stop, give it around five more seconds . . . And back down. Make sure you have a firm grip, sometimes they buck a little. And stay out of the way of the legs, they kick too . . . Now you have a subject you're ready to work with: he's wet, he's tired and he's scared.

The next piece of equipment you want to have on hand is a nice big metal work table about so wide, so deep. *(Indicates with hands)* . . . I suggest metal just because it lasts longer. Nice big working surface . . . Get your subject up onto the worktable, strap down the arms, the legs, the head. Piece of gaffer's tape, duct tape, over the mouth—and you have him where you want him. Just pinch the nostrils and he can't breathe. He's completely at your disposal. Fingertip control.

OK. So how do we begin? Myself, I like to start with a simple psychological device—kind of a trademark of mine. I'm a smoker, OK? Bad habit, I know I should quit. Anyway, I like to just take the cigarette out—everybody's afraid of fire—take the cigarette out *(Indicates with his cigarette)* and just push it right into the navel, soft like, wax . . . Oh, it hurts. It hurts . . . I'm sure any of you who were in 'Nam or Korea came across this baby once or twice. Just leave it in there. Kind of an hors d'oeuvre.

What do we want to do for the main course? Well, some people like to work with rubber truncheons, knitting needles, plastic bags over the head, breaking fingers, twisting arms. *Hey!* We're not in the Dark Ages. We have electricity. Electricity when properly applied will achieve whatever ends you desire. Simply take your two electrodes, nothing more than a couple of bare wires hooked up to a generator. Just take the two wires and press them firmly up against the palms of the hands, the soles of the feet, inside the ear, the eyelids, the nostrils, lips, gums . . . of course, any cavities or fillings you may find . . . The armpits, the nipples, the genitalia. All very effective. Of course, I know a lot of you have worked with electricity before. So I won't go into a lot of detail.

However, one point I always stress whenever I'm talking about electricity to training groups such as this, is that you have a licensed physician on hand, a medical doctor. For two reasons: First of all, he can tell you exactly how much electricity is needed to get the job done. That's his area of expertise, his job. Use him, ask him questions. Secondly, you have a lot of people working around the area, around water and electricity. You don't want anyone to get hurt.

We'll finish up the seminar tomorrow evening. Until then, if you have any questions, please talk to your commanding officer.

21

STARVING CHILDREN

A man strides around the stage with evangelical purpose, addressing the audience with a microphone:

WHAT ARE YOU AFRAID OF? . . . What are you afraid of? . . . "The only thing you have to fear is fear itself . . ."

So many people write to me, they write to the station, they stop me in the street, they call me on the telephone. They call me and they say: "Reverend Tim . . . Reverend Tim, I have a problem. My husband's out of work and he's been drinking." "Reverend Tim, I have a problem. My daughter crashed the car up and I think maybe she lost her virginity." "Reverend Tim, I got no job." "Reverend Tim, I got no money." "Reverend Tim, I'm sick." Problems, problems, problems! And people write to me about them.

I got a letter the other day from a Mrs. R in Seattle that I would like to share with you right now. Mrs. R has a problem that I would like to share with you because I think it tells us so much about how God can help each and every one of us. She wrote me and she said:

"Reverend Tim, I watch your show every day and you are an inspiration to me, Reverend Tim. But, Reverend Tim, I have a problem: Ten years ago my boy got back from Vietnam and he was missing a leg. And ever since that time he's been down and lonely and depressed. And now, Reverend Tim, I think he's using heroin, Reverend Tim. And the other day he went out and bought a shotgun, Reverend Tim, and I'm afraid he might hurt somebody, Reverend Tim. Maybe he's gonna kill somebody, Reverend Tim. Maybe he's gonna kill himself, Reverend Tim! Reverend Tim, I'm afraid! Reverend Tim. I'm scared! I'm afraid, I'm scared!"

I read that letter . . . and I got a little angry . . . because I thought to myself: Where is the faith? WHERE IS THE FAITH!?! You know we are God's children, we are His sheep. God is our teacher. He's up there to lead us, to help us. God is just settin' up in Heaven every day just thinking up new ways to teach us, new ways to test us, new ways to SHOW US HIS LOVE! He just sits up there all day long thinking. (He's got nothing better to do.) He just says to Himself: Now what kind of obstacle can I put in their path today that will lead 'em on the right road? What kind of weight can I put on their shoulder that will teach 'em a thing or two? *(Indicates dropping heavy weights on a tiny individual standing next to him)* "How's he doing with that? Hmmmm, maybe a little bit more? Just a little bit more . . ."

AS IT SAYS IN THE BIBLE: "HE WHO CARRIES THE GREATEST BURDEN, HE SHALL KNOW THE GREATEST TRUTH"! Now think about that for a second . . . It also says: "God helps him who helps himself"!

(Addressing the camera over the audience) Mrs. R, sure, times are tough; sure, life is difficult. Sure, you got "problems": your boy's handicapped, he's on drugs, maybe he's gonna kill himself . . . maybe he's gonna kill you . . . but Mrs. R . . . if you've got FAITH, if you've got WILLPOWER . . . you can make it . . . I know you can. *(To the audience)* I know we all can.

(Pause.)

Well, so much for our petty personal problems . . .

I would like to talk to you right now about some little children who carry a burden much greater than any we'll ever know. I'm talking, of course, about the millions upon millions of starving little children in Southeast Asia, in Africa, in South America. Millions upon millions of starving little children.

(To the camera) If you're watching at home you can see pictures of them on your TV set. *(To the audience)* Those of you in our audience here can see them up in the monitors. Look at 'em all you want. Aren't they cute? They're starving . . . and they're little.

I want you to think about those starving little children for just a minute. And then I want you to think about that extra piece of pie you had with dinner last night. You weren't even hungry and you had to have that second helping of pie. That extra slice of pie! . . . I want you to think about that MOVIE you went to see, filled with sex and violence. What did it cost you? Five dollars, and who knows how much for the hot buttered popcorn! I want you to think about that popcorn. I want you to think about that slice of pie!

And then I want you to think about those little, starving children. And I want you . . . to take out your checkbook . . . and I want you to write me . . . a check for eighteen dollars. And next month I want you to write me another check. And the month after that and the month after that . . . Eighteen dollars a month! And you'll be doing everything you can . . . everything you possibly can . . . to help ME do everything I can . . . to help those millions upon millions of starving . . . little . . . children!

Eighteen dollars a month, and you can end starvation in the whole world today. Eighteen dollars a month, and the next time you want an extra slice of pie, just go ahead and eat all you want! The next time you see some poor beggar on the street with his hand up to you begging for a dime, begging for a quarter . . . you can walk on by with a clear conscience 'cause you sent me eighteen bucks! . . . The next time you see some starvin' little baby on the TV set, all withered and bony, with his little stomach stickin' out, you can look all you want and say to yourself: It's not my fault!

You know, there are two kinds of people in the world: the haves and the have-nots . . . And among the haves, there are two kinds of haves: there are those who take out the checkbook, and then there are those who just turn off the TV . . . Which one are you?

22

CALAMARI

A man sits at a table, speaks in a growly, inner-city voice:

Every time I have fried calamari, I feel like I'm gonna blow up! . . . Vincent, be a good boy and pour your uncle a cup of coffee there . . . Just a half a cup, no sugar, I'm having a diet . . .

So Vincent, you go visit Frank in the hospital? How's he doing, he's doing OK, right? Just gallstones, right? I was gonna go visit him last week but I got home from work and I couldn't move! I even bought him a geranium for his room there, but I left it on the Mr. Coffee machine in the office and it got all burnt up!

So how's he doing? He's doing all right, huh? Just gallstones, huh? Gallstones is nothing! I saw the whole operation on *Marcus Welby, MD*. Right on TV they showed it. Very simple operation, I could do it myself. They just make a little cut in the stomach like this . . . then they got this thing, uh, like, it's like a grapefruit spoon, OK? They take this grapefruit spoon and they dig out those gallstones. That's all . . . and then they throw 'em away. Throw 'em away right in the garbage. They don't even keep 'em. You figure for the amount of money you pay for that operation

they'd at least give you the gallstones to take home . . . show 'em
to the kids . . . give 'em to the dog to play with . . . Forgetaboutit!
. . . Merv Griffin had those gallstones one time—he was back on
the show in two weeks.

Gallstones is nothing. Of course, when Frank went in, he
thought he was gonna DIE! First he thinks he's got appendicitis,
then he thinks he's got a heart attack, then, then they tell him he
might be gettin' cancer! And with his mother passing away last
year cancer and his brother two years ago cancer! Everybody in
that family's dying of cancer! Even the dog died. Remember that
little dog they used ta have? The poodle? What was his name
there? That cute dog? What was—?

(Interrupting himself, shouting off) ANGIE! ANGIE! . . . WHAT
WAS THE NAME OF FRANK'S DOG? *(Pause)* YEAH, THE
ONE THAT DIED! *(Longer pause)* . . . Snowball! Snowball! That
was it. *(Back to Vincent)* Remember little Snowball? Little pink
poodle, they used to dye him all pink, remember that? Lick ya
hand? Yeah, he died . . .

Listen, Vincent, let me have a little piece of that pie there,
will you please? Yeah, just a thin piece. Just a thin . . . well, bigger
than that for crying out loud, what are you trying to do, starve me
to death, come on! . . . And put some whipped cream on top! . . .
I don't know what it is, I can't eat a piece of pie without whipped
cream, it . . . it just doesn't taste right. I think you need the cream
to lubricate the crumbs, make 'em go down smoother.

Thank you . . . Huh? . . . What operation? I didn't have no
operation. That was an "exploratory," Vincent! An exploratory is
not an operation. Exploratory they just open you up, look around
inside and close you up again. They don't change nothing. They said
I was in perfect health. All I have is a little benign tumor . . . No,
Vincent! Benign! You're thinking of a *malignant* tumor. Malignant
and benign are two different things. Look, malignant tumors are
very, very bad for you. But benign tumors . . . benign tumors . . .
you can have all the benign tumors you want, they don't hurt ya . . .
they're good for ya.

What are you going to do about it anyway? Everybody gets
cancer these days, it's in the food you eat, it's in the water you
drink . . . that disoksin stuff and the DDT and the PCB and the

acid rain. Every day they think of some new thing put in the food, gives you cancer.

You know, Vincent, it wasn't like this when we was kids! We didn't have all this poison in everything you eat and drink all over the place . . . Take asbestos. When we was kids we used to have asbestos all over the place. Nobody ever died from asbestos. We used to *play* in asbestos! Nowadays, nowadays, you go down to the drugstore to buy yourself some aspirin, some Tylenol, and some maniac put cyanide in the bottle! You take it home and you drop dead! Buy yourself some baby food, it's got ground glass in it! You don't know what you're eatin' anymore . . .

And if you don't eat nothin', you don't eat nothin', you get that starvation disease . . . uh, you know . . . that starvation disease . . . they uh . . . *(Shouting off again)* ANGIE! ANGIE! . . . Well, turn the water off for crying out loud, I gotta ask you an important question! . . . *(To Vincent)* What's she doing in there, washing the dishes twenty-four hours a day! . . . *(Off)* WHAT WAS THE NAME OF THE DISEASE THAT KAREN CARPENTER GIRL DIED FROM? . . . IT WAS IN THE *PEOPLE* MAGAZINE . . . THE ONE IN THE BATHROOM! . . . YEAH . . . *(To Vincent)* The anorexia, you get the anorexia! See what I'm saying, Vincent? If you eat you die and if you don't eat you die! I'd rather eat.

Huh? No, I'm not going, I'm not going. Look, I went to the wake, I went to the funeral, enough of these social functions. I mean, Louie was a nice guy and everything, but all we're gonna do is go over to that house and sit around with Mary and talk and eat, and besides all Mary's got is a black-and-white TV set! Louie was too cheap when he was alive to buy a color TV and now look what's happened! Mary's stuck with black-and-white for the rest of her life!

Besides, there's a show on TV I want to watch that night . . . A Charles Bronson movie . . . uh, you know the one . . . the good one, where he's got that big gun and he goes all over New York City and kills all those Puerto Ricans . . . Yeah, it's a good movie . . . Nah, I got it on the cable-TV, on the cable.

You know what they say, Vince. When you got cable-TV you never got to go out. What do I got to go out for? I got everything

I need right here: my color TV set, hundred and five stations; my own sofa, nice and soft; my own kitchen, plenty of food in the ice-box; my own bathroom, plenty of toilet paper. What do I gotta go out for? Stay home, it's safer, it's cleaner, it's more sanitary. Stay in the house, lock the door, piece of Sara Lee cake, turn on the TV. That's livin'. What else you want from life?

Plus, I just got the videotape machine. Yeah, it's in the bedroom, come on, I'll show it to ya. You can watch whatever you wanna watch whenever you wanna watch it. *(Stands)* Like last week Ronald Reagan was on TV, gave that big speech? I recorded the whole thing on my videotape machine! Anytime I wanna watch Ronald Reagan, anytime at all, day or night, middle of the night—BANG! *(Hits table)* Ronald Reagan on TV! You can't beat it!

Plus Angie's got that Jane Fonda exercise tape, you know the one? . . . What, me? Forgetaboutit. I'll tell you something though, that Jane Fonda, I wouldn't kick her outta bed! Uh???? *(He starts laughing as he turns to exit. The laughter turns into racking coughs . . .)*

23

HONEY, I'M HOME!

Lying on the floor, singing in a raspy voice:

"God bless America! Land that I love! Stand beside her . . . and guide her . . ." *(Pause)* . . . Blah, blah, blah, blah, blah, blah, blah, blah!

(He starts coughing, turns onto his side and notices a bystander.)

Hey! Hey, buddy, can you give me a hand here? I just slipped and fell down for a second, could you help me out please? Buddy, pal? How about helping out an old veteran! I served in Korea, buddy! I helped save this country from communism. Whaddya say? "Ask not what your country can do for you . . . ask what you can do for your country . . ."

Remember that one? JFK said that . . . They blew *his* brains out!

Hey, buddy, what do you say? Am I invisible or something? What, am I talking to the fire hydrant here? You! Mister! The guy with the *New York Times* under his arm, how about it? It'll only take you a second . . . What's a matter, afraid you're gonna miss your bus to Connecticut??? What, do you have to rush home and skim the pool, is that it? Drive the wife to the Amnesty International meeting? Is that why you can't help me up here for a second?

I know you can hear me! I know you can hear me! Don't act like you can't hear me, buddy! I know all about guys like you! Guys like you don't give a fuck about nobody, do ya? Do ya? You're just a bunch of bums, aren't ya? No good to nobody . . . You think you're something special 'cause you got a Gold American Express card . . . and 'cause you drink "fine wines." . . . Well, I drink wine too, buddy, nothing special about that! . . .

What are you gonna do? Go home now and have a nice little dinner with the wife and the kids and the dog and gerbil?!? Nice little roast beef dinner, is that what you're gonna have? Roast beef and gravy??? And little baked potatoes . . . Maybe some little . . . asparagus tips! Nice little asparagus tips . . . Is that what you're gonna have tonight? Is that why you can't pick me up? Because you're gonna have asparagus tips tonight?????

(He begins to get to his feet, very shakily.)

I know all about guys like you! With your London Fog raincoat! And the briefcase that your wife gave you for Christmas with your initials on it and the combination lock! *(Pause)* What do you need a combination lock for, you a secret agent or something?

You're all the same, you go home, you walk in the front door and you all say the same damn thing:

(Standing now, mimicking the man . . . in a hoarse voice:)

Honey, I'm home! Honey, I'm home! Honey, I'm home!

24

THE PACER

A man paces and stops, paces and stops, throughout the monologue, talking to himself. He speaks to the audience more directly as the monologue goes on.

Yeah, yeah, yeah, yeah, they're always telling you the same old story, always giving you the same old story: One plus one equals two, two plus two equals four, you reap what you sow. It always starts the same way, it always ends the same way . . . I don't, I don't, I don't got any answers . . . I don't know what the answer is . . .

You're coming and you're going, you're coming and you're going, you take it or you leave it. You make it or you need it. It's human nature, it's human nature, the same old story: Man against man, man against nature, man against himself!

Beginning, middle, end. Climax . . . anticlimax . . . Subplot! . . . But you gotta read between the lines . . . you can't win the way things are now. Oh, yeah, sure, sure, sure, sure, sure, it used to be all different. Sure when I was a kid, when I was a kid everything was different: Bread, ten cents a loaf. Eggs, fifty cents. No plastic bags. No plastic bags! NO PLASTIC BAGS! Waxed paper! No pollution, no conspiracy.

Everything was different. Easy to understand. I can't understand . . . I can't, I can't, I can't make any sense out of it. And then
the guy, the guy, the guy, the guy says, "Get out of here! Get out
of here!" . . . "*You* get out of here," that's what I should of said to
him! "*You* get out of here!" I got no place to go! No place to go!
It's crazy, it's a madhouse, a funhouse . . .

It's dog eat dog, man eat man, eat or be eaten, hunt or be
hunted! It's the letter of the law, the law of the land, and the land
is a jungle! . . . You see what I'm saying, you follow what I'm talking about??? Now, now look, look, look, look . . . I gotta look after
myself first. They want you to give to the taxes, give to the starving children, the abandoned babies, the blind people, the poor
people!

I can't worry about those poor people! I gotta worry about
me first! . . . And then, then they say, "Don't worry about it! Don't
worry about it! We'll take care of you. Everything's gonna be all
right! Everything's gonna be terrific! We got a safety net for you!
A safety net for you! Jump in the safety net! Go ahead, jump in the
safety net . . . Go ahead, jump. And here's some free cheese to go
with you . . . and here's a space shuttle!" . . . I don't want no space
shuttle! I just want a cup of coffee!

. . . I give up, I'm gonna give it up! It's just gettin' harder and
harder, every day, day in, day out . . . You gotta stand in line, you
gotta stand in line for hours and hours and hours . . . And then
you get to the end of the line, you get to the end of the line and
they say, "No more! No more! We don't got no more for you! . . .
No more for you!" For who? For who? Who's gettin' it? Who's
gettin' it? I'm not! I'm not gettin' it!

You're either winnin' or you're losin', you're either sinkin' or
you're swimmin' . . . and I'm sinkin', see! I'm in a little lifeboat
with no oars and I'm sinkin' in the ocean . . .

(Indicates by his posture) I'm on a little piece of ice, just gettin'
smaller and smaller and smaller day by day by day, goin' into the
water . . . and that water's polluted, it's dirty, it's disgusting . . . and
I can't swim! I can't swim!

Sink or swim, fish or cut bait! You're either part of the problem or you're part of the solution . . . And what's the solution?
What's the solution? The bomb? The bomb? Drop the bomb.

Go ahead, drop it! I don't care! I'm not waiting for any packages!
I got no all-paid vacation coming up! I'm no Little Orphan Annie.
(Sings in a cracked voice) "Tomorrow! Tomorrow! Tomorrow!" . . .
Where's the tomorrow? You know where tomorrow is? You got a
tomorrow? I don't got no tomorrow . . . OH!!! I know what you're
gonna say now . . . *More! More!* Tomorrow is more . . . that's what
tomorrow is . . . More money. We make more money, everything
will be all right, that's it. Let's all make some more money . . . all
go to work and make more money . . . and then we can make more
kids . . . more people, we need a lot more people! What do we
need more people for? What's wrong with me?

More people, more radio stations, we need a lot more radio
stations . . . and TV stations, we gotta have more TV stations!
Lots more TV stations . . . UHF, VHF, cable-TV, satellite-TV,
mini, maxi, tape deck, PBS, CBS . . .

*(A loud voice-over of a rock radio deejay comes over the sound system,
getting louder and louder:)*

"Hey, this is John Cummings on WXXX, the home of HEAVY
METAL! I'm gonna give away ten thousand dollars in the next
hour . . . ten thousand dollars in our MADNESS contest. Bet
you could use that money, huh? Well, who knows, maybe you'll
win! On the other hand, maybe you won't. *(Laughs)* Then you'll
just have to SUFFER! And while you're burning in your own pri-
vate hell, we've got the new AC/DC album for ya right here at
WXXX, twenty-four hours a day ROCK-AND-ROLLLLLLL!"

(The voice-over ends. Music begins.)

. . . It never stops, day in, day out. In the subway, the kids with
their boxes—*boom, boom, boom!* In the supermarket, they never
shut it off. In the streets. In the elevators. The noise. It never
stops. What are they talking about? In my apartment, the people upstairs, always playing that music! *(Shouts to the people)* Hey!
Turn it down. Hey! I'm trying to think down here! Hey come on!

(He goes into a mad dance, which segues into an air-guitar dance.)

25

SHINING STAR

A man is sitting at a table, leaning forward and speaking into a micro-phone. His hands are behind his back. Perhaps he is handcuffed. He is lit by a single instrument shining directly into his eyes.

Yeah, yeah, yeah, yeah . . . I got something to say. I got a few "last words." This is what I got to say: You don't know. You don't know anything about me, you don't know anything about the world, about reality, got it? I mean, who the hell are you people? Who are you to say, "He dies"? What gives you that right? My "peers"? My "jury of peers"? You're not my peers, 'cause I look down on you. You and your fat-ass existence. You and your TV brains. You never been anywhere, you don't know nothin' . . . All you know is what some idiot on the boob tube tells you.

So maybe I killed those girls . . . So what? I didn't. But what if I did? Insignificant people die all the time. You don't seem to be too concerned when there's a war going on or there's children starving in Africa. What about that, huh? You're responsible for that and you're responsible for putting me away! I mean, first of all, I'm innocent, OK? But second of all, I'm somebody 'cause I have seen the world. I have been in the desert, man, I have seen the "shining star." I have rode with the Kings, man, and I have rode with the best!

I know what the truth is, and the truth is that I count and you don't. It's like when you're a little kid and you step on ants on the sidewalk. You know they don't count. Well, it's the same with me. You're just a bunch of ants. You're not even alive as far as I know. You could just be a bunch of robots. You might be robots filled with blood and guts but you're still robots, see?

See, I can see that . . . I understand that. 'Cause I have seen the shining star in the desert, man. I have rode a Harley at a hundred and fifty miles per hour and I have seen reality go by! I have been through it. I have tripped in places you don't even know exist! I have shot dope in the Mekong, man. I have looked death right in the eyes, and I saw the Stars and Stripes!

And no one can dispute me! Those who have tried are very sorry now. They're not around to talk about it. 'Cause I'm always ready . . . There's a war comin' on and this is only the beginning. Only the strong will survive. It's gonna be kill or be killed. Hand to hand. Mind to mind. And I'm ready, see? I'm ready for anything, anything. I passed every test.

See, I will survive 'cause it all passes through me. It's up to me to hold it all together. I am the center. It's like cosmic. Like Oriental. You got to go all the way out and come all the way back and keep your center. Like if there was a candle here right now, I could put my hand over it and I wouldn't get burned. I wouldn't. I wouldn't feel any pain at all. 'Cause I can take it, see. I'm just testin' myself harder and harder, goin' out further and further to the shining star . . .

You people, you people livin' out your safe, protected little lives. You think you know about things? You think you can tell me about things? You can't tell me about nothing, man, 'cause I have seen it all. I have shook hands with the devil!

And you wanna come here and you wanna fight with me and you will lose, man, you will lose! 'Cause I am the stronger one, and the stronger one always wins, that's the law of the jungle. That's survival of the fittest. And I am the stronger. I am the stronger physically, mentally and spiritually . . . *(Laughs to himself)*

See, that's the big joke, see? You're just here 'cause I'm here! You just came here tonight to see me! I'm the one! I'm sittin' up here, and you're just sittin' out there scared: "There's the killer. We gotta kill the killer." You're afraid of me—like Jesus! And you think you can just put me away and that's the end of it, and that's where you're wrong, man! You can't get rid of me!

'Cause I'm everywhere! I'm in the air, I'm in the ground, I'm inside you. See, 'cause the shining star, it doesn't go away. It's always there in my brain, burnin', shinin' in my head . . . And when everything's gone, when everything is blowed away . . . I'll still be here!

(Fade to black.)

FROM "DRINKING IN AMERICA"

(1986)

26

JOURNAL

A man explains that the journal he's holding was found with some college memorabilia, then he reads:

April 11, 1971

Today I began to understand one of the immutable truths with regard to my own existence. Today I discovered that I am not a being surrounded by walls and barriers, but part of a continuum with all other things, those living and even those inanimate. I feel a new surge of desire for life, for living now, for getting out and becoming part of everything around me. I want to change the world and I know I can do it. I'm like a newborn baby taking his first steps. I was blind before to my inner self, my true desires, my own special powers and the universe itself. So many people live lives of pointless desperation, unable to appreciate that life is life to be lived for today, in every flower, in a cloud . . . in a smile.

I also realized today that Linda and I have to break up. I realize now that her lack of imagination has been holding me back. She's been trying to mold me into someone I will never be. She's too somber, too materialistic, too straight. She thinks that life must be lived in the straight and narrow, but she's wrong and

I learned that today. Today I learned that life is an adventure for people with courage.

I guess I should back up for a minute here. I don't really know where to start. I guess everything began when I dropped that acid Mike gave me for my birthday. When I got off, I decided to take a bath, and I was watching the water, just thinking about how beautiful it looked, how I've never really noticed how beautiful bathwater looked before, when out of nowhere I heard this incredible music, like chimes.

Eventually I realized that it was the front doorbell. And then I thought, I better go answer it, you never know. And I stood up and realized that I was wet and naked. And then I thought, Hey, so what? What difference does it make, really, in the grand scheme of things? So I went to the door, and it was this girl from down the street who I have never met before, and I forgot what she wanted, but I invited her in, and—this is the really strange part—she came in.

So there we were in my parents' living room and I'm naked and she's beautiful so I made some tea. It took me around an hour to do it. Then we just sat and talked about everything and I realized that I have this incredible power over people. Almost messianic. She sat there and listened with these big beautiful brown eyes. And then I kissed her. And we were kissing and I was naked and I had this erection and she looked at it and suddenly she said she had to leave.

And I said, "Why?" And then we met each other's eyes for a long time and she said because she realized that I was a very special person and that she didn't want to ruin a special moment with something as common as sex. And I understood deep down what she meant. I understood that she meant that we were connecting in a much deeper way, that it was all too much for right now.

And she left, and I started to think . . . that I must be the kind of man that women find irresistible, that I am special, that I have powers others don't have, and that I can't let myself be hindered. I must connect with everything in this world that wants me. So, I just lay down on the floor, naked, tripping, and I could feel the power moving through me, as if the whole world lay under me just to hold me up. I was literally on top of the world. I felt like GOD.

That was around five hours ago and I'm pretty straight now. After I write this down, I'm going to call Linda and tell her it's over between us. Then I'm going to wait for my parents and tell them I'm dropping out of Boston University. There's really no point to a liberal arts degree now, with all the potential I have within me. I've decided to take my savings, a thousand dollars, and move to Portland, Oregon, for a while. I think that will be a good place to begin.

Until tomorrow . . .
SHANTI.

27

AMERICAN DREAMER

A man knocks back an entire pint of wine in three big gulps. He addresses passing cars:

Hey, bro! Hey, bro! Bro! My MAN! How you doin' today? How you doin'?

I like dat car you're drivin', man . . . dat's a nice car. I like your car, man, I like your car. It's a nice car, man, how you doin' today? All right? ALL RIGHT!

I like your ol' lady sittin' dere too, man. HOW YOU DOIN', MAMA? Feelin' good? You're a beautiful lady, anybody ever tell you dat before? Bet *he* never tells you dat!

(Pulls his crotch) How about you and me, we go aroun' da corner, drink a li'l bit more a dis T-Bird, I got a drop lef' here. How about it, whuddyousay? You and me gonna party all night. Come on, baby! Come on!

Huh?

Say what? Hey, watch your mouth, sucker. You don't know who you talkin' to. You don't know who you talkin' to . . . Come over here and say dat, bro, come on, right now, come over here!

Hey. Hey. Hey. I was jus' sayin' dat shit to her, make her feel better, man . . . 'cause she's stuck wid YOU! . . .

Huh? Get outta da car. I don't have to take dat shit from you! Come on, get out . . .

Gowan back to New Jersey, wherever you come from, man. Go fill some teeth, whatever you do. Get outta here . . . You think you such a big deal . . . wid your rusty ol' Cadillac. Huh! And your flea-bitten ol' lady. Ugly ol' lady.

I DON'T NEED YOUR OL' LADY! What do I need her for?

Shit! Huh! Shit!

What do I need your ol' lady for? Got me plenty a ol' ladies!

Man, I got me so many ol' ladies . . . had to buy me a whole 'partment building jus' to fill it up wid my ladies, man! I got ladies in ev'ry 'partment. Fashion models. Blonds, brunettes, redheads. Look like dey jus' come outta *Vogue* magazine . . . all sittin' aroun' in der 'partments, polishin' der nails, sittin' waitin' aroun', waitin' aroun' fo' ME, man! Dey get up in da mornin', dey say to demselves, Where is he? Where is my MAN! When's he gonna come see me? I need my KISS! Dat's what dey say!

And I'm up on da top, in da penthouse, smokin' a cigarette, eatin' some Doritos, watchin' *Donahue* . . . I need me a lady, I want me a *taste*, a little *squeeze*. Shit! I got me an *intercom* system. I press on my intercom system: "BUUUUUUP! Yo! Renetta, get your butt up here, I wanna *talk* to you!"

See what I'm sayin'? I got ladies all day long . . . all day long . . .

Don't need your car neither. Got me plenty a cars. Got me . . . shit . . . got me a whole parkin' garage full a cars down da bottom a my buildin' . . . Got me Mercedes, Lamborghinis, Maseratis, Volares . . . all dem kind a cars . . . Don't even drive 'em. Jus' look at 'em.

I wanna drive aroun'. I got me a limousine, bro. Stretch limousine. Long stretch limousine . . . Long, long, loooonng stretch limousine. Ladies like 'em long. I got a long one, man.

Got me a chauffeur . . . he hates me, takes him all day to buff down one side a da limousine . . . all day he polishes one side . . . next day, he goes down de other side, dat's how long it is!

Got me a TV set in my limousine . . . 'frigerator, swimmin' pool, bar . . . fully stocked bar in my limousine . . . wid whiskey, good whiskey: Ol' Crow, Ol' Grand-Dad . . . all da good kind, da old kind . . . COLT 45 . . . ON TAP! . . . Perrier, dat Perrier shit . . . Got it, don't drink it.

Got me toothpicks, napkins wid jokes on 'em, ice cubes . . . li'l plastic cups wid de chopped-up limes, chopped-up lemons, li'l red cherries . . . all dat shit. Got it. FRENCH WINE . . . from FRANCE!

(He stumbles and falls to the floor. Sits, unable to get up.)

I . . . I sit in da back a my limousine . . . *(Lies down)* . . . I lay down in da back a my limousine, I like dat even better . . . I lay down . . . da ladies, dey all come down outta da building . . . lie on me in da back a da limousine . . . lie down next to me, lie down on top a me . . . piled up, stacked up, squishin' me flat . . . HUGE pile a ladies like a bowl a Jell-O!

We drive aroun' . . . Got me a hookah . . . smoke my hookah: opium, hashish, cheebah, all dat shit packed in my hookah dere . . . I smoke it up . . .

I get stoned . . . stoned . . . stoned outta my brain . . . and if I get too stoned out, I put my head back and da ladies dey sprinkle cocaine right down into my nostrils . . . jus' like dat! Right down dere. GOOD cocaine too. None a dat New Jersey dentist cocaine, man, I got da good kind . . . da kind da cops does, dat Miami cocaine . . . fill me right up, can't even breathe . . .

Den I put out my arm . . . dey gimme de French wine . . . intravenously . . . right down dere in my arm . . . Open up da sky roof, watch da clouds . . . da birds flyin' aroun' up dere. We drive aroun' . . . turn on da TV set, see what's on *Wheel a Fortune* dere, see how Vanna be doin' . . . drive aroun' wid my ladies, I say, ". . . Ohhhhhhhhhhhhhhhhhh Yeah!"

Dat's what I do! I don't NEED your ol' lady . . . Got my own thing goin' here, I got da American Dream, see, I do what I wanna do, I do what EVERYBODY wants to do . . . I drive aroun' all day long . . . in my limousine . . . I get high . . . put my head back . . . watch da clouds . . . and I . . . pass out . . . I pass out. *(Closes his eyes)*

28

CERAMIC TILE

A man is standing, arms outstretched, holding a champagne bottle.

Whoooeeee! I'm feelin' good tonight, I'm feelin' fine tonight. Come here, come here, come here, come, darling . . . come on, come on, give Daddy, give Daddy a kiss . . . give me a kiss . . . Come on. Come on. Come on . . . Do ya love me? Do ya love me? Do ya love me? Sure ya do . . . Come on, have some more champagne, here, darlin'. You gotta have yourself some more champagne! Come on . . .

(He launches a big woozy kiss, and rocks on his heels.)

YEAH? WHO IS IT? COME ON IN, DOOR'S UNLOCKED! . . . Yeah . . . just a, just, OK, just put it, bring it on into the room there, that's OK. Just put it over by the bed there, that'll be fine. Yeah. OK. Ummmm. Looks delicious. Yessir. Heh heh. All right. OK. Yeah . . . Look, buddy, I'll sign for it later, give yourself five bucks, OK? Thank you, too. All right. OK. All right. I will. OK. Heh heh . . . Oysters do do that . . . Yeah. Thanks a lot. Good

night, buddy. Yeah, all right, I'm a little busy now so . . . all right . . .
OK . . . Lock the door on your way out . . . Thank you, too. OK.
All right. LOCK THE DOOR!

Where were we? Oh yeah, you gotta have some more of
this good champagne here, darling. You don't have some more
champagne, I'm gonna have to drink it all myself! I drink it all
myself, I'm gonna throw up all over your pretty party dress there.
WHOOOOOEEEEEE! I'm feeling good tonight! I'm feelin'
fine tonight.

(Coughs, slumps in a chair.)

Michelle. Michelle? . . . Michelle! See, I told you I'd remember
your name!

Turn around for me a second, Michelle, lemme take a look at
you . . . Lemme take a look at you, go ahead, turn around. Yeah . . .
You're one hell of a good-looking girl, aren't you darlin'? You're
just about the most beautiful girl I seen . . . the last twenty-four
hours. You know that? You are.

You got beautiful breasts. You got a beautiful behind. You got
everything right where it belongs and plenty of it, don't you, huh?
(Drinks) You can stop turning around now, Michelle.

How old you say you were? . . . Just a babe outta the woods,
eh? . . . Guess. Go ahead, guess . . . Forty-seven years old. My wife
says I look like I'm sixty. She says being on the road all the time
makes you get older faster. She thinks I enjoy being on the road.
I hate being on the road . . .

Tell you a secret. Tomorrow's my daughter's fourteenth birthday . . . and I can't be there. Can't be there at my own little girl's
birthday party 'cause I gotta be here at this convention.

You know why I gotta be at this convention, Michelle?
Because I am an industrial ceramic-tile salesman . . . And when
you're an industrial ceramic-tile salesman you gotta do one thing
and you gotta do it real well. You gotta sell industrial ceramic
tile. That's what I do, see, I sell tile . . . I sell tile all the way from
Tampa to San Diego. I sell tile and I sell a lot of it. I go to every
little sales meeting, every convention, I go out there and bust my
ass . . .

It's a dog-eat-dog world out there, Michelle, and I go out there and I bite . . . I bite as hard as I can and I don't let go till I make a sale. 'Cause I'm good. 'Cause I'm the best.

I work hard, Michelle. I work hard, you work hard. Everybody in the world works hard. Everybody in the whole world works hard . . . except my wife. My wife, my wife thinks money grows in checkbooks . . . she thinks her job is spending the money I earn. She thinks it's easy for me to go out there on the road, kill myself to bring back a couple of bucks so she can sit by the poolside flipping through her Saks Fifth Avenue catalog picking out sterling-silver eggcups and fur-lined Cuisinarts . . . She just sits there all day trying to figure out where to waste my money next. She thinks that's her job and— What am I talking about her for when I'm here with you, right?

What do you do when you're not doing this, Michelle? . . . Uh-huh. Good. You keep going to school. It's important to go to school. No future in this escort business, I'll tell you that. You keep going to school, Michelle, because . . . I want you to. You're a beautiful, sensitive girl and I wanna see good things happen to you, so you keep going to—

WHAT'S THAT LOOK? What's that look? I know, I know, I know what you're thinking . . . I know what you're thinking . . . You think I'm bullshitting you, don't you? You're looking at me, you're thinking: Here's another middle-aged, overweight, half-drunk . . . ceramic-tile salesman . . . I know, I know . . . Well, let me tell you something, little girl, I may be middle-aged and I may be a little round at the edges and I may be feeling pretty good tonight . . . but I'm very different than the rest of these idiots you see here at this convention . . . don't confuse me with these salesmen guys. I'm nothing like them, and I'll tell you why . . . Because . . . see . . . I . . . you're looking at . . . you're in the same room with . . . the NUMBER ONE ceramic-tile salesman in the United States of America. Numero uno. I sell more tile than all these guys put together. I sell more tile than anybody in the whole United States of America . . . I probably sell more tile than anybody in the whole world!

Now think about that . . . that's a lot of tile. And I sell it all. Because I'm good, I'm the best, I'm special. And the reason why I'm special is . . . 'cause I care about people. I do. And I care about you, Michelle. Because you're special, too . . .

You know, tonight, when I came into the hotel, I thought to myself: I'm just gonna have a couple of drinks, go up to my room, pass out. But I saw you standing down there in the lobby, and I said to myself: There is a beautiful, sensitive, intelligent, sophisticated girl . . . a beautiful girl with beautiful blue eyes—green eyes, beautiful green eyes—there's a girl I could talk to tonight. That's what I said to myself. There's a girl I can talk to.

Because I'll be honest with you, Michelle, I just need a little companionship. I'm just a lonely guy . . . just a lonely little cowboy . . .

You know, every morning I wake up, I'm in a different hotel room . . . The first thing I hear is the alarm clock ringing by the bed, the first thing I see . . . the toilet . . . then I see the cable-TV set down by the end of the bed . . . luggage on the floor, maid knockin' on the door, I got a headache and a hangover and I don't know where the hell I am!

Now if I don't know where I am, how the hell's anybody else supposed to know where I am? I feel like I'm the last man left in the whole world . . . and I get lonely, Michelle . . . I get real lonely . . .

Come here, come here, come here, baby, don't stand there all night, come here and give Daddy a hug. Come on.

Oh yeah . . . ummmm that's nice . . .

SHIT! I'm jus' about gonna pass out on you here, Michelle!

(He slumps in his chair.)

Lissen, Michelle, it was great talkin' to you. I want to tell you, you're one hell of a stimulating conversationalist, you know . . . and I'll let you get out of here now . . . and I just want to tell you it was great . . . and uh . . . Michelle, before you go, though, uh . . . jus' so that hundred bucks don't go to a total waste, do you think you could do a little something for me right now . . . jus' so, jus' so your boss knows you're working? *(Wink)* Huh? She tell you what I like, right? Think you could do a little bit of that for me right now? Huh? Just a quick one? Just a nice slow quick one?

Yeah, you got the idea . . . oh! Ummmmmmm. That's it. Yes. Oh, I feel better already . . . Oh . . . I'll tell you something, Michelle . . . nothing worse . . . than being . . . lonely . . .

29

COMMERCIAL

A man stands before a microphone. He holds a piece of paper in his hand. A voice addresses him from a raspy loudspeaker:

VOICE *(Click)*: What do you think, Eric? *(Click)*

ERIC: Looks good . . .

VOICE *(Click)*: Yeah, uh . . . you wanna try it for me one time here, just throw something off? *(Click)*

ERIC: We laid down more than one before. Which one did you like?

VOICE *(Click)*: I'm sorry, what was that? *(Click)*

ERIC: We did more than one take, which one did you like?

VOICE *(Click)*: Uh . . . I think we liked the third one. *(Click)*

ERIC: Warm?

VOICE *(Click)*: Macho. But with a smile. You're selling virility. *(Click)*

ERIC: Gotcha. I think I can do that.

VOICE *(Click)*: Good . . . uh, you wanna give Jimmy a level? *(Click)*

ERIC: Sure. *(Reading)* Kronen-Bräu. Kronen-Bräu. Kronen-Bräu. Kronen-Bräu. Kronen-Bräu. Kronen—

VOICE *(Click)*: That's fine. OK. So, uh, let's try it once, OK? *(Click)*

ERIC: I'm ready.

VOICE *(Click)*: Remember, Eric, this is the voice inside your head. The guy wants to get laid and you've got the secret. *(Click)*

ERIC: Wants to be part-of-the-crowd kind of guy.

VOICE *(Click)*: Right. OK? Jimmy will give you the cue. No slate. *(Click)*

ERIC: You've worked hard to get . . . I'm sorry, can we start over again? I'm not . . . concentrating . . .

VOICE *(Click)*: OK. We're still running. *(Click)*

ERIC: You've worked hard to get where you are today and you've still got a long way to go before you get to the top . . . You want your life to be *good* . . . so you surround yourself with the best . . . the very best . . . in clothes, in food, in people . . . You know you're going to get there some day . . . and when you do, you'll say "good-bye" to your companions of a less prosperous time. But there is one thing you will never leave behind . . . And that's your beer: Kronen-Bräu . . . always superb, always fulfilling, always the best . . . because *you're* the best . . . Just taste it and feel its *strength* fill you . . . Ahhhh . . . Kronen-Bräu. The thing you have before everything else. Kronen-Bräu. The beer of kings.

VOICE *(Click)*: OK, Eric, sounds good. Nice and warm, but macho, I'll buy it . . . Just gimme the tag three times, OK? And then we'll uh . . . play it back. I think we'll be all done for the day . . . I think that's all right . . . We're gonna, we're gonna keep it . . . *(Click)*

ERIC: That's it? Great. OK, tag three times . . .

(Clears throat.)

(Normal voice) Ahhhhhh . . . Kronen-Bräu. The thing you have before everything else. Kronen-Bräu. The beer of kings. *(Peppy voice)* Ahhhhh . . . Kronen-Bräu. The thing you have before everything else. Kronen-Bräu. The beer of kings. *(Deep voice)* Ahhhhh . . . Kronen-Bräu. The thing you have before everything else. Kronen-Bräu. The beer of kings.

(Looks up for approval.)

30

MELTING POT

A man in a V-neck T-shirt gesticulates with his arms, gesturing and shouting. He has an Eastern Mediterranean accent.

LISA! LISA! Get this guy over here . . . *(Addressing the man he's been pointing to)* What you want? What you want? Huh? Cup of coffee? What else? That's it, cup of coffee? . . . LISA, get this bum cup of coffee . . .

Where the hell is Jesus? *(Pronounced "Hey-soose.")* JESUS! JESUS! What are you doing down there? . . . Shooting up? Jerking off? Come on, come out of there . . . What rat? . . . Leave the rat, if it's dead leave it . . . Come up here now, come on, come here, I want to show you something.

OK, come here . . . What is this? Huh? What is this mess? French fries in the fat, french fries on the floor, french fries in the sink, everyplace french fries. Mess, mess, mess, mess, mess, mess. Eh? Huh? Look at me when I'm talking to you! Look at me. Don't look at girl over there, look at me . . .

Who teach you to make mess like this? I don't teach you to make mess. You want Health Department come in here, they close us up, they say, "George, too dirty, close up!"?

71

I show you how to make french fries, you don't make no more mess, all right . . .

Yeah, yeah, yeah, yeah, yeah . . . I know you know, I know you know, you know everything, you genius! . . . George show you how to make french fries, no more mistake, all right? No more messy. Yeah, yeah, you watch me, mister . . .

Take bag, all right, cut corner on bag, all right? Yeah, I know you know, smart guy . . . Einstein, you watch me. Take bag, put in basket, all right? *(His arms flail wildly)* In . . . in . . . not all over . . . in the basket. One shake. Put back, take basket, put in fat, all right? *(Shakes the frying basket)* Cooking . . . Cooking . . . Cooking . . . Easy, nothing to it! . . . Cooking . . . Cooking . . .

Then shake, shake, bim, bim, boom, boom, zip, zip! Back in. Cooking . . . Cooking . . . Cooking . . . All right, take it out . . . brown, white, don't make no difference, nobody eat it anyway . . .

All right, now you show me. Show me, I want to see, come on. I don't got all day here, please, I'm busy . . .

(Watching) All right, OK, yaaaaa, ummmmm, all right, put it in, ummmmm, yaaaaaa, OK.

You know, I don't have to hire you, you know. Lisa, she tell me you good. That Chinese guy, he was great! Buck an hour that guy, huh? . . . Too bad he die on me . . .

Come on, come on, put it back now, you're spilling, you're spilling! . . .

You know what your problem is, Jesus? You Puerto Rican. You go back whenever you want to go back. You come, you go, you don't need green card, you be citizen when you want be citizen. I can't go back. I have to stay in America. You want to stay in America, you have to work all the time . . .

I want to be big success in America. I work sometimes twenty-four hours a day, I work. Sometimes I don't eat, I don't sleep, I don't piss. Nothing. Working all the time. That's it. You know what I'm saying?

You don't work all the time, you know what's gonna happen to you? You gonna be like all these these these bums, these junkies, these winos . . . they come in here, they hang around all the time, night and day: "Gimme cup a coffee. Gimme cup a coffee.

Gimme glass a water—I wanna shoot up. I wanna throw up! Cup a coffee. Glass a water. Cup a coffee. Glass a water . . ."

You want cup a coffee? You want glass a water? You go back to Puerto Rico. They got water there, they got coffee, all day long. You want to be in America, you *work*. That's it. Working all the time. All right? That's it. Work.

No time for this . . . wine . . . this drugs . . . this hanging around, pinball, disco, girlfriends, TV, movies . . . *bullshit.*

(Pounds chest) WORK! WORK! WORK! WORK! WORK!

You work, you make money, you buy house . . . you go in melting pot, you *melt.* That's the American way. You know what I'm saying? Think about these things. All right. All right.

Come on, OK, that's good. A little burn, but OK. All right, that be your lunch today . . . Double order french fries. Is good for you. Lots of vitamins . . . *(Pats Jesus on the back)* Don't worry. Don't worry. Don't cry. You learn how to make french fries, don't worry . . . two, three years you make as good as George. Good boy.

LISA! LISA! Take over for me, I'm going to the bank, I gotta make deposit . . . *(Walks off)*

31

OUR GANG

A tough guy, holding a beer bottle, T-shirt, sleeves rolled up, struts onstage. Talking to someone off:

Tony, you goin' to the store? Get me a pack a cigarettes, will ya? Marlboro . . . hard pack. And get me a RingDing too, I'm hungry . . . Get me a Diet Pepsi too, I'm starved. Didn' have no breakfast or nothin' . . . Please? Please? Come on, man, I got a hangover, man, I'm disabled. I'll pay ya back later . . . Yer a saint, man . . .

(Sipping his beer) I'm all right . . . I'm all right . . . Where were you last night, Joe? We was lookin' all over the place for you. It was FUCKIN' GREAT, man! You missed the whole fuckin' thing. Me and Frankie and Sally and Joanie, we had these 'ludes, Frankie got 'em outta the drugstore where he works . . . So we took these 'ludes. I figure let's take the 'ludes, take my car, drive up the highway, smoke a couple a J's, drink a couple a beers, listen to some Bruce on the radio, you know, make a quiet night of it, stay outta trouble, right? Right.

So we're drivin' around, I'm not gettin' off on the 'ludes, right? So I turns to Frankie, I says, "Frankie, I'm not gettin' off on these 'ludes." Frankie turns to me, he says, "Don't worry, man, you will . . ." You know with that, like, wisdom that Frankie's got, he just knows stuff . . .

So I'm drivin', I'm drivin', waitin' for the 'ludes to kick in and I looks down and I see I got this little piece a dirt on my shoe. And you know me, I'm neat and clean, I don't like gettin' nothin' on my clothes or nothin'. So I'm drivin', I keep lookin' down at this piece a dirt . . . piece a dirt's drivin' me crazy. It's like me and this piece a dirt we got this thing goin' on here between us . . . I'm lookin' down I keep seein' this piece a dirt. It's lookin' at me, I'm lookin' at it. Back and forth, drivin' me nuts. I'm mesmerized by the dirt. So, I start scratchin' the dirt off my shoe . . . I'm scratchin', I'm scratchin' . . . Got my hand on the wheel, drivin' the car, not fuckin' aroun' or nothin'.

Scratchin', scratchin' . . . all of a sudden . . . out a fuckin' no place—BANG! This guard rail comes up the front a the car! Car starts spinnin' aroun', chicks is screamin' in the backseat, cars honkin' their horns all around me and shit—BOOM! We run over the guard rail, we're on the other side of the highway now, goin' down the highway . . . cars blinkin' their headlights at me and shit . . . you know, like I don't know I'm on the wrong side of the road?! People are so stupid—BANG! We go down the side of the road, into this you know, valley-gully thing, down by the side of the road—ZING! Car comes to a stop.

I gets outta the car. Frankie gets outta the car. Sally gets outta the car. Joanie gets outta . . . everybody gets outta the car. Everybody's cool, everybody's fine, everybody's healthy, right? Great . . . The car, Joe. You had to see the car, man. Everything was gone from the outside of the car, you know? The bumpers was gone, and the headlights was gone, and the handles was gone, and the license plate . . . the car was one big scrape. It looked like, it looked like . . . you know ET? Little fuckin' ET? It looked like fuckin' ET's head. *(Laughs)*

Frankie comes . . . Frankie comes over to the car, he comes over. He looks at the car like this, he says, "Fuck the fuckin' car, man, the fuckin' car's fucked!" Right? *(Laughs)* With that razor wit of his, you know—ZING! The guy's a fuckin' word master . . . thinkin' all the time . . .

All right, so I figure, let's ditch the car, we're holdin' 'ludes, let's get outta here before the cops show . . . so we start hitchin' down the highway . . .

Nobody's pickin' us up . . . I don't know why . . . Joanie's just got a little blood runnin' down her face, that's it. Nothin'. So we're standin' there. Finally, this van rolls up. Big peace sign painted on the side, flowers painted . . . Yeah, yeah, that's it, a hippie van, like outta prehistoric times . . . Door pops open, guy drivin' the van, Joe, you had ta see this guy. He's got hair down to his butt, he's got a headband on, incense, flowers, beads, Grateful Dead music on the tape player, you know, complete asshole . . .

We figure, what the hell, why not? So we all jumps inside this guy's van. Joanie gets in the front seat, the rest of us gets in the backseat. We start drivin'.

Joe. The guy starts rollin' these joints. You had to see these joints, they were huge, the size of ya dick. No—even bigger—the size of MY dick, enormous! *(Laughs)* Monster joints, made outta some kind of weed, I never smoked weed like this before in my life. The strongest weed I ever smoked. Like from one of those weird Oriental places, like Taiwan . . . Taiwan weed, that's what it was. Taiwan weed, all right . . . Smoke one toke a this shit, ya blind for the rest of ya life! Good weed, strong weed.

Me and Frankie, we each roll up a monster joint of this stuff and we're in the backseat, blowin' smoke rings around each other's head. Like getting completely wasted, just wasted outta our brains, vaporized. Meltin'-into-the-upholstery kind of thing . . . oxygen-tent time, you know? We're doin' experiments on our brain cells . . . like how many can you kill in one toke? *(Laughs)*

Totally, totally screwed into the fuckin' ground, blown inside out, comatose, right? Even the Grateful Dead music's startin' ta sound good . . . "Truckin' with da Doo-Dah Man"! *(Laughs, then starts coughing)* Blasted! Then . . . then the 'ludes kick in!

All right. Now, check this out. Party time, right? OK. So we're drivin' along, havin' this good time, and all of a sudden this guy, this hippie guy, he reaches over, he puts his hand on Joanie's leg! Frankie's sittin' in the backseat. He goes like, "Hey, man, take ya hand off my girlfriend's leg!" Right?

The guy turns around to Frankie. He says, "Hey, man . . ." *(Raises his middle finger)* ". . . Fuck you!" Right? To Frankie he says this . . .

So what's Frankie gonna do? He takes his knife out, he opens it up, he goes, "No, man, *fuck you!*" Right?

The guy reaches into the glove compartment, pulls out a *handgun*, points it at Frankie's *head*. He says, "No, man, FUCK *YOU!*"

I'm fuckin' shittin' my pants, right, 'cause you do not fuckin' fuck with Frankie! . . . You know what I'm talkin' about? We're in a movin' vehicle here, we've got a loaded gun here, I'm not feelin' good about this . . .

Frankie's sittin' there like a stick a dynamite, just vibratin', right? The guy turns around ta look at the road for one second, Frankie takes the knife—*Bing!* Cuts the guy behind the ear . . . Little tiny cut, nothin' cut, hardly bleedin'.

Guy gets pissed off. Pulls the van to the side of the road. Says, "Everybody outta the van right now!" The van's stopped by the side of the road. He's wavin' the gun around in front a Frankie's face . . .

What's Frankie gonna do? He takes his knife, closes it up nice . . . *(Punches)* BANG! BANG! BANG! BANG! BANG! BANG! BANG! The guy's head . . . *(Kicks)* BOOM! BOOM! BOOM! BOOM! BOOM! BOOM! Kicks the guy outta the van. WHAM! WHAM! WHAM! WHAM! WHAM! WHAM! In the ribs, guy's on the ground. Frankie just bends over, picks up the gun, gets back in the van, we're outta there. FRANKIE!!! *(Laughs)*

We leave the guy in the middle of the highway lookin' like the Woodstock revolution or somethin'. "GET A HAIRCUT, HIPPIE!" *(Laughs)*

So now we got the guy's van . . . So Frankie's drivin', he takes the van down off the highway, so no cops, right? There's a little road down into these woods. Frankie's drivin' . . . real careful: "Oh, there's a tree!" BANG! "Oh, there's another tree!" CRASH! "There's a rock!" BOOM! Beatin' the hell outta this guy's van . . . CRACK! We break the axle . . .

We're in the middle of the woods, we don't know where we are . . . Frankie gets outta the van, he looks at the axle, he goes, "Don't worry, man, I can fix it!"

He gets in the back of the van, he looks around, finds a can of gasoline and starts splashin' the gasoline all over the inside of the van . . . He turns to me, he says, "Richie, can I see ya cigarette fa a second?" I couldn't figure out what he wants my cigarette for . . . He takes one puff outta my cigarette, flips it in the van—BOOM!—the van blows up! Joe, you had to see this thing, man, it was nice, man. It was really nice . . . Fireball, ten, fifteen feet high . . . like this . . . colors in it and everything. It was beautiful, one of the most beautiful things I ever seen . . . Plus we's in the woods, right? You ever been in the woods before, real woods? Nice in the woods . . . Not like Central Park . . .

This fireball's burnin' like this in the middle of the woods, and we're in this clearin' and all around us you got, like . . . trees, you know, with leaves on 'em and stuff. And like the flames, they're like reflectin' up on the leaves, you know. Then up over ya head, ya got like stars . . . and it's quiet, ya know, real quiet in the woods. You don't hear nothin' . . . just, like, maybe a headlight poppin' or the windshield wipers meltin' onto the hood . . . nice, you know, quiet . . .

And I'm just standin' there, the fire's burnin', the stars, the 'ludes, my friends standin' next ta me . . . it was like *spiritual* or somethin'. I never felt so calm in my life . . .

Joanie was lookin' in the flames, she said she could see Jim Morrison's face like floatin' in there.

Frankie's totally into it. Frankie's spiritual, you know. Ever talk to Frankie about Satan? He knows all about Satan. He says he's *met* Satan.

He turns to me, he goes like this, he goes, "Here, man, take this." I says, "Frankie, I can't take any more shit, I'm gonna fall down!" He says, "Take it, man, take it. Trust me, it'll wake you up . . ." So I takes the stuff, I figures it's crystal or speed or pep pills, somethin' harmless like that. —It's triple-strength LSD! Acid, we're doin' acid. I haven't done acid for at least three . . . weeks—ZOOOOOOM!—everything's meltin' and weird and stuff . . . Plus it's the woods, so you got trees and rocks and crazy shit like that, right? Not like in the city where everything's nice, easy to figure out . . . You're walkin' along, smashed outta ya brains . . . a little squirrel runs out . . . looks like a fuckin' rhinoceros! *(He jumps)*

And Frankie, he's still got the guy's gun, right? So he's walkin' along—BANG, BANG, BANG, BANG, BANG!—shootin' in the air, trying to see how far up the bullet goes . . .

Anyways, to make a long story short, we ends up comin' to this big field . . . Beautiful field with like a beautiful farmhouse in the middle of it, the kind of farmhouse, like, the Pepperidge Farm guy, he'd live in that farmhouse, right? Nice farmhouse . . .

Frankie says, "Check this out." He goes up to the farmhouse. *(Laughs)* He's such a practical joker . . . Goes right up to the front door . . . doo-doo-doo-doo-doo . . . rings the doorbell . . . and this little old lady comes to the front door. And like, Frankie, he takes the gun, he goes . . . he goes like this, "Helter-skelter, run fa shelter, let us in!" *(Laughs)*

We go waltzing into these people's house, we're like completely bonked outta our brains, we don't know where we are or nothin'.

This old guy's like comin' down the stairs puttin' on his bathrobe, doin' this, like, you know, "What's goin' on down here?" kind of thing, right? "Can I help you boys?" He's tryin' to tretten *(threaten)* us or somethin', right?

Frankie takes the gun, he wasn't gonna hurt the guy or nothin', he just takes the gun, goofin' aroun', takes the gun and goes up to the old guy like this, he goes, *(Pointing his finger)* "Say one more word, Grampa, I'll blow ya brains all over the wallpaper!" *(Laughs)* ". . . blow ya brains all over the wallpaper!"? Where does Frankie get this shit? He's so funny!

Anyways, we gets the guy and the old lady, we put 'em on the floor, we cut their phone wires, tie 'em up with the phone wire, like on *Kojak*. Frankie's still into it. He's standin' over them with the gun, "We're the Charles Manson gang. If you tell anybody about us, we're gonna come back and burn ya house down!" I'm like, "Come on, Frankie, time to get outta here, man. You don't want to give these people the wrong impression about us or nothin'. Enough's enough!"

So anyway, we take their car keys, we take some booze, we hightail it outta there over ta Frankie's father's house. It's like four o'clock in the morning or somethin' . . . Huh? Nah, his dad ain't home at four in the morning! His dad's an alcoholic, man, he's on the street all night drinking his face off. You ever meet his dad? . . .

Aw, yeah, it's pathetic, he's got like a beer in one hand and a whiskey in the other. Yeah, I feel bad for Frankie, his father's so fucked up.

Anyway, so we like got the stereo on full blast, we're dancin', we're partyin', me and Frankie and everybody, we're havin' a great time . . . Joanie's in the bathroom throwin' up, 'cause she's got lousy tolerance. Couple a 'ludes, acid, it goes to her head.

OK. Now Sally starts comin' on to me, right? I been tryin' to make this chick for three months or somethin' and now she's standin' in front a me doin' this, like, "Richie, Richie, I really want to go home with you, I need you, I want you. I love you. Take me home right now . . . uh-uh-uh-uh-uh!" Like this, right?

I'm standin' there, I'm lookin' at her thinkin' to myself, She's beautiful . . . she's stoned . . . she don't know what she's sayin' . . . her eyes aren't even open, fah cryin' out loud. *(Pause)* What the hell, go for it!

So I take the car keys, I start drivin' her home . . . She's hot! She's got her hands down my pants, she's got her tongue in my ear, she's drivin' me crazy . . . I'm drivin' as fast as I can . . . six, seven miles an hour at least. *(Laughs)*

I finally get in front of her parents' house and, when I turns to her to, like, start romanticizing her and shit, you know, I turns and . . . she's passed out! She's on the floor, curled up in a ball under the glove compartment, she's under there . . .

So what am I gonna do? I'm a gentleman, I don't mess with unconscious broads . . . So I gets outta the car, I go around, I pulls her outta the car . . .

I brings her up to the front door of her parents' house, and her parents, they got like a regular front door and they got a screen door, you know? So I opens up the screen door, and I like wedge her up between the two doors . . . knock on the door, ring the doorbell . . . get the hell outta there! *(Laughs, slaps hands with Joe)*

(He unzips his fly, turns his back to the audience, looks down, pees.)

So anyways, listen, Joe, we're goin' out again tonight, man. You should come along with us . . . It's a lot of fun . . . You know, it'd be a good time. Frankie likes you and everything . . . *(Zips back up)* Oh, yeah, Frankie wanted me to ask you one thing . . . uh . . . you got a car?

32

NO PROBLEMS

A man walks to center stage and addresses the audience:

I have no problems. I'm happy with life. Things are fine as far as I'm concerned. I know some people have problems, some people have quite a few. I, fortunately, have none.

First of all, I'm in perfect health. I just got back from the doctor's office, he gave me a completely clean bill of health. He checked me from top to bottom. He couldn't believe what great shape I'm in. I guess all that jogging and bran paid off. He even checked my teeth . . . no cavities . . . so I'm in perfect health.

I have a good job. It's a, uh . . . I guess you would call it a "semi-creative" job, very little pressure to perform. I put in about forty hours a week . . . when I want to. I have the weekends off every week, three weeks' paid vacation in the summer. I get paid very well for what I do. It's a good job. I like it.

My wife and I have been married fifteen years. We're very loving and have a very supportive relationship. My wife's a very attractive, a very lovely lady. We have a great sex life, if you must know. I don't fool around. Wasn't it Paul Newman who said,

"Why go out for hamburger when you can have steak at home?" I subscribe to that theory.

Our daughter's eleven and she's doing very well in school. She gets very high grades, has a lot of friends. Besides her school work she also uh . . . she's also studying modern dance, violin. Next month she starts her Latin lessons. She's a very precocious, very pretty little girl. We like her very much.

Our parents are alive on both sides and uh . . . we all like each other. None of this "mother-in-law" stuff in our household. We all enjoy each other's company. They're all retired now. They worked hard and saved during their active years and now they're enjoying a . . . "golden harvest" so to speak. Certainly no burden on us, we're very proud of them.

Our friends are all happy and healthy as far as we know. We usually see them around once a week. We go over to their house and . . . uh . . . have dinner over at their house. Or at our house. I like to cook. I'm kind of a gourmet chef. I like to cook things like . . . uh . . . I don't know . . . uh, tortellini with sun-dried tomatoes or . . . uh . . . arugula salad with endives, something you wouldn't think of . . . that's my cooking style. Or we go out and see a movie . . . something with Meryl Streep in it or . . . uh . . . a play, a Sam Shepard play usually, or one of those one-person shows or magic or juggling plays. We like them, there's so many to choose from . . . Or we go bowling. We all like to bowl. They're very nice people, we've had a lot of good times with them.

So that's it, uh . . . our neighborhood is safe and clean. We have an excellent town council, an activist school committee (and that's important!). Ummm . . . fire department, police department, garbage disposal . . . all top-rated.

The house is in good shape, just had a new boiler put in last year, there's nothing wrong with the house. The Volvo's running smoothly, nothing wrong with the car. So uh . . .

I mean, there are times when . . . uh . . . I mean, I'll be honest . . . there are times when I am concerned about all the . . . uh . . . you know, all the trouble there is in the world these days. You know, you turn on the news and . . . uh . . . it's disturbing, you know . . . and nobody likes being disturbed. I make myself watch it because I know I should. For their sake.

And I worry about it all. But then I just think to myself, There's always been trouble, we didn't invent it, you know, and . . . uh . . . I should just be thankful for all the good things I have in my life. Those people are doing their thing out there, whatever it is and . . . uh . . . well anyway, I . . . I guess this isn't really the point . . .

The future . . . looks good. We're going to have the house paid off in ten years. We're buying a little condo down by the water, kind of as an investment/vacation/retirement thing. We're really excited about that . . .

Ummmm, we've got money in a pension fund, so we're cool there . . . insurance . . . some stock.

Like I said, I have no problems. None. I'm happy. I'm healthy. I love my wife, I love my kid . . . good job . . . no problems.

That's what it's all about . . . I guess.

33

GODHEAD

Speaking slowly in a guttural voice:

The way I see it, it's a fucked-up world, it's not going anyplace, nothing good is happening to nobody, you think about it these days and nothing good is happening to anybody and if something good is happening to anybody, it's not happening to me, it's not happening to myself.

The way I see it, there be this man, some man sitting in a chair behind a desk in a room somewhere down in Washington, DC. See, and this man, he be sitting there, he be thinking about what we should do about crime rate, air pollution, space race . . . Whatever this guy supposed to be thinking about. And this guy, he be sitting down there and thinking, and he be thinking about what's happenin' in *my* life . . . he be deciding on food stamps, and work programs, and the welfare, and the medical aid and the hospitals, whether I be working today. Makin' all kinds a decisions for me. He be worrying about how I spen' my time! Then he lean back in his ol' leather chair, he start thinkin' about da nukular bomb. He be deciding whether I live or die today!

Nobody makes those decisions for me. That's for me to decide.

I decide when I want to get up in da mornin', when I want to work, when I want to play, when I want to do shit! That's my decision. I'm free. When I die, that's up to God or somebody, not some guy sittin' in a chair. See?

I just wanna live my life. I don't hurt nobody. I turn on the TV set, I see the way everybody be livin'. With their swimming pools and their cars and houses and living room with the fireplace in the living room . . . There's a fire burnin' in the fireplace, a rug in front of the fireplace. Lady. She be lyin' on the rug, evenin' gown on . . . jewelry, sippin' a glass o' cognac . . . She be lookin' in the fire, watchin' the branches burnin' up . . . thinkin' about things. Thinkin'. Thinkin'. What's she thinkin' about?

I jus' wanna live my life. I don't ask for too much. I got my room . . . got my bed . . . my chair, my TV set . . . my needle, my spoon, I'm OK, see? I'm OK.

I get up in the mornin' I combs my hair, I wash my face. I go out. I hustle me up a couple a bags a D . . . new works if I can find it. I take it back to my room, I take that hairwon. I cook it up good in the spoon there . . . I fill my needle up. Then I tie my arm . . . *(Caressing his arm)* . . . I use a necktie, it's a pretty necktie, my daughter gave it to me . . . Tie it tight . . . pump my arm . . . then I take the needle, I stick it up into my arm . . . find the hit . . . blood . . . Then I undoes the tie . . . I push down on that needle . . . *(Pause)* . . . and I got everything any man ever had in the history of this world. Jus' sittin' in my chair . . .

(Voice lower) I got love and I got blood. That's all you need. I can feel that blood all going up behind my knees, into my stomach, in my mouth I can taste it . . . Sometimes it goes back down my arm, come out the hole . . . stain my shirt . . .

I know . . . I know there's people who can't handle it. Maybe I can't handle it. Maybe I'm gonna get all strung out and fucked up . . . Even if I get all strung out and fucked up, don't make no difference to me . . . Even I get that hepatitis and the broken veins and the ulcers on my arms . . . addicted. Don't make no difference to me. I was all strung out and fucked up in the first place . . .

Life is a monkey on my back. You ride aroun' in your car, swim in your warm swimming pool. Watch the fire . . . I don't mind. I don't mind at all. Just let me have my taste. Have my peace. Just leave me be. Just leave me be. *(Turns in toward the dark)*

34

THE LAW

A man walks across the stage with a microphone, addressing the audience. He's some sort of preacher.

What has happened to our country? Will somebody answer that question for me, please? We are in trouble. We are in serious trouble. Look around you, what do you see? Crime, perversion, decay, apathy. We are living in a nightmare.

You can't walk down the street for fear of being assaulted. You can't ride in an airplane for fear of being hijacked or blown up. Every corner newsstand openly sells vicious pornography. Every doctor's office is perfectly happy to perform an abortion on you . . . or your daughter . . . Our children! Our children are subjected daily to the perversions of their schoolteachers and when they come home from school they have nothing better to do than to take drugs or alcohol, watch television, learn how to become homosexuals and rapists . . .

What a lovely situation, is it not? It is the world we live in today.

In the Bible . . . they tell us of two cities. The worst cities that God had ever seen. They did everything in these cities. They committed every act, natural and unnatural . . . And God, He looked down on these cities . . . and He saw sin. And He destroyed these cities.

Now you know what cities I'm talkin' about! I'm talkin', of course, about the cities of Sodom and Gomorrah . . . and friends, I regret to inform all of you here tonight . . . that everything they did in those cities of Sodom and Gomorrah . . . they do today . . . they do today. And more. And God destroyed those cities . . .

Now friends, we have to be honest with ourselves, we have to ask ourselves: From whence have come these plagues? And isn't the answer right before our eyes? Do you really have to go to the fountainhead to tell me that the water is poisoned? Well, if you do, go ahead . . . go into the inner cities. Take a look at the Negroes and the Latins congregating on every street corner . . . Take a look at the homos and dykes openly strutting up and down the avenues . . . Take a look at the pimps and prostitutes and the junkies, conspiring with the Jewish slumlords, the Arab bankers and the Italian Mafioso . . . cutting this country up and destroying it piece by piece!

Don't look to the churches to save you! Don't look to the government to save you! Don't look to the corporations to save you! There's only one place to look for salvation, friends, and that's within yourselves . . . In your hearts! In your hearts, you know the truth. In your hearts, that's where God is! God's inside your heart, He's a little voice inside you.

When you walk down the street and you see something terrible, you can't believe it and you think to yourself, What a horrible thing! That's the voice of God inside you. When you see something and you think to yourself, How can I stop this? What can I do to stop this? I have to stop this, I have to stop this now! That's the voice of God inside you. I know you have this voice . . . I know you feel it . . . We can feel it, we can ALL feel it . . . deep inside . . . burning . . . the truth is burning . . .

Just as it burned in the heart of Bernie Goetz when he took out that handgun and shot down those Negro subway criminals, he knew the truth. He knew that we are in a war for our souls! . . . And he who will not protect what is his . . . is condemned to lose it!

We must continue to put pressure on these Satanic abortion clinics, on these Negro subway criminals, on these Jewish media personalities, like Alan Berg, who only understand the discipline of the bullet. These pornographers, like Larry Flynt, who only understand the discipline of the bullet. These homosexual politicians, like Harvey Milk, who only understand the discipline of the bullet. We must show them, we must teach them. God needs our help!

(He looks the audience in the eyes) These people . . . these people . . . these people have sold their souls to the Devil . . . and if you don't believe me, you go down to Skid Row, take a look at the fallen bodies of the hopeless lost souls, their outstretched filthy hands still trying to reach out and pick up that empty wine bottle! This is the Devil's work right there for you to see! Go down to the red-light district, take a look at some of that porno, take a look at some of those magazines with the young girls on the cover, showing what they should never show anybody, the Devil dancin' in their eyes . . . these girls are lost! Go down to the city morgue, have 'em show you the dead bodies of the junkies, cold and stiff, lost and forgotten, lying on those metal tables . . . These people have no souls . . .

You go down to the city hospital, you have them show you the AIDS ward . . . go ahead and take a look . . . take a good look . . . and tell me what you see . . .

This is Satan's work! This is the work of the Devil. The Devil is in the world today! He's sittin' here with us right now. He's sittin' here, and he's laughin'. He's laughin' at us because he seduced us with a life of plenty and he invited us into Hell.

And we all went, didn't we? We took him up on it, didn't we? And we're all goin' down to Hell . . . You're goin' and you're goin' and you and you! And your children are goin' and your children's babies.

As the blind lead the blind, as the damned lead the damned, onward into oblivion we're goin'. We're goin' down to Hell, unless we do what we know is right! Unless we do what God wants us to do! Unless we do what that little voice inside tells us to do!

If you have to take a bottle, fill it up with gasoline, light it on fire, throw it into one of these abortion clinics, then you do it! If you have to take a handgun, load it up, shoot down one of these black urban barbarians, then you do it! If you have to take a nuclear device and cast it into some country filled with nothing but bearded, terrorist heathens, then you do it.

You do what you have to do! You do what you know is right.

Because this is the world where Satan walks, where Satan walks and where Satan laughs . . . Where Satan says to himself, I WON. I BEAT 'EM. I BEAT 'EM ALL.

There's a few of us who don't agree with Mr. Satan. There's a few of us who are going to do everything we can, everything within our power . . . to stop him, to do the Lord's work . . . and make America—and hopefully the rest of the world—free of sin . . . again.

Are you with us? Thank you. Amen.

35

FRIED-EGG DEAL

A man lies on the floor.

(Singing) "... We are the world ... we are the children!"

   (Rolls over and speaks to someone in the first row of the theater)
Hey there, buddy! How you doin' there, bud? You're my buddy,
huh? You got a quarter there for me, bud? You got a quarter for
me? Hmmmm?

   (Standing) I'm sorry. I'm sorry. I didn't mean to bother you,
I'm sorry, I didn't see ... you're all dressed up ... you're out
for a good time ... you don't want to be bothered by me ... I'll
leave you alone ... *(Turns away, then turns back)* ... You're here
with the little lady, she's a beautiful little lady, you're together ...
You're a together guy ... GOOD FOR YOU! That's what I say.
God bless you, that's what I say! Somebody's gotta make it in this
world, it might as well be you, right? Good for you, that's what
... I'll leave you, I'll leave ... I'll get outta here. All right. I'll get
outta here. *(Turns away again, then turns back)* See, buddy, people
like me ... I'm a loser ... Always been a loser, always gonna be
a loser. I'm a loser, 'cause I'm a drunk ... Always been a drunk.
When I was a kid, I was a drunk ... When I was a baby, I was a

baby drunk. I'm a good-for-nothin' drunken bum, you shouldn't even look at me. Don't even waste your time. Put me in the trash can and flush it, that's what I say. Just get rid of me . . . Don't even listen to me, OK, bud? I'm sorry, I didn't mean to . . . I just wanna say: "GOOD FOR YOU!"

You work hard, you deserve everything you got . . . 'cause you beat them at their own game . . . you know? 'Cause you know what? They never give you a straight deal in this world . . . never do. You know what they give you in this world? They give you a fried-egg deal. That's what they give you. A fried-egg deal. You know what I mean, fried-egg deal? *(Flips his hand)* They flip you this way, they flip you that way . . . just like a fried egg, you never know which side you're ending up on. That's the deal, right there. You wake up one morning, you're sunny side up . . . The next day, you're all scrambled up again, you don't know what's coming next . . .

And you beat 'em, and I say, "GOOD FOR YOU!" Good for you, buddy. Me, I'm good for nothin'. I'm good for nothin' . . . I'll leave you alone . . .

. . . But you know, I'm good for somethin', buddy. You know why I'm good? I'm . . . good because if . . . if I wasn't where I was . . . you couldn't be where you was . . . 'cause, you know, 'cause *(Illustrating, his hands flipping)* you can't have a top without a bottom. It's impossible. It can't be done. You're on the top and I'm on the bottom. We're like two sides of the same coin. See? And you never know which way that coin's gonna flip . . . *(Staring at his flipping hand)* You never know which way that coin's gonna go . . . That coin there . . . *(Empty hand outstretched)* . . . Gotta coin there for me, buddy? *(Laughs)*

That's OK, I gotta get goin', I gotta get outta here. It was just a joke, I was just jokin' . . . I got a limo waiting for me around the corner, don't want him to wait too long . . . Thanks a lot for listenin' to me, buddy, thanks a lot. God bless you . . . You're a good guy . . .

FROM "TALK RADIO"

(1987)

36

IT'S NOT HOW MUCH YOU MAKE, IT'S HOW MUCH YOU TAKE HOME

Lights up on Sidney Greenberg at the console in a radio studio, wearing a headset, talking into his mike. He speaks rapidly and mellifluously.

SID: . . . so we're back. Richard, you still with me?

RICHARD: Uh-huh.

SID: OK, now with the cash you have in hand from the second mortgage on the first property, the lake-view property, you've either taken a second mortgage or completely refinanced that property with an ARM. You have cash in hand. Whaddya gonna do with that cash?

RICHARD: Uh . . .

SID: Figuring the property's worth roughly in the neighborhood of two hundred thou, you pay off the existing mortgage of ten thou with a hundred-and-seventy-five-thousand-dollar refinancing loan. Simple arithmetic leaves you with a hundred and sixty-five thousand dollars. Now you *could* pocket that money. You could go nuts. Buy a Cadillac, go to Hawaii. But that isn't going to get you . . . *anywhere*. 'Cause you're not *using* the money. And the last thing you want to do is SELL and take the profit, because that means *capital gains tax* and *that* means you gotta send a check down to . . . yeah, you guessed it . . . our fat UNCLE down in Washington, DC . . . Don't wanna do that, so you hold on to that property! Now . . . Richard, you still with me?

RICHARD: I think so.

SID: Good. 'Cause now we're going to make you some money! Richard! Grab a paper and pencil and write all this down, because you're gonna take that hundred and sixty-five thou, fly to Florida and find yourself a mid-priced office building in the one-two-million range. Use that hundred and sixty-five thou AND the fifty your Uncle Harry left you . . .

RICHARD: Henry . . .

SID: What?

RICHARD: Henry. My Uncle Henry.

SID: AND the fifty your Uncle Harry left you AND you take the hundred thou you're gonna make off the second mortgage on your primary residence, put all that together and use that three hundred and fifteen thou as a DOWN PAYMENT on the office building in, let's say, Cocoa Beach.

RICHARD: Florida?

SID: Of course, Florida! You like oranges, don't ya? Drink a glass of juice every day, you'll never die. Now—you take the income you make on the rentals in your new office building, pay off your monthly finance payments and USE that excess income to buy either zero-coupon bonds or T-bills . . .

RICHARD: What about a Ginnie Mae?

SID: Ginnie Maes, Fanny Maes, Willy Mays, you'll be sitting pretty with a tax break in Florida, two places to go on vacation, and get this, Richard, over two million dollars worth of property! Unbelievable, but guess what, Richard? Using my method, you've just become a millionaire. How 'bout that?

RICHARD: But wait, I don't understand—

SID: Alrightee, the big clock on the wall tells me it's time to wrap up this episode of "Your Taxes and You" for this evening. Stay tuned for news and weather, followed by some stimulating conversation with a man who has no peer, my esteemed colleague, Mr. Barry Champlain! I'm Sidney Greenberg reminding you: "It's not how much you make, it's how much you take . . . home." *(Throws off his headset and stands)*

37

DENISE

A woman phones in to Barry's radio talk show:

I'm scared, Barry.

Nothing specifically, but on the other hand . . . you know, it's like everywhere I go.

Well, like, Barry, you know, like we've got a garbage disposal in our sink in the kitchen, I mean, my mother's kitchen . . .

And sometimes a teaspoon will fall into the garbage disposal?

So like, you know how you feel when you have to reach down . . . into that guck and you have to feel around down there for that teaspoon? Who knows what's down there? Could be garbage, a piece of something, so much stuff goes down there . . . or germs, which you can't even see.

If they're gonna be anywhere, they're gonna be down that disposal. They grow there, see? They come back up the pipes. Salmonella, yeast, viruses, flu, even cancer, who knows? But Barry, even without all that, what if, and I'm just saying "what if," what if the garbage disposal came on while your hand was down there?

I get so scared of thinking about it that I usually leave the teaspoon down there. I don't even try to get it out. But then I'm afraid that my mother will get mad if she finds it down there, so I turn the disposal on, trying to make it go down the drain. But all it does is make a huge racket. And I stand in the middle of the kitchen and the spoon goes around and around and I get sort of paralyzed, you know? It makes a lot of noise, because I know the teaspoon is getting destroyed and annihilated and that's good 'cause I hate that teaspoon for scaring me like that . . .

Well, it's not just the garbage disposal, it's everything. What about insects? Termites. Hornets. Spiders. Ants. Centipedes. Bedbugs. Roaches. Mites. You can't even see mites. They're like the germs. Tiny, impossible to see! I like things to be clean. Dirty ashtrays bother me . . . Just one more unknown. Just like the houses on our street. Used to be we knew who lived on our street. But that was years ago. Now all kinds of different people live on our street. Foreigners. People with accents. What are they doing on our street? What are their habits? Are they clean? Are they sanitary?

That would be a great idea to just go to somebody's house and knock on the door. Who knows who's behind that door? Maybe a serial murderer? What if Ted Bundy or the Boston Strangler was living there, just sitting inside watching television, and I came to the door? Great! Come on in, Denise! That's why I don't go to strange people's houses anymore. I keep the doors locked at all times. But that isn't going to solve anything. You're not going to stop a plane from crashing into your house, now are you?

The mailman brings me unsolicited mail, I mean, the postage stamp could have been licked by someone with AIDS. Right? My mother is a threat to my life just by persisting to go out there . . . Barry, did you know that there's this dust storm in California that has these fungus spores in it? And these spores get into people's lungs and it goes into their bloodstreams and grows inside them and kills them! Strange air . . . strange air . . . you have to . . . Oh! There's my mother. She'll kill me if she finds out I used the phone!

38

I'M HERE. I'M HERE EVERY NIGHT

Barry speaks into the in-studio mike:

Kill it, Spike. *(On the air)* I'm here. I'm here every night, I come up here every night. This is my job, this is what I do for a living. I come up here and I do the best I can. I give you the best I can. I can't do better than this. I can't. I'm only a human being up here. I'm not God. Ummm. A lot of you out there are not . . . I may not be the most popular guy in the world. That's not the point. I really don't care what you think of me. I mean, who the hell are you anyways? *(Beat)* You—audience—you call me up and you try to tell me things about myself. You don't know me. You don't know anything about me. You've never seen me. You don't know what I look like. You don't know who I am. What I want. What I like, what I don't like in this world. I'm just a voice. A voice crying in the wilderness. And you, like a pack of baying wolves, descend on me, because you can't stand facing what it is you are and what you've made. Yes, the world is a terrible place. Yes, cancer and garbage disposals will get you! Yes, a war is coming. Yes, the world is shot to hell and you're all goners. Everything's screwed up and you like it that way, don't you? You're fascinated by the gory details. You're mesmerized by your own fear! You revel in floods and car accidents and terrorist attacks and unstoppable diseases. You're happiest when others are in pain. And that's where I come in, isn't it? I'm here to lead you by the hand through the dark forest of your own hatred and anger and humiliation. I'm providing a public service. You're so *scared*. You're like little children under the covers afraid of the bogeyman, but you can't live without him. Your fear, your own lives have become your entertainment. *(Beat)* Monday night, millions of people are going to be listening to this show. AND YOU HAVE NOTHING TO SAY. NOTHING TO TALK ABOUT. Marvelous technology is at our disposal and instead of reaching up for new heights, we try to see how far down we can go. How deep into the muck we can immerse ourselves. What do you want to talk about? Baseball scores? Your pets? Orgasms? You're pathetic. I despise each and every one of you. You've got nothing. Nothing. Absolutely nothing. No brains. No power. No future. No hope. No God. *(Beat)* The only thing you believe in, is me. What are you, if you don't have me? Because I'm not afraid, see. I come up here every night. And I make my case. I make my point. I say what I believe in. I have to. I have no choice. You frighten me. So I come up here and I try to tell you the truth. I tear into you. I abuse you. I insult you. And you just keep calling. Why do you keep coming back? What's wrong with you? I don't want to hear any more. I've had enough. Stop talking. Don't call anymore. Go away. Bunch of yellow-bellied, spineless, bigoted, quivering, drunken, insomniac, paranoid, disgusting, perverted, voyeuristic, little obscene phone callers. That's what you are. *(Beat)* Well to hell with ya . . . I don't need your fear and your stupidity. You don't get it. It's wasted on you. Pearls before swine! *(Beat)* If just one person out there had any idea what I'm talking about! —Fred, you're on.

FROM "SEX, DRUGS, ROCK & ROLL"

(1991)

39

GRACE OF GOD

A man hobbles on a cane, holding an empty paper cup; he addresses the audience:

Good afternoon, ladies and gentlemen. I only want a few minutes of your time. It doesn't cost you anything to listen. Please be patient with me.

I just got released from Riker's Island, where I was unjustly incarcerated for thirty days for acts I committed during a nervous breakdown due to a situation beyond my control. I am *not* a drug addict.

This is the situation: I need your money. I could be out robbing and stealing right now; I *don't* want to be doing that. I could be holding a knife up to your throat right now; I *don't* want to be doing that . . . And I'm sure you don't want that, either.

I didn't choose this life. I want to work. But I can't. My medication costs over two thousand dollars a week, of which Medicaid only pays one-third. I am forced to go down to the Lower East Side and buy illegal drugs to stop the pain. I am not a drug addict.

If you give me money, if you help me out, I might be able to find someplace to live. I might be able to get my life back together. It's really all up to you.

Bad things happen to good people. Bad situations beyond my control forced me onto the streets into a life of crime. I won't bore you with the details right now. But if you don't believe me, you can call my parole officer, Mr. Vincent Gardello. His home number is 555-1768.

The only difference between you and me is that you're on the ups and I'm on the downs. Underneath it all, we're exactly the same. We're both human beings. I'm a human being.

I'm a victim of a sick society. I come from a dysfunctional family. My father was an alcoholic. My mother tried to control me. My sister thinks she's an actress. You wouldn't want the childhood that I had.

The world is really screwed up. Things get worse every day. Now is your chance to *do* something about it . . . help out somebody standing right in front of you instead of worrying about some skinny African ten thousand miles away. Believe me when I tell you God is watching you when you help someone less fortunate than yourself, a *human being*, like me.

I'm sorry my clothes aren't clean. I'm sorry I'm homeless. I'm sorry I don't have a job. I'm sorry I have to interrupt your afternoon. But I have no choice, I have to ask for help. I can't change my life—you can. Please, please look into your hearts and do the right thing! . . . Thank you.

(He addresses people in the front row, begging to one or two, while holding out his cup, saying, "Thank you very much," "God bless you," repeatedly. If money is given, he says, "Stay guilty." If money is withheld, he says, "I really feel sorry for you, man." Finally, he leaves, repeating over and over again, "Thank you," "God bless you" . . .)

40

BENEFIT

"Thank you," etc., from the last segment continues to a man addressing an imaginary "host" onstage. The man then seats himself in a chair. His accent is "British."

Thank you, Bill, thank you . . . nice to be back.

(Sits, attaches lavaliere microphone to shirt.)

Yes, yes, yes, yes, yes, yes . . . we're very excited about the success of the new album. It's nice having a number-one album again, you know, considering the band really hasn't done anything for about ten years . . . it's a real breath of fresh air . . .

(Picks up a glass of water from a small table on his left, sips the water.)

No . . . I don't, Bill . . . and I'm glad you asked me that question . . .

(Returns the glass of water to the table, then takes out a pack of cigarettes and a lighter. He taps out a cigarette as he speaks.)

I used to do quite a few drugs . . . But you know, Bill, drugs are no good for anybody. I've seen a lot of people get really messed up on drugs, I've seen people *die* on drugs . . .

(Lights cigarette, inhales deeply.)

I was saying to Trevor just the other day. I said, "Trevor, how is it that we managed to survive?" After Jimi died and Janis died and John died, I said to myself, Why didn't *we* die? We shoulda died. All the stuff we used to do.

Yes, Bill, I was. I was a bona fide drug addict. I used drugs every single day for five years.

What was it like? Well, I tell you, Bill. I used to get up every morning, before I even brushed my teeth, I would smoke a joint. While I was smoking the joint, I'd pop a beer. While I was sipping the beer, I'd cook up a spoon of cocaine, heroin—whatever was lying around. Shoot it right into my arm, get completely wasted . . . Flip on the telly, get high some more . . . maybe order up some lunch . . . have some girls over, get high with them . . . fool around with the girls, get high some more.

I did that every single day for five years.

It was horrible . . . it was horrible . . . I mean, it was wonderful, too, in its own way. I won't lie to you, Bill—my life is based on honesty today.

Yes, we did . . . we saw many tragic consequences. People very close to us. We had a sound engineer who had major problems with drugs . . . "Hoover" we called him. His problem was that he wasn't just our sound engineer, he was also in charge of getting the drugs for the band, because we always used to get very high whenever we cut an album. And I'll never forget, we were cutting the *Wild Horses* album, and Hoover shows up—

Oh, thank you, Bill . . . yes, it is a great album. A real rock classic.

. . . So we're cutting *Wild Horses*, and Hoover shows up with a coffee can full of the most amazing white flake Peruvian cocaine . . . absolutely pure, very wonderful . . . I don't know if you've ever done white flake Peruvian, Bill, but it's an experience. Wouldn't mind having a little bit of it right now! *(Laughs loudly; then remembers the audience)* Just joking, just joking!

So we took that can of cocaine, dumped it onto a table in the middle of the studio, cut out some lines, two, three feet long . . . Hoover would do three or four in each nostril—what a beast! Don't know where he had room in his skull for the stuff. And we started to play . . .

Of course, in those days we didn't just do coke. We did everything—it was heaven! Trevor was smoking Afghani hash 'round the clock. Nigel was in his crystal meth period, so we had that. Ronnie showed up with a large bottle of NyQuil. We were blind, we were so high . . . completely wasted.

And we started to play, and you know, Bill, we never played better. It was like we all had ESP; it was historic . . . Myself, I looked down at my fingers and I'm thinking, It's not me playing this guitar, it's not me playing this guitar. It's *God* playing . . . It was awe-inspiring.

(Loses his train of thought.)

What was I talking about? . . . Oh right—Hoover!

So we're playing this brilliant music for about an hour, and I happened to look up and there's Hoover in the sound booth, and well . . . he was smashing his head up against the glass. Blood is running down off his forehead all over his nose. His nose is all red with blood. Cocaine is shooting out of his nostrils onto his beard. His beard was all white. He looked like a deranged Sandy Claus.

Well, see, the thing is, the thing is, he forgot to push the "record" button. And he went completely stark raving mad. They had to take him away in a straitjacket. Took him to a sanitarium.

And the sad thing is, Bill, he was one of my closest friends in the whole world.

(Puts out his cigarette.)

What's that? . . . No . . . no . . . I don't know where he is today. I know he's somewhere. Probably still in an institution somewhere . . . Maybe he's watching right now. *(To camera)* Hoover, if you're watching . . . *(Makes a thumbs-up sign; then laughs)*

You see, Bill, that's the insidious thing about drugs—you don't realize . . . uh . . . I mean, you're having such a good time, you don't realize what a bad time you're having.

I got straight while I was on tour. Woke up one morning . . . typical tour situation: luxury hotel room, I don't even know where I am . . . beautiful naked girl lying next to me in the bed—don't know who she is, I don't know how she got there—champagne bottles all over the floor, cocaine on every horizontal surface. I hardly have the strength to lift my head. So I pick up the remote control and I flip on the telly.

And I was saved, Bill, I was saved.

You have a man on in this country, on TV all the time. Saved my life. White hair. A genius . . . Dr. Phil, Dr. Phil was on . . . What he said really hit me. He said: "If you haven't met your full potential in this life, you're not really alive." The profoundness struck me like a thunderbolt. I thought, That man is talking about me. He's talking about me.

Because here I was, young, talented, intelligent, wealthy, good-looking, very intelligent . . . and what am I doing with my life? I'm on drugs, day and night. I mean, I can understand if you're talking about some Negro guy or Puerto Rican guy in the ghetto on drugs—I can understand that. But in my case it was such a tragedy when you think about it. Such a waste of human potential. Such a waste.

Because, Bill, you can have your caviar breakfast, lunch and dinner, you can have your stretch limousines, your Concorde flights back and forth to London. Wads of cash, everyone treating you like God. Women willing to do whatever you want them to do . . . *whenever* you want them to do it. House in London, house in L.A., apartment in New York . . . home in the Bahamas . . . Bill, if it doesn't mean anything, what's the point? You know what I'm saying? Maybe not.

I straightened up and went cold turkey. Had all my blood changed. And I feel like I've been reborn. I can say today, "I like myself today. I'm not such a bad guy. In fact, I'm an amazingly wonderful human being." I'm honest enough to say that today. I've really come to terms with my own brilliance—it's not a burden anymore.

The rest of the band got straight, too, and today, we're just one big happy family. We just want to help other people.

Yes, yes . . . Well, that's why we're doing the benefit to aid the Amazonian Indians. I think they're Indians . . . the people down there in the Amazon . . . that we're helping . . . in the jungle . . . *(Calls off)* Billy? Are they Indians? . . . well whatever . . .

Yes! Well, Trevor has a home down in Rio, we go there every winter when it's summer down there. He has this lovely house-boy takes care of the house for him—"Nacho," we call him. He's actually not a boy; he's about fifty or so . . . lovely little guy, very brown, always smiling, very helpful.

Nacho knew we were into the environment, so he hired a boat to take us up the Amazon, take a look at the birds and the trees and the flowers and all that shit . . . So we're going along in this boat and we come to a turn in the river and there was this clearing, turned out it was an Indian village . . . whatever, and we all got out and took a walk around.

Bill, I've never seen such depressing poverty . . . children running around barefoot with the dogs in the dirt, no shoes . . . the women, half naked, breast-feeding their infants straight from their breasts . . . No running water. Couldn't even get a glass of water. I was parched. No Coke, no Pepsi.

The chief of the whole village came out to greet us. Man owned no clothing whatsoever. Completely naked—everything's showing, his willy hanging out and everything. All he had on was this carved piece of wood on his head with a feather sticking out. Couldn't even speak the Queen's English. It was heartbreaking.

I turned to Trevor and I said, "Trevor, we have to do something about this. We have to help these people. It's up to us, after all—'We are the world,' so to speak."

And so we decided to do the benefit. Now, I hate to say this, but so many of these benefits, they're just ego trips. They raise the money and just throw it at these people. Well, these poor buggers are primitive people—they've never seen money before. They don't know what to *do* with money. We found when we were down there that there were many things we had they really liked: digital wristwatches, Sony Walkmans, cigarette lighters, cigarettes . . . they *love* cigarettes.

So we're going to be buying these things for them up here with the money. Shipping them down. Try to improve their lives in a substantial way. Do some good for a change.

Thank you, Bill, thank you. It's nothing . . .

So I hope everyone watching can tune in when we're on MTV. Brought to you by Kronen-Bräu Beer, Remington Cigarettes . . . Have to say it, Bill, have to say it—sorry! The cigarette people have been fantastic, donated a truckload of cigarettes to hand out to the Indians . . . Or buy the album when it comes out. And remember that for every dollar you donate, fully twenty percent goes directly to the Amazonian Indians.

Bill, I'd like to say one more thing about drugs if I may. A lot of the kids watching right now buy our albums, learn the lyrics, memorize them, live their lives by them. So I know that everything I have to say is very, very important. And I'd like to say this about drugs: *(He looks directly and "meaningfully" at the audience)* I've done a lot of drugs. I had a lot of adventures on drugs. Some of my music has been inspired by drugs. In fact, I think it's safe to say I had some of the best times of my life on drugs. That doesn't mean *you* have to do them.

We were recently invited to the White House to do a special concert for Vice President Quayle and his lovely wife, Marilyn.

Oh, yes, she's hot . . . she's very hot. *(Aside)* I'll tell you a little story when we get off the air . . .

He's a wonderful man who, whatever you think of him publicly, in person, is a very caring, very sensitive, very intelligent man. He shared something with us that I would like to share with all of you tonight: The next time someone offers you drugs, remember you can always just . . . turn them in.

Thank you, Bill. Good night. *(He stands and gives the peace sign)* Cheers.

(He walks off.)

41

DIRT

A man shuffles and rants, scratching and coughing, grumbling in a gruff voice:

Fuckin' ya shit fuck piss, ya shit fuck piss, ya shit fuck piss . . . *(Coughs and spits, points at the ground)* What's that? What's that? It's shit, that's what it is . . . Shit on the ground, shit in the air, it's a bunch of shit if you ask me! You know what I'm talking about, you know what I'm talking about—we're living in a human garbage can, that's what I'm talking about . . . we're living in a human sewer . . .

(He picks at the seat of his pants, talking continuously to the audience:)

You can't walk down the street without stepping in some garbage, some dog mess, lumps and smears everywhere ya go . . . some cat piss . . . everything's drenched in piss. Pools of piss. Streams of piss. Rivers of piss. Rivers . . . rivers, the rivers! The rivers are polluted. They are! You know what I'm talking about . . . And where do the rivers come from, huh? They come out of the mountains, and the mountains are full of hikers and hunters and cross-country skiers. What are they doing? Pissing on every tree, shitting behind every bush. What do they care? Trees are gonna die from the acid rain anyway!

But you know what happens? You know what happens?

(He demostrates his storytelling with a kind of energetic mime:)

The acid rain, the acid rain runs down the tree and mixes with the piss and it makes a little brook and the little brooks flow into little streams. And the streams—where's the stream go, huh? Streams go down by the condos, where the pipes come out filled with more piss and shit and soap suds and tampons and puke from the drunken parties they have on Saturday night 'cause the houses are so ugly they have to be drunk just to live in 'em.

And the streams pour into the rivers and the rivers go by the factories, where they got bigger pipes spewing out chemicals and compounds and compost and arsenic and . . . and NutraSweet . . . and all that goes into the river.

And then the river gets bigger and it goes by the *city*, where they got even bigger pipes choked with all the slop from millions of toilets and garbage disposals and hospital bed pans and laundromats and car washes and fried-chicken places and pizza parlors and whorehouses and Ukrainian restaurants . . . And all this goes into the river, and the river goes down to the ocean.

And the ocean! What's the ocean? The ocean is just one big oil slick with all this shit being poured into it. But if that isn't enough—no, no, no! . . . *(Scratches and coughs)* . . . They gotta drag out these giant garbage scows filled with tons of burning plastic bags of garbage—they drag those around for a couple of months until they stink and are full of maggots and mildew, and dump those in, too.

And then rich guys ride around in their pleasure boats with their fishing poles, and they're drinking their beers and getting drunk and throwin' the empties over the side and pissing over the side and then they get seasick and puke up their steak tartare and caviar and crème brulée and their pâté! *(He pretends to vomit over the edge of the stage) Braaaaaahhhhhhh!!!!!* And all this stuff is going into the water!

And what else is in the water? Huh? Fishies, that's what. Millions and millions of little fishies are swimming around trying to get past the chicken bones and the orange peels and the syringes, and the little balled-up pieces of toilet paper floating by get stuck in their eye! They can't even see, there's so much stuff down there!

And they want to wipe their eyes but they can't 'cause they don't got hands, they got fins . . . So they go up to the top of the water to look around and they get all covered with oil and it goes in their gills and their hair, and they get all greasy and they drown . . .

And this seagull is flying by and he sees this greasy little fish floating there, so he comes down to get a free meal—oooops! Now he's stuck in the oil, too! And then a seal, he sees the seagull, now he's stuck in the oil, too—he drowns! Then the polar bear, he sees the seal, comes to eat him, he's stuck in the oil, too! Then . . . then the lion comes to eat the polar bear, he gets stuck in the oil, too . . .

And there you have it! That's the ocean: just a giant vat of oil, garbage and dead animals . . . just sloshing around there.

And then a hurricane comes. Then a tidal wave comes. And the whole mess splashes all over the beaches. And there you've got it. That's it. Millions and millions of dead fishes all over the beaches . . .

(Pause.)

And then you know what happens? The rats come, the rats come and they eat the fishies . . . and then, then the cats come and they eat the rats! And then the dogs come and they eat the cats! And then the dogs—you know what the dogs do? You know what they do! They shit all over the place, that's what they do!

Dog shit, horse shit, pigeon shit, rat shit. You can't go down the street without steppin' in something! *(Mumbling)* Fuckin' shit fuck piss. Shit fuck piss . . .

(He notices something on his foot, scrapes his foot on the edge of the stage.)

We're living in a human cesspool, we're living in a human septic tank. Living in a human toilet.

You know what I say? Flush the toilet, that's what I say! Flush the toilet! Flush the toilet! That's what I say!

(He hobbles upstage, his back to the audience.)

That's what I say . . .

(In the darkness, he vomits.)

BRAAAHHHHHHHHHGGGGGH!

42

THE STUD

A man speaks directly to the audience in a slow, easygoing drawl. He's drinking from a long-necked beer bottle.

— Sometimes, when I'm in a bar, having a drink with some fellas, one will make an idle comment like, "How does that guy do it? He always gets the girls!" I remain quiet when I hear such remarks. I like to keep a low profile with regard to my "extracurricular activities." I don't need to advertise. I know what I've got. And the ladies . . . hell, they know better than I do.

— I'm not so good-lookin'. I was athletic when I was younger, but I'm no Mr. Universe. I'm medium height, medium weight. Never really excelled at anything, certainly not school. As far as my job goes, they can all screw themselves.

— But you know what? I don't give a shit. 'Cause I've got what every guy—and every woman—wants. And all the looks, brains, money in the world can't buy it.

I'm "endowed."

(Takes a swig from his bottle.)

I've got a long, thick, well-shaped prick. The kind girls die for.

You're laughing. So what? Fuck you. Facts are facts. I'll hang out in some bar down on Wall Street around six o'clock, and in they all come, the guys with their health-club bodies and expensive Italian suits. Trying to compensate. The women—smart, fresh, pretty. I especially like the ones with the stiletto heels.

I pick out the prettiest one in the room. We start talking about this or that. I act like I'm going to buy her a drink, then save myself the money and say, "Why don't we get the hell out of here?"

Two hours later, I'm in some strange bedroom, blowin' smoke rings at the ceiling.

(He takes a swig from the bottle, places it on the floor.)

They love to tell me about their boyfriends and husbands. What wonderful men they are. So nice, so gentle, so dependable . . . so boring.

And they love to tell me what a wonderful cock I've got. So big, so hard, so unlike anything they've got at home. And they love to beg for more . . . and I love to give it to 'em.

Ever see a girl cry 'cause she's so happy? Ever have a lady beg to tear your clothes off? Ever see a woman faint because she's had such an intense orgasm? *(Scans the audience, looking for an answer)* I have.

It's like in school—that Greek guy—what was his name?—Plato, said everything in the world has a perfect example after which it is modeled. That's my sex life. Platonic perfection.

I know what you're thinking. This guy is pretty screwed up. He's lonely. He's obsessed. He's got no love in his life.

Don't tell me about love. I got love. I always keep the choicest for a daily visit . . . that's love. Right? Same as you, same as everybody.

But the point is, I got love, and I got all the others too. I see a girl walkin' down the street, I like the way she smiles—bingo—she's mine.

Some of 'em get scared after a while, go back to their boyfriends. That's fine with me. I understand—it's a lot to handle. Some get addicted, I get rid of them too.

But most of the time, they are very cool about it. Whenever I call 'em up, they drop whatever they're doin', whatever they're doin', and come to me. A couple of times, girls stopped screwing their boyfriends when I gave 'em a ring. They understand that this kind of quality and quantity is in limited supply . . .

Let's be honest—sex is what everyone is basically interested in. Great sex with great-looking great fucks. There are only so many to go around . . . I am one.

Sometimes I feel sorry for other people. *(Adjusts his crotch)* Sometimes I feel guilty. It's like I'm living in a color movie, everybody else is living in black-and-white. But then I think, Someone has to live out the dream. Somebody's got to have it all. Might as well be me.

43

STAG

A man, wearing a T-shirt, sleeves rolled-up, stands in the middle of the stage, a beer in one hand, an imaginary football in the other. He's about to throw the ball.

Terry! Terry! Go out for a long one! Go back! Go back! Go way back! *(Throws the ball)* Hey, watch out for the truck, man, watch out for the—oh . . . shhhhh—I told you to watch out for the truck! . . . Hey, I can't help it if you're uncoordinated . . . Yo, Terry, Terry, Terry, Terry, if you're goin' to the store to get bandages, get me a pack of cigarettes, please? Winston, hard pack . . . *(Contorting his posture)* Come on, man, *pleeeeeeassse!* . . . Thank you.

(He sips from his beer as he walks across the stage. Then he notices someone behind him. He spins around, giving a high-five.)

Hey, Joey, my man, that pot was great last night, man—you got to get us some more! Yeah, we smoked it all up . . . half pound only goes so far . . . Aaah, the party was great, it was great! You shoulda been there! Me and Frankie, we goes down the corner, we grabs Louie, we kidnaps him. We brings him up to the apartment. We got five cases of beer, three cases of champagne, four bottles of

Jack Daniels, an ounce of blow, and the half pound of pot. For the three of us, right?

Louie looks around, he goes, "What's all this?" I says, "What's all this?"! You're gettin' married tomorrow, man—this is your surprise stag party!"

Louie's lookin' around . . . He goes, "I gotta be at the church by ten o'clock—I can't get too wasted." And Frankie—Frankie's so funny, man, he's cutting lines on the counter, he's cutting lines and he goes, "Don't worry, man, we won't get you *too* wasted." *(Laughs a long, horsey laugh)*

Then Frankie—Frankie's so cool, man, he just goes like this . . . *(Snaps his fingers)* The bedroom door opens up and these three beautiful babes come waltzing out of the bedroom wearing bikinis . . . *(Laughs)* You shoulda seen Louie's face. He looked like he was gonna cry! . . . Yeah, yeah, they're friends of Frankie's— he told 'em if they hung out for the night he'd introduce 'em to Bruce Springsteen. I didn't even know he *knew* Bruce Springsteen. *(Pause)* Oh, he doesn't? Oh . . . So anyways . . .

So we start partying, man . . . champagne, cocaine . . . Frankie gets out these porno tapes, to warm up the ladies? The nice ones, man—the kind with, like, stories in 'em? One of 'em was so funny, man. How'd it go? Oh, yeah . . . There's this girl, right? And, uh, this chick, she's in her house, ironing her clothes, and there's a knock on the door and the guy goes, "It's the milkman—I have something for you!" Right? And he comes in . . . I don't think it was a real milkman . . . and they start screwing right on the ironing board. Very sensuous, very nicely done . . .

So then he leaves, and there's another knock on the door. And she goes, "Who is it?" And the guy outside goes, "It's—" Wait a minute . . . oh, yeah . . . "It's UPS, I have something for you!" And this guy comes in and he's holding this package like this, *(Indicates carrying a heavy box)* and she opens it up and—*his dick's inside*! Joe, what a riot! I never woulda guessed it in a million years. Huh? There was a hole in the box! And they do it . . . Then he leaves . . . takes his dick with him . . . And there's another knock on the door . . . and she says, "Who is it?" And . . . there's no answer.

So she goes over to look out the door—there's nobody there! She opens the door—there's nobody there! She looks down,

Joey—there's a *dog* out there! The dog comes trotting in . . . starts licking her feet, licking her legs . . . I can't watch it . . . I mean, what am I gonna tell the priest in confession? "Oh, yeah, I was watchin' dog porno tapes." "That's fifteen million Hail Marys, twenty million Our Fathers . . ." Hey, man, I don't got the time!

But listen, Joe . . . the girl I'm sittin' with? She's watchin' the whole thing! Oh, yeah, man . . . she's watchin' it. I turns to her, I says, "This stuff turn you on?" She says, "Sure. Why not?" Like it's the most normal thing in the world. The rest of the night, man, I'm like checking myself out for fleas!

Great party, man—we had food. I got the food together. You know how you always run out of potato chips? I bought *fifty* bags of potato chips. The ripple kind, the good kind? Clam dip . . . from the 7-Eleven . . . We spared no expense.

I'm sittin' there on the couch, man, and I'm thinkin' to myself, This is the best party I ever been to, man. I'm doing everything I love to do in the whole world! I got a beautiful girl sitting next to me . . . I'm watchin' TV . . . I'm eating clam dip . . . with a rippled potato chip! I'm smoking joints, I'm snortin' coke, I'm tossin'shots of Jack Daniels and I'm chasin' 'em with glasses of champagne! I'm thinking to myself, This is civilized! The president, the president doesn't get better than this. What more could you want?

And all of a sudden I got depressed, man. You know why? Because I looked over and I saw Louie on the couch and I thought to myself, He's never gonna have it like this again for the rest of his life. Really, man—think about it. Guys get married and they never have any fun anymore. Might as well shoot 'em in the head and bury 'em . . . No, come on, Joey. I'm gonna call up Louie six months from now and you know what he's gonna say? I'm gonna call him up and say, "Louie, come on, let's go out, let's play some pool or something." And he's gonna say, "No, I can't . . . I gotta go up to the mall with my wife, look for towels and sheets." Guy's had one towel, one sheet, for twenty-five years, now he needs new towels and sheets . . . Who puts those ideas in a guy's head? You know who! *(Sips beer)* You know fucking who!

So me and Frankie, we're getting wasted. Playing all the old party games—you know: who can snort the most coke, who can make his nose bleed first, who can toss the most shots, who can see double first . . . Getting totally hammered. You know when you're like *(Indicates)* this close to puking, but you don't puke? We were *there*, man—we were there all fucking night. Just sitting there feeling the brain cells die . . . "Oh, there goes the right side of my brain! *I'm a moron!*" *(Laughs)*

It was nice, man. Blacked-out three times! Woke up: Louie's over with this babe we hooked him up with, this Angela, he's kissing her, he's got his tongue in her ear, his hand up her shirt . . . Next thing we know, he's going in the bedroom with her . . . Hey, OK with me—he's not married yet, he's normal, he's got hormones. Go in the bedroom.

So I'm hungry, so I goes into the kitchen. I always get really hungry whenever I'm doing 'ludes, so I'm frying up these steaks. *(Mimes frying the steaks)* Joey, the whole trick to frying up steaks when you're on 'ludes is keeping your face outta the frying pan. *(Mimes nodding into the frying pan)* "Whoooooa! Keep burnin' my nose!"

Five minutes goes by . . . Angela comes tearing out of the bedroom, she says, "You guys gotta do something about your friend in there." "What? What?!"

Me and Frankie go running into the bedroom . . . Louie's sitting in the middle of the bedroom floor, shit-faced, crying his eyes out. No, Joey—really crying. He's sitting there going: "I changed my mind . . . I changed my mind . . . I don't want to get married anymore." I says, "Louie, Louie, you gotta get married, they already hired the hall . . . You gotta get married, Louie—ya grandmother made lasagne for four hundred people!" "I don't care! I don't care! I'm in love with *her!*" *(Points)*

He's in love with this Angela! Great! I'm trying to figure this thing out, I'm getting one of those brain tumor headaches . . . All of a sudden, I smell my steaks burning! We runs into the kitchen—and the kitchen, Joe, the kitchen was all like . . . fire . . . all different kinds of fire, burning everything up! So we're taking, like, champagne, we're pouring that on it, we're throwin' beer on it. Frankie goes and gets the TV set, throws that on it . . .

We finally get the fire out, right? The place stinks, it smells . . . Steaks stuck to the wall with clam dip . . . place is wrecked . . . Frankie goes, he goes, *(Laughing)* "Fuck the fuckin' party, man, the fuckin' party's fucked."

How does he think up those lines, man? He's funny—he should be on TV . . .

I says, "Wait a minute—apartment's finished, but the party's not finished! Let's go somewhere, have a nice sit-down dinner, have our party there."

So anyways, make a long story short, we decide to go down to the new McDonald's. So we walks into the McDonald's. First thing I see, four Hell's Angels sitting over there having something to eat. Fine, great. We sit over here . . . The girls are fooling around—you know the way girls get when they're drunk—they get silly. Louie, he's not eatin', he's in love with Angela, he's never gonna eat again for the rest of his life. Frankie, he's not eatin' 'cause every time he gets near Hell's Angels, that scar next to his eye starts to throb.

Me, I'm eatin'. I'm in a McDonald's, I'm gonna eat, I'm not gonna miss the opportunity.

So one of the girls, she takes my ketchup thing—you know, those things of ketchup, whatever you call 'em, ketchup bag—and she squeezes it, and the ketchup goes way up in the air, comes down, goes all over Frankie's shirt. She starts laughin' like this is the funniest thing she ever saw in her whole life. Right? Now all the girls, they start going hysterical.

The Hell's Angels, they see what happened, they start laughin', the manager of the McDonald's, he starts laughin', everybody who works there, they're all laughin'. People out in the parking lot, they're laughin'. Everybody in the whole world is laughin' at Frankie. Great, let's make an atom bomb while we're at it.

I goes over to Frankie. I says, "Frankie, let's go out and get some fresh air." He says, "In a minute." I says, "Frankie, there's four of them, there's three of us, let's get out of here now." He says, "In a minute."

Frankie stands up, he walks over to the biggest Hell's Angel. Guy isn't even a human being, he's just this side of a mountain, sitting there. Guy's got a shaved head, a tattoo of like Satan or Jesus or some fuck on his forehead, big bushy beard, ring through his nose. Guy's just sitting there, *(Imitates the Angel)* "Rah-blah-

blah." Frankie goes up to him like this: "Yo, chief . . . you lose this?" And he's got one of those like ketchup things in his hand. He just goes *spllllllt, frllllillt* . . . right in the guy's face!

Before the guy can even shake his head, Frankie's like *BANG! BANG! BANG!* right in the guy's face, kickin' his ass. Fortunately I thought ahead—I picked up one of those Ronald fucking McDonald trash cans. I toss it into the teeth of the guy sitting next to him. So I'm standing there crunching this guy's head. Louie comes over, he's good for nothing, falls on a guy. The girls, they're throwing french fries, hamburgers. The manager of the McDonald's, he comes running out with a fire extinguisher, sticks it in my ear, turns it on! Like I started it or something! What a rush! Frankie, he jumps over the counter, runs in the back, gets a big potful of that hot french-fry grease, throws it all over these guys . . .

Me, Frankie and Louie, we go running out to my car . . . Frankie jumps in, tries to start my car, trying to start the car, car won't start—as usual—gotta get a new starter. I'm sitting there, I'm praying . . . Louie's in the backseat, he's got the door wide open, hanging out the door, he's goin', "*Angela!* ANGELA!" I says, "Louie, get inside the car, lock the door, come on!"

And that guy, that inhuman mountain guy? Like nothing even happened to him, Joey. He just stands up, starts walkin' right at us in the car, *(Mimes a Frankenstein-style walk)* right through the plate glass window of the McDonald's, man! Boom!

We're just about to take off, the guy reaches out, grabs Louie's leg. Louie grabs me around the neck. Frankie hits the gas, we're pulling this whale all over the parkin' lot. Frankie's trying to scrape the guy off on trash cans, the curb, over those little McDonald bushes they got everywhere. Nothing's workin'. I'm going, "Louie, Louie, hit the guy, kick him, do something!" And Louie—I don't know if he did it on purpose or what—he just turns around, pukes all over the guy's face . . . *(Laughs)* He let go of him *then*, man!

Louie passes out into the backseat of the car. We slam the door shut, take off like a bat outta hell! *(Laughs, really enjoying himself)* It was fuckin' great, man!

(Catches his breath.)

But you know what was really great, man? What was like the icing on the gravy? We're driving, we're like five miles away, the action's behind us. We're not even going that fast—maybe seventy, seventy-five. And I turns to Frankie and I says, "Frankie, why'd you start all that shit, man? I mean, we coulda gotten killed back there!" And you know what he says, Joey? He doesn't even look at me—he just keeps drivin'—and he goes, "Sometimes you gotta spit in the devil's eye . . . just to make sure you're alive." *(Slow smile)* Think about that. Hit my brain like a rock.

I'm sitting there and I looks at Louie passed out in the backseat, dreamin' about towels and sheets . . . I looks at Frankie drivin' the car, smokin' a joint, a beer between his legs, the music's blastin', and I thinks to myself, Yeah, man, yeah—this guy knows what he's talking about. He's never gonna sell out. He's gonna live until the day he dies. *(Raises his fist)* Rock on, man, no surrender!

We drove all the way out to the beach, man . . . we made a little fire on the beach and we just stayed up all night smokin' joints. Smoked up that whole half pound of pot, man. Didn't even talk. I thought about what he said all night, man. It was heavy.

Watched the sun come up. And I thought about all the water in the ocean. There's a lot of water out there. And that water's just little drops. And I'm like a little drop of water in the world. So I might as well party, man. Might as well party. *(Laughs)* Sun comes up and Louie wakes up, stumbles down to the beach. He goes: "I gotta be at the church at ten o'clock."

He's got puke all over him, he wants to go to church!

So we throw Louie in the backseat of the car, we start driving to the church, run outta gas a mile down the road . . . Huh? Naw, we got there, we got there. A little late . . . around twelve-thirty . . .

Yeah, they gotta postpone it to next Saturday. Big deal. It's OK. Louie's OK . . . Louie's grandmother got one of those little heart attacks.

But listen, Joey—next week, Friday night, we're gonna have another surprise stag party for Louie. Don't tell nobody . . .

Listen, Joey—one thing. *(He turns and pees against the back wall, then turns back, zips up)* . . . If you're gonna come . . . no girls . . . They cause too much trouble . . .

44

BOTTLEMAN

A man talks quickly, nervously, rarely looking up. He constantly hitches his pants and pats his hair. His over-cheerful manner covers his fear. He's making conversation with an imaginary listener. He begins by talking to the wall.

I don't like to complain. I'm not a complaining kind of guy. I'm a happy kind of guy—runs in my family—happiness. Never been sick in my life. Not one day. Unless you count broken bones, which I don't. But I like to stay positive. Stay on the sunny side of the street. You give me a pack of cigarettes, egg salad sandwich, cup of coffee, a newspaper, someplace to sit down, and I'm happy—I'm happy.

(Turns, paces, then stops.)

I don't even need the cigarettes. I should quit anyway. It's a dirty habit. Unhealthy. Expensive. Of course you can always find cigarettes. People always have cigarettes—they'll give 'em to you. Food's another subject altogether. People aren't exactly walking around with an egg salad sandwich in their pocket—unless they're crazy! And you figure, egg salad sandwich's gonna run you maybe seventy–eighty bottles. I'm findin' maybe fifty bottles a day— you're talking a shortfall of about twenty bottles . . . or cans . . . bottles or cans, it doesn't make much difference.

(Walks in another direction, paces, stops.)

Back in the old days, I used to weigh a lot more than I do now. Used to be on a diet all the time. Always trying to lose weight. I don't have that problem anymore. I'm on the egg salad sandwich diet now. One egg salad sandwich every two days . . . you lose weight like crazy. The fat just flies off . . . and it stays off. I'm gonna patent it. Get a copyright and put an ad in the newspaper. Make a little money.

See, newspapers—newspapers, you can get. You can always find a newspaper, people just leave 'em around. And I read 'em. I wanna know about the world.

(His pacing has brought him completely upstage, his back to the audience.)

It's important to stay informed. I read about a train in Japan goes three hundred miles an hour, gets you there in no time. They got hotels for cockroaches now, hotels for mice. I stay away from hotels. Too much money—who's got that kinda money? Ten bucks a night—forget it. You figure that's two hundred bottles—bottles or cans—and that's not in my budget.

(He faces the audience, talking to them in a detached way:)

But it's not a problem. You can always find someplace—there's always someplace to stay. You wedge yourself in someplace. The real problem is the concrete. The stone. They make everything out of rocks and cement! Too hard. What ever happened to wood? Used to be all the buildings were made out of wood. Used to make benches outta wood. But no more. Because they make wood outta trees, and trees, they don't got them no more.

I saw this tree . . . there was this tree, beautiful tree . . . they dug a hole and put it in the sidewalk. Every day I come to say hello. And this guy was backing up his truck. The truck was making that beep sound—*beep-beep-beep-beep*—right over the tree, 'cause, see, the tree can't hear that. See? That was it for the tree. That was it. What are you gonna do? It's just in the nature of a tree that if you run 'em over they die. They're not like people—they can't take the abuse.

Take a tree, replace it with a metal pole, then there's no problem. Truck hits the pole, that's it. But you lose the leaves. You lose the leaves and the twigs. You lose the wood. Wood is good.

(Paces.)

(Suddenly) Dogs like wood. I know. I used to have a dog. Walked him every day. I used to say, *(Miming walking the dog)* "Come on! Come on! . . . Who takes care of you? Who takes care of you? *I* take care of you . . . Who's gonna take care of *me* in my old age? Who's gonna take care of me?" That's what I used to ask him.

He ran away. But that's OK—they gotta eat, too, the little ones. Everybody's gotta eat, sooner or later. It's human nature. It's human nature. I like to eat. I like to eat. Kind of a habit of mine, food. *(Holds an imaginary sandwich in front of his face)* Nice egg salad sandwich. Cup a coffee . . . Cream. Sugar.

I'm cutting down on the coffee. I don't drink much coffee these days. Sixty cents a cup. Where did they come up with that figure? That's the question I want to ask. Should be ten cents! But they got ya, see, they got ya. 'Cause they got the beans. They got the beans. You got no choice. They got a cartel. This OPEC.

But I don't need coffee. I don't need the coffee. People drink coffee to stay awake—I don't need to stay awake. I'm awake! I'm awake! When I'm asleep I'm awake. You gotta keep your eyes open when you're sleeping, 'cause you find a place to lie down and you don't keep your eyes open and a guy comes back with a baseball bat and that's it—*bang bang*—you're dead!

No more coffee, no more cigarettes—that's it!

See, these guys on the street, they like to fight. I don't got that luxury. I'm on my second set of teeth. I'm missing a kneecap. I can't hear in one ear. I'm like the bionic man without the hardware. I'm no Cassius Clay. I'm no Cassius Clay.

But I stay on the sunny side of the street. I stay on the sunny side of the street. A guy once told me, "Life is like a half a glass of water . . . half a glass of water . . ."

(He loses his train of thought: his hand starts shaking, holding an imaginary glass.)

"You got a half a glass a water . . ." And . . . uh . . . "You should drink the water." That's what he said . . .

(Sheepish—he didn't get the saying right—he turns away, then laughs at himself.)

No, that isn't what he said . . . He said . . . he said . . . "Half a glass of water is better than no water at all"! That's it. "Half a glass of water is better than no water . . ."

(Pulls himself together.)

I look at it this way—I could be living in Ethiopia. Those poor people got it terrible. They got nothing to eat. Starving all the time. They just sit in the sand all day long . . . It's too sunny, too many flies . . . it's not for me. It's not my bag. I prefer it here . . . it's better here.

    (Lost in thought, convincing himself) It's good here, it's good. It's good. Thank God!

(He stands there, staring at the ground. Then he snaps out of it, and is sunny and cheerful again. He addresses the audience:)

Well, I gotta get going, got to get to work. You know what they say: "The early bird catches the can!" Or bottles . . . bottles or cans, it don't make no difference . . .

    (He turns away, walking upstage) It don't make no difference at all . . .

45

CANDY

The sound of a push-button phone being dialed; then a recorded sexy voice is heard:

Hi, I'm Candy. I'm glad you called. I was just about to take a really, really erotic bath, and I thought, Wouldn't it be nice if a really, really horny guy called up so I could tell him all about it while he plays with himself? . . . I can't think of anything sexier than having a really, really horny guy listening to my deepest and most . . . intimate . . . erotic fantasies . . . It gets me sooooo excited, I feel all tingly and pink, it makes me just want to pull off all my clothes and dance around the room, listening to some really, really hard rock. Ooooooh, I get goose bumps just thinking about it! Sometimes when I'm really, really horny I have to call just two or three of my best girlfriends up and they come over and we get super naked and rub olive oil all over each other and then do really really vigorous aerobics while listening to Steely Dan! Wow, just thinking about it is getting me all sweaty! I better take a bath! Ohhhh, my bathtub's all filled up, and I'm ready to jump in and scrub myself all over. But wait! Now I'm all sudsy, so I better take a long shower and loofah myself in all my intimate places.

And NOW I'm going to get out the fluffiest towel I can find and just rub and rub and rub-a-dub-dub. How's that sound? Fun? You bet! And then I get dressed again! How cool is that?

If you want to "come" along, call me back and press two on your touch-tone phone for more erotic adventures. I can't wait.

46

ROCK LAW

Lights up on a man sitting in an office chair, rolling across the stage. He jumps out of the chair, shouting into a hand-held phone. He paces as he yells into the phone:

Frank, Frank, Frank . . . what did he say? He's gonna sue me? He's gonna sue me? Did you tell him who he's messing with here, Frank? Did you tell him who he's *fucking* with here, Frank? He's fucking with *God*, Frank—did you tell him that? Did you tell him what God *does* when he gets fucked with, Frank? Ever hear of Sodom and Gomorrah, Frank? That's what I'm gonna do to his *face*!

No, no, no, no, no, Frank—I don't want to hear it. Sue me? Sue me? I'm gonna blow him away, Frank, I'm gonna peel his skin off, I'm gonna chew his bones, I'm gonna drink his blood, I'm gonna *eat his children*, Frank!

And I'm gonna enjoy myself. You wanna know why? Because he's a schmuck, a schlemiel, and a shithead for fucking with me, that's why! He should know better! . . .

No, no, no, Frank—I'm not listening to another word! *(Sings loudly)* La-la-la-la, la-la-la-la! Sue me? *Sue me?* Call him back right now and tell him . . . tell him . . . *Wait*—don't call him back, don't call him . . . Call his children, call his children, and tell them to *get ready to be eaten*! Good-bye, Frank!

(He yells into an intercom:)

DIANE! DIANE! Who's on line one? . . . My wife? Put her on hold . . . What's for lunch? I'm starving to death . . . I don't care. Anything . . . I don't care, Diane, anything—*I am starving to death*! *(Pause)* No, I don't want that! *(Pause)* No, I don't want that, either . . . No monkfish . . . no monkfish, no arugula, no sun-dried tomatoes, no whole-wheat tortellini . . . I want *food*, Diane—you know what I mean when I say "food"? Diane, unlike you, I am a human being, I need food, I need coffee—please get me some . . . Call Jeff Cavanaugh, put him on line two—call Dave Simpson, put him on line three . . . *Thank you!*

(Taps a button on his hand-held phone, becomes cordial and familiar:)

Hi, honey . . . I know! I tell her time and time again, "Don't put my wife on hold," she puts you on hold. I'm sorry. What did you do today? . . . That's nice—how much did that cost? . . . No, no, no! Spend the money—that's what it's there for . . . That's what it's there for . . . *(Rubs his forehead)* How's Jeremy? . . . Why did he do that? No, no—why did he bite the kid, Sonia? . . . I told him to? I did not tell him to bite anybody . . . Sonia, I did not tell him— Don't tell me what I tell him . . . I told him— Can I talk, please? I told him, "The next time a little boy does something to you, do twice as much back to him." That's what I told him . . . I don't care what his therapist says! I don't care what his therapist says—his therapist is a co-dependent dysfunctional fraud! . . . No, no, wait—you know what I'm going to tell Jeremy? I'm gonna say, "Jeremy, bite your therapist!" Let him work on that for a while.

What else? . . . —How did she do that? How did she get it in the microwave, Sonia? . . . No, wait, that's what?—three microwave ovens in two years? . . . We have to buy another microwave now? . . . No, no, I just want to say something: If you hired people who came from a country where they had electricity, we wouldn't have this problem . . . Well, you gotta tell her . . . What do you mean, "She'll quit"? . . . She won't quit—she's got it great. She spends all day in a luxury New York apartment! I spend all day in this office killing myself so she can spend all day in my luxury New York apartment! She spends more time there than I do! I AM NOT SHOUTING! *(Lowers his voice)* I am not . . . This is not shouting . . . Am I shouting? Now wait a minute, am I shouting? Is this shouting? This is not shouting—this is discussing. We are discussing . . . we are having a discussion. *(Patronizing)* Well, obviously you're too agitated to have a normal conversation right now, so why don't we wait until I get home . . . I'm gonna be a little late tonight . . . Around nine . . . I have a lot of work to do! Sonia, do you think I like slaving and sweating here all hours of the night and day so that you and Jeremy can be safe and free? Do you? It hasn't been two weeks . . . It hasn't been two weeks, we just did it the other— OK, OK . . . we'll have sex tomorrow night, all right? . . . I won't forget—I'll put it in my book!

Listen, honey, I've been working very hard. Next month, we'll go down to St. Barth's, we'll get a place by the beach, we'll make love every day on the beach . . . You won't get sand in your skootchie! Look, I gotta get off, I got twenty people on hold . . . Huh? . . . No, don't color your hair—no, don't cut your hair, either! Nothing with your hair . . . Don't start with the hair blackmail now . . . No henna, nothing! I want you to look the same when I get home tonight as you did when I left this morning, that's what I want . . . I gotta get off . . . Give Jeremy a kiss good night for me, OK? Say hi to your mother for me, too . . . OK, all right . . . What?! . . . Orange juice. Fine. OK . . . I love you, too . . . I'll be home around ten-thirty . . . Bye!

(Goes over to the intercom:)

Diane, what are you doing in there, *growing the food*?! Come on! I feel like a poster child for Ethiopian Relief. My ribs are sticking out, flies are crawling all over me, I'm gonna be dead in five minutes—come on!

(He punches a button on his phone, starts to speak, then relaxes into his chair. He begins to have a very casual conversation:)

Jeff? Hey, man, how they hanging? . . . Not bad, not bad . . . Yeah, I finished that deal yesterday . . . No, I made twenty grand—chump change. Listen to this, man—this morning I cut a deal I made seventy-five grand. You know what they say: "A hundred grand here, a hundred grand there—pretty soon you're talking real money." . . . I don't know—maybe I'll buy a Porsche for the country house, park it in front of the tennis court, piss off my neighbors. Not even drive it, just leave it there all the time . . . Huh? No, I can't drive it—I don't drive a stick . . . That's an idea—Range Rover, they're good. Very ecological, right? Maybe I'll get one of those . . . Naw, I can't, not tonight. I'm doin' something . . . *Who* am I doin'? I'm not telling you. Jeff, I tell you, you're gonna tell Nadine and she'll tell Sonia . . . Very beautiful . . . Better . . . Better than her . . . Better than her . . . Yeah, she has breasts—yeah, she has legs, she has arms, she has a head. I got the whole package. Jeff, the closest you ever came to a girl this beautiful is that time you bought the scratch-and-sniff picture of Britney Spears . . . ha-ha . . . And get this—she's an artist. She's very, very sensitive. She picked me up in a bar—how could I say no? . . . Jeff, unlike you, I am still committed to my idealism. I'm still committed to experience and exploration . . . Unfortunately, you gave up the struggle a long time ago; but for me, it's a matter of principle.

Why don't we get together tomorrow night, play some handball, have a couple of pops over at my club? . . . No, *my* club, my club, Jeff. My club is nicer than your club—it's safer, it's cleaner, it's more exclusive . . . *(Stands up)* OK? I gotta get off the phone, I have a lot of work to do, unlike you . . . Thank you . . . thank you. I am a genius. I am the best. No one can get close to me. I'll let *you* get close to me, Jeff, you can blow me . . . Bye!

(Pushes more buttons on his phone and keeps talking, with a more aggressive, impatient tone, pacing once again:)

Dave, Dave, can I say just one thing here? I agree with you one hundred and fifty percent! . . . No, no, Dave, the man is a wonderful human being, he's a mensch, he's a lovely person . . . I love him, I felt terrible having to let him go . . . Yes, I understand that, I know he's fifty-eight years old . . . I know he's gonna lose his pension . . . I understand that, but Dave, Dave, Dave, Dave! . . . There's two sides to this argument—don't forget the human side of the equation! . . . Now, when I first came to work at this company, this man was like a father to me—he's like my own father, this guy. I love him—we're like blood relatives . . . It broke my heart to *have to fire him*, Dave! . . . Yes, yes, yes . . . I know he's going in for major surgery next week—that's not my problem, I'm not his doctor, Dave, I'm his boss . . . No . . . no . . . no . . . but—but—but—but Dave! Dave! Now you've been talking for five minutes straight, can I get a word in edgewise here? The guy . . . the guy is not performing anymore. He's not hustling anymore. He's easy-listening and this place is rock-and-roll! I need heavy metal here, Dave—I need production—I need performance! . . . Yes, but Dave, Dave, Dave! Let me make it a little clearer for you: You like your Mercedes station wagon? You like your country house? You like your swimming pool? You like skiing in Aspen? You like long lunches, your car phone, that horsey school you send your daughter to? What pays for those things, Dave? Now, wait—what do you think pays for those things? . . . Profits, that's what—say "profits," Dave! Say "profits" . . . I just want to hear you say it . . . Say it! Thank you . . .

Now, now, now, Dave, when the profit ax comes down, anybody's head can roll. I could lose my job tomorrow, you could lose your job tomorrow. You could lose your job today, you could lose your job in the next five minutes if we keep up this stupid conversation. Because, to tell you the truth, Dave, I want to get rid of the guy even more now, because now he's wasting *your* time as well as mine. You're wasting your time, I'm wasting my time, all these people in this company are wasting their time around here, and I have to say to myself, What's the point? What's the point, Dave? What's the point? What is your fucking goddamn point?! WILL YOU TELL ME WHAT YOUR FUCKING GODDAMN POINT IS, PLEASE?

Dave? . . .

You're not sure? Well, let me ask you this: Are you happy working for this company? . . . No, I mean, are you happy working for this company? . . . You are? Good, because I just want you to be happy . . . so get back to work.

(Suddenly laughs) OK . . . All right . . . No, no—no hard feelings. We've all been working hard . . . OK . . . All right, I understand . . . Call anytime . . . Say hi to Judy for me . . . Janet? . . . Say
hi to Janet . . . OK . . . All right . . . Take care.

(He switches off, then yells into the intercom:)

DIANE, LET ME MAKE IT EASY FOR YOU: TAKE YOUR
HAND, PUT IT IN THE MICROWAVE, GRILL IT, BRING
IT IN TO ME! WHO'S ON LINE FOUR? . . .
　　I GOT IT.

(Pushes more buttons on his phone; then, very relaxed, sultry:)

Hi . . . Nothing . . . I'm making money—what else do I do? . . . I'm
working very hard . . . now that you called, it's getting harder and
harder . . . Um-hmmmm . . . You being a good girl? . . . Oh, yeah?
What are you doing? . . . Making a sculpture, that's interesting.
What kind of sculpture? . . . You made a sculpture of a horse and
you wrote the word "horse" all over it? That's very conceptual,
Yvette . . .

(He checks his watch, stifles a yawn.)

What do you mean, I sound bored? Of course I'm not bored,
I love talking about your art! I was just telling someone ten minutes ago what wonderful art you have . . . Yvette, Yvette, can
I just say something? . . . No, can I say something? . . . If you
were ninety-five years old and you were in a wheelchair, I would
still love you, and you want to know why? Because I love your
art, that's why . . . Of course I mean it, of course I mean it—and
when you say these mean things to me I get all angry and confused
. . . and . . . and I feel like coming over there and . . . giving you a
good spanking!

*(The serious look on his face melts into pleasure as he listens to what she's
going to do to him.)*

Ooohhh . . . that would hurt! All over my body! And then what are you going to do? . . . The whole thing?! The phone is heating up, Yvette—stop it! . . . No, not that! Anything but that . . . *(Laughs)*

What did I do to deserve all this attention? I am a pretty nice guy, aren't I? . . . Um-hmm . . . I love you, too. I love you, too . . . Of course I mean it. Yvette, when I say I love you, I mean I love you. No one else in the whole world knows what love means the way that I know what love means when I say from me to you: "I love you." No one was ever loved before the way that I love when I love you. Because my life would have no meaning if I didn't love you.

(Through all of the above, he has become fascinated with a smudge of dirt on his shoe. He's been picking at it as he speaks, and now is totally engrossed in the smudge, but he keeps talking without missing a beat.)

Of course I mean it, of course I mean it. Would I lie to you? . . . *(Checks his watch)* Listen, Yvette, the boss just walked in—I gotta get off . . . When am I going to see you? . . . Around six? At the loft? OK . . . I will . . . Keep making those sculptures . . . Ciao to you, too.

(He blows her a noisy kiss over the phone, switches off, then lurches at the intercom:)

Diane, cut the food, cut the coffee. Send in the Maalox, the shoe-shine boy, and hold my calls. Thank you!

(Blackout.)

47

X-BLOW

A man in silhouette declaims to a rap beat:

I'm a child of nature, born to lose—
people call me "Poison" but that's no news.
When I wake up in the morning, I see what I see,
I look into the mirror, what I see is me:
A player, a winner, an unrepentant sinner—
if you mess with me, I'll eat you for dinner.
There are those that rule and those that serve,
I'm the boss, baby, 'cause I got the nerve
to take what I want, take what I need,
cut you first, sucker, and make you bleed.
'Cause life's a bitch, that I know.
Don't misunderstand me or then you'll go
to your grave in a rocket, nothing in your pocket,
if you got a gun, you better not cock it,
'cause then you'll die, that I know,
what's left of you away will blow
and you will spend eternity

praying to God you never met me!
Huh-huh-huh-huh-huh!

(He steps into the light and addresses the audience, telling his story in a friendly manner:)

Sucker dissed me, man, he dissed me! I had no choice. He showed me his gun, so I walked up to him, I stuck my screwdriver into his belly, and I ran it right tru his heart. He looked surprised, man. Skinny kid like me, killing him like dat. Hah. Didn't even bleed.

Felt good, man, felt better than gettin' laid on a sunny day. And I like to feel good. Feeling good makes me feel good. Don't need no sucker drugs to feel good.

'Fore they locked me up I used to get up every morning and I had me two problems: How to find money, how to spend it. All the rest was gravy. Like the man says, "Don't worry, be happy."

That was the Reagan years, and the Reagan years is over, man, and I miss 'em! Ronnie Reagan, he was my main man. He had that cowboys-and-Indians shit down. Now he's out in L.A. sitting on a horse and we're sitting in the shit he left behind. But it's OK he's gone. New man's in charge! *Batman!* Batman is my man!

Gonna be beaming around like Kirk and Scotty, like the Jetsons, man! Just beaming around, beaming around. Jump into my Batmobile, get behind some smoked bulletproof windshield, stick in the CD, flip the dial to ten, rock the engine, burn the brakes . . . Man, that's living . . . you can smoke that shit!

You only live once, you gotta grab that gusto shit.

My best friend in school went to work at McDonald's—worked hard too! First he 'came 'sistant manager, then he 'came manager. Guess he figured if he worked hard enough, one day he's gonna be president of McDonald's. Making four-fifty a week, had it nice, man. Had himself a duplex rental 'partment and a Ford Escort.

One Friday night some homeboys came in with a .38-special, greased him for the receipts, man . . . Bang, bang in the back of the head—execution style!

Sucker! He missed the whole point! He's standing on that platform and that train be gone!

See, you wanna play the game, you gotta think about the big guy, you gotta think about God! God made man same as hisself. You wanna learn how to live, live like God! Check the big guy out!

God, man, he gets up every morning, he don't smoke no crack, he don't shoot no dope. God don't flip no burgers. No, man— he gets up and he looks down on the world and he says, *(Hands on hips)* "World, what am I gonna do with you today?" *(Stretches out his arms)* "Lessee, how about this, I will make an earthquake today . . ." "Or how about dis, a tidal wave?" "Or, lessee, maybe I'm a little bored, I think I will crack up some trains in India, kill me up some dot-heads . . ." "Or maybe I'm feeling a little evil, maybe I jus' burn down an elementree school, fry up some nine year olds . . ." "Or maybe I'm feeling real evil, I'll mix up some new disease, sprinkle it all over them homosexual faggots, fuck 'em up, make 'em miserable, make 'em cry and die a slow evil death!"

See, God's a player, he likes the action! God likes to rock, he likes to get high . . . But God don't shoot no dope, he don't shoot no dope—he lets the dopes shoot each other!

Man, I *know* how he feels! . . . 'Fore I was in the joint, used to get me a ten-gauge shotgun, shoot me up some sewer rats. You hit one square, they just vaporize. Like with a ray gun! Makes a nice sound too—BOOM! That must be what it's like to be God, lots of noise and destruction and fun!

See—people, they don't *understand* God. Last summer I was running down the street in my home neighborhood. Typical day for me—guy's chasing me, wants to put a bullet in my head . . . So I jumps inside of this church, middle of the day . . . and there be this buncha little kids in the church with their teacher. Prayin'. In the middle of the day. Little tiny heads, little tiny butts. I said, "Yo, teacher, whachoo be doin' in this here church for in the middle of the day?" She says, "Boy, we's in here prayin'—we's prayin' for peace, we's praying against nuclear disarmament."

Hah! I starts laughin'. I says, "Baby, you be prayin' in the wrong place! This here's God's house. You best go pray someplace else. Who you think make all that war shit up in the first place? Who you think make that nuclear bomb up, made up the poison gas and dynamite, rockets and bombs? They's his toys, baby!" I's laughin' so hard, I fell right down on the *floor* of the church, my gun fell outta my pocket, went off, shot a hole right true the cross on the altar!

See you gotta figure: You wanna run with the big guy, you gotta think big. That's what I do—I think bigger every day. 'Cause God, that's where all the power is. I want to get closer to the power, I want to get more and more spiritual, get closer to God.

That's why next time I gets out, I'm gonna get me some new wheels and an Uzi, man.

Peoples, you gotta wake up, smell the coffee.

(Turns to go.)

"What goes around comes around." If you can't dig that shit, you better get out of Gotham City. *(Walks off)*

48

LIVE

A man walks to the edge of the stage, cigar in hand. He stands erect, chest thrust forward. Gruff, New Jersey accent:

JIMMY! I'm out in the backyard, here! Come out to the backyard!

(Feels his belly) Ugghhh . . . every time I have the fried calamari with the hot sauce, I feel like I'm gonna blow up!

So what do you think? . . . Olympic size, Olympic size! I said to the guy, "I want the best pool you got—gimme the biggest, the best pool you got! I don't care what it cost!"

I got a motto, Jimmy, very simple: "Take care of the luxuries, the necessities will take care of themselves." You only live once, Jimmy—you gotta go for the best in this life, you gotta grab all the gusto you can.

I dunno, one hundred grand? It's not important. It's like when I was buying my BMW . . . I says to myself, I can buy the 750 or I can save a little money, buy a 535 . . . But then I thinks to myself, I buy the 535, I'm in the middle of the highway someplace, 750 passes me, I'm gonna get pissed off! Another eight hundred, nine hundred bucks a month—why waste the aggravation, buy the 750!

You should get yourself a BMW, Jimmy . . . What do you mean you can't afford it, of course you can afford it, don't give me that crap! . . . You know what's wrong with people like you, Jimmy?—and I'm just trying to be helpful here—you're full of crap, see? The only thing that's stopping you from having the car of your dreams is fear. You're afraid. You're afraid to have, you're afraid to own, you're afraid to live.

How much are you making now a year? Nineteen grand a year? Twenty-two grand a year? Get yourself a BMW! What are you afraid of? . . . You gotta live, Jimmy—that's what life is all about. I want to buy something, I buy it! I want to go someplace, I go there!

See this cigar? This is a Havana cigar. Why do I smoke Havana cigars? Because it's the best cigar, that's why. I could smoke something else. I could save myself fifteen bucks a pop, I could smoke something else. Why should I? So somebody else can smoke this cigar? Fuck him, it's my cigar . . . It's my cigar—it's my life and I'm living it.

I exercise. Now we got the pool, I come out here every morning, I jump in the pool, I swim a whole lap. Then I go in the house, I have a healthy breakfast. I eat those oat bran muffins. I can't stand 'em, but I eat 'em, they're supposed to be good for you . . . I have four or five muffins, scrambled eggs, bacon, sausage . . . big pot of black coffee, and I'm alive, Jimmy, I'm alive!

I'm sixty-one years old—I still make love to my wife like it's our wedding night. I know guys ten years younger than me, they don't even know they got a dick! They're in the shower in the morning: "La . . . la . . . la, la—oh! What's that?" They think it's a growth sticking out of their body!

(Smokes his cigar, contemplates the horizon:)

See that there—you know what that is? That's a gazebo. Guy who sold me the pool, he says you gotta have a gazebo if you're gonna have a swimming pool. That's the best one they make—cost me five grand. I don't even know what it is.

(Puffs contentedly on his cigar.)

See, perfect example of what I'm saying here . . . Vito Schipletti! Never did nothing in his life. He never smoked, he never drank, he never chased skirts, never gambled, never walked when it said: "Don't walk"! You know where he is today with all his money in the bank? He stands in front of the old candy store from nine o'clock in the morning till nine o'clock at night. He lived his life so good, he forgot to live . . . What's the point of being alive like him? You might as well be dead!

Jimmy, they tell you cigars take three years off your life. What three years? What three years? Eighty-six to eighty-nine? Who needs 'em! Gimme the cigars!

There are people, Jimmy, all over the world, starving to death, in Africa and Asia, Armenia, they sit around all day starving . . . just sitting in the dirt. Those people, all they got is dreams. They dream, "What would it be like to live in America? What would it be like to have a car, a house, food, a swimming pool . . ." Jimmy, I can't let those people down . . . I'm here, I'm living it, I might as well enjoy it . . .

I read in a magazine about a new resort in Hawaii where you can swim with the dolphins—*Bingo!*—I'm there. They open a new casino down Atlantic City, I'm there the first day it opens . . . They make a new TV set, ten feet wide, two stories high, I buy it. 'Cause it's my life, Jimmy, it's my life. If I don't live it, who's gonna? I'm gonna live until the day I die, then I can rest.

(Moves to the edge of the stage, very close to Jimmy) You know what you need, Jimmy? You need a nice swim in my new swimming pool . . . Put on your suit, come on! Snap out of it! *(Bends over the edge of the stage and tests the "water")* The water's not cold—jump in!

49

DOG CHAMELEON

A man sits in a chair, talking into a microphone with suppressed anger. He tries to be pleasant.

Hey, I want to be normal, just like every other guy! Don't leave me out, come on! There's got to be more to life than worrying about the price of cigarettes, getting a job, what's on TV. I know—I know about normalcy. Don't tell me about normalcy!

I want to drive a station wagon with a bunch of kids singing Christmas carols in the backseat. I want to go to the supermarket and compare prices. I want to lose weight while I sleep. I want to buy life insurance. I want to wear pajamas and a bathrobe, sneak into the kitchen in the middle of the night and steal a drumstick out of the refrigerator. Worry about my dog's nutrition. Or maybe just order something from the L. L. Bean catalog . . . a nice down parka maybe, a flannel shirt . . . something in corduroy!

I know all about normalcy!

I want to yell at my wife when she goes on a spending spree! I want to help my kids with their grades! I want to fertilize my lawn. I want to order my hamburger *my way*! I want to donate money to impoverished minorities!

But all that stuff costs money. Being normal is expensive, you know.

(Short pause.)

There was this rat scratching inside my wall the other night. After a while it sounded like it was inside my head. And I said, *"Wait a minute! Wait one minute! I'm white, I'm an American! I'm a male! I should be doing better than this!"*

Ozzie and Harriet didn't have rats in the wall. There were no roaches in the Beaver's room! Even Mister Ed had *heat*! WHAT THE FUCK IS THIS?

The rat kept scratching and I realized something: Times have changed. It's a race to the death now. Anyone waiting around for the good life to show up is a *fool*! Anyone who thinks that playing fair will get you anywhere is *blind*!

Then I said, *"Calm down, calm down, you're getting all excited about nothing. Sure you're poor, you're an artist! You have an artistic sensibility! Artists are supposed to be poor."*

And the rat-scratch voice inside my head said, "Fuck that!" I want to be rich. And I want to be famous. These are normal desires, that should not be thwarted. If you thwart them, if you repress them, you get cancer.

Shit, I want *fame*! Look at *me*, man! Fame is what counts. Fame with money. Any jerk can go to the top of some tower with a scope rifle and start shooting at people. That's shitty fame. I want the good kind. The kind with lots and lots of money. Any slob can win the lottery, it takes *skill* and *brains* to get the fame and the money *at the same time* . . . that's success, man. So everyone looks at you, wherever you go, and they say: "That guy, he did it. He got everybody to look at him, admire him and give him money, their money, at the same time!"

I heard about this guy, he made four hundred million dollars. Four *hundred* million dollars! I'd be happy with *fifty* million. Most people would still think I was a success, even if I wasn't as successful as that guy. I don't care what they think! I wouldn't even tell them how much money I have! I'd just ride around in my stretch limousine, and when I got tired of that I'd go home and I'd have this enormous mansion with fifty rooms . . . And . . . and I'd have this room with a trench around it full of pit bulls, and I'd have a chair that tilts back and a TV set with remote control and a big bowl of potato chips!

And I'd just watch TV all day and change the channels. Maybe I'd just sit in a large bathtub with lots of bubbles. Smoke a cigar like Al Pacino in *Scarface* . . . But I wouldn't take drugs or have sex. Too dangerous. Just gimme the money, and the food, and the dark room . . . and the TV set. And a gun—so I can shoot the TV set when somebody I don't like comes on.

I hate people. They get in the way of a good time. Just when everything's getting good, they want something from you!

But I want you all to love *me*. Even though I hate all of you. Just to confirm my deep-seated feeling that you're all scum compared to my beneficence.

Just joking. Just joking. Don't get all excited. Nothing to get excited about. Just love me. Tell me I'm great. And pay me. And then we'll be even. For all the shit you've given me my whole fucking life! I know, I know what you're all thinking: What a jerk. All he does is talk about himself. Yeah? And what do you do? LISTEN!

I was wronged when I was little. I never really got what I wanted. Now it's time to even the score. Even if I tell you my plans you can't stop me. I'm gonna become so rich and powerful, no one will touch me.

And all those rich fucks who lorded over me, all those muscular jocks who kicked sand in my face, all those big-boobed blondies who laughed at me when I asked them for a date, all those sanctimonious paternal patronizing administrators at school and at the unemployment office and at the IRS and the police station . . . you'll all be sorry. You have no idea what I've got in store for you. Hah!

You know what it means to be really, really rich? You walk into a store and the jerk behind the counter gives you some kind of shit like . . . like, I don't know, smirking at you because he thinks you can't afford the most expensive watch in the case . . . You know the look they give you, they humor you: "Yes, sir, may I help you?" He doesn't want to help me, he doesn't want to help anybody—he just wants to laugh at me! Won't show me the watch, won't take it out, won't even tell me the price . . .

Well, when I make it, I'm going to go back to that store and I'm not going to buy *one* watch, I'm not going to buy *ten* watches—I'm going to buy the whole store, and then I'm going to fire that patronizing jerk for laughing at me . . . And then, I'm going to find out where he lives and I'm going to buy his apartment building and I'm going to have him evicted . . . one more pathetic homeless person walking the streets in a state of permanent depression!

Or those big thugs that push into you when you're walking down the street and don't say they're sorry or nothing. Why? Because they think I can't fight back. They think I'm afraid of them. Well, when I make it, I'm gonna get me some bodyguards. They'll walk with me when I'm going down the street. And some fucker pushes into me and I'll just step aside and there's my boy with the sock filled with marbles. Or the straight razor. Or the .38. He won't know what's hit 'im. He'll just end up on the ground, bleeding, looking up at me with glazed eyes, and I'll just lean over and step over 'im and say, "Excuse me." *(Laughs)*

You think I should be ashamed of myself? I HAVE NO GUILT! Because I am not a man. I am a dog. *(Barks a long howl)*

You know what I find fascinating? Human nature. The nature of human beings . . . what they like, what they don't like, what turns them on, what turns them off. What incredible appetites they have. Night after night they stay glued to their TV sets watching some pinheaded newscaster going on and on about today's grisly murder or vicious rape. They munch on popcorn and suck up TV dinners as they absorb the minutiae pertaining to the day's massive mud slide or exploding chemical plant.

(Mimicking the newscaster) "Thousands dead and dying! Hundreds blinded!"

Munch . . . munch . . . "Carol, get some more salt while you're in the kitchen! . . . Oh, wait, wait, come here, you have to see this—they're completely buried! Come on, you'll miss it, there's a commercial coming on!"

Then, these same people watch shows on educational TV about dolphins, *then* they cry . . . Then they stay up late to watch some old Christmas movie with Jimmy Stewart standing on a bridge on Christmas Eve; *then* they go berserk!

The next morning, they jump into their sporty compact cars, drink ten cups of coffee, and race each other on the highway while they sing along with some ardent rock singer screaming and yelling about emaciated, dark-skinned, hopeless people turning to dung half a world away.

So they feel so guilty they race home and write out a check for five dollars and mail it to some post office box in New York City and then they feel so good about themselves they go to bed with each other, and they kiss and they lick and they suck each other and they hold each other really really tight, because they really, really care . . .

(Pause.)

I know I'm negative. I know I'm not a nice guy. I know you all hate me. But I don't care. Because at least I realize I'm a shit, and for that tiny fragment of truth, I respect myself. That's why normalcy is so far out of my reach. Because you have to be blind to be normal. You have to like yourself, and the thought of that is so repellent to me that I'm ecstatic to be in the depressing place that I am!

50

ARTIST

A man sits cross-legged in the middle of a pool of light, downstage center. He is smoking a joint and passing it to an unseen companion.

It's like if a tree falls in the forest—you know what I'm saying, man? It's like if everybody already knows everything, then nothing means anything. Everything's a cliché.

That's why I stopped making art.

(Takes the joint and tokes.)

You know what's wrong with the world today? Why everything's screwed up and you can't do anything about it? Because we don't live in a human world—we live in a machine world.

(Passes the joint.)

There's this guy, I can see him from my apartment, down in his apartment across the street. All night long, every night, he lies on his couch, doesn't move for hours on end, his eyes wide open . . . Now if I didn't know that guy was watching TV, I'd think there was something seriously wrong with him, like he was paralyzed or hypnotized or something . . . All night long he lies there, and messages from outer space beam into his brain: "Buy a new car," "Use deodorant," "Work harder," "Your dog has bad breath," "Buy a microwave oven . . ." All night long, man, into his brain.

(Takes the joint and tokes.)

I mean, what's a microwave oven, man? Everybody's got one, nobody knows what it does, nobody knows how it works, everybody's got one. Why? Why does everybody have a microwave oven? . . . Because the TV set told 'em to buy it, that's why.

(Tokes again and passes it.)

I'm telling you, man, the government is building this computer, biggest computer they ever built. Spending billions and billions of dollars. It's a secret project, but I read about it . . . When they finish this computer we're all gonna be dead, man . . . 'Cause they're gonna hook this huge computer up to everybody's TV set. Then they're gonna reverse the TV set so it can watch you in your house doing your thing? Computer's gonna watch you, man, and if you do something the computer doesn't like, it's gonna send a message to the TV set. TV set's gonna send a message to the microwave oven, door's gonna pop open, you're gonna be *ashes*, man . . .

Don't believe me? Go in a store, pick something up, pick anything up, take a look . . . everything's got those little computer lines on 'em now. Everything. What do those little lines mean, man? . . . Nobody knows. Nobody knows what they say—it's not English, it's computer. All these computers are talking to each other, man, nobody knows what they're saying. It's like we're living in an occupied country, man.

All day and all night long, the computers are talking to each other on the internet and the fax machines and the satellite linkups. All day and all night. What are they talking about? What are they talking about? I'll tell you what they're talking about.

They're talking about you and me . . . how to use us more efficiently . . .

See, they don't have feelings, man, they're just machines. All they care about is efficiency.

The worst human being who ever lived had feelings, man. Genghis Khan had feelings. Adolf Hitler had feelings. Every once in a while he'd get a little bummed out. Computers never get bummed out, man, never.

(Tokes again and passes it back.)

You know how they make bacon? . . . No, I mean, you know how they make bacon? They got these giant meat-packing plants out in Idaho . . . Ohio . . . Iowa . . . one of those places . . . run by robots and computers. And way down at the bottom of the assembly line they have to have a human being to hold the meat? 'Cause every piece of meat is different. And these twenty-four razor-sharp blades come down, slice through the meat, and that's how you get a slab of bacon.

So some dude comes into work, isn't thinking about what he's doing—maybe he had a fight with his old lady the night before, whatever—sits down at his spot, down come the twenty-four razor-sharp blades, and instead of a hand, he's got a half pound of sliced and smoked Armour Star.

(Tokes.)

Bummer, right?

Happens about once a week. And nobody does anything about it. Nobody cares. Who's to care? Machines run everything now, man.

Every day the machines put more oil in the water, more poison in the air, they chop down more jungles. What do they care? They don't breathe air, they don't drink water.

We do.

(He looks at the joint, considers it for a moment, then swallows it. A strange look comes over his face.)

Stoned, man.

Wish we had some music to listen to. I used to love to listen to rock when I got high. All the great old bands—the Jefferson Airplane, the Stones, the Who.

They're all dead now.

. . . What, those bands touring around? You think that's the Stones, man? You think that's the Who? . . . Robots, man. They gotta be robots. Listen to the words. The old bands, what did they sing about? Love, Peace, Anarchy, Freedom, Revolution, Get High . . . What do the new bands sing about? Fear, Paranoia, Work Harder, Buy a Microwave Oven . . .

They're just trying to brainwash us, man. They're just part of the system—if they weren't part of the system, you'd never even hear about 'em. All the bands that fought the system—Janis, Jimi, Morrison—they killed 'em all, made it look like accidents. They're all gone now, man, all that's left is the system.

The system only has one message, man—fear. That's all they tell us all day long—fear. Because we're like little mice in our cages, man, running on our wheels as fast as we can, because we're so afraid.

Every day, get up seven A.M., drink two cups of caffeine, jump in the car, get stuck in traffic, get to work, get yelled at by the boss, make a deadline, drink more caffeine, get back in the car, get stuck in traffic again, get home, pay bills you can't afford, eat your microwave dinner, jump into bed . . . Oh, wait, wait, I forgot the most important thing—watch a little TV—gotta get those messages in the head!

Get up the next morning, do it over again, get up the next morning, do it over again. Do it over again, do it over again, over again, over again . . .

They call that "being responsible," man. Everybody's scared, man—they're afraid they don't do what they're supposed to do— BANG—they're homeless.

That's what the homeless people are, man. They're the warning to all of us, "Stay in your cage, don't rock the boat."

Ever talk to any of those guys on the street, man? Everybody says they're crazy. You live on the street for a while, see what kind of ideas *you* come up with. You don't go crazy, man—you start to see the truth. You start seeing the truth, you start telling the truth, you start talking about the way things *really* are.

That's why they keep those guys out on the street, man. The system's afraid of them. Afraid of their freedom. Freedom is the opposite of responsibility. Freedom is a threat to the system.

That's why nobody smokes pot anymore—everybody's afraid of the freedom. They're afraid they're going to smoke some pot, get high, think a thought or two, realize what bullshit their life is . . . and freak out.

That's why I stopped making art, man. It's hopeless. What can you say about this situation?

You write a book, best book ever written, makes best-seller list, everybody reads it. Two years later, it's a movie and now it's about George Clooney's big brown eyes. You write a song, beautiful song, makes Top 40. Next thing you know, it's a jingle in a beer commercial. You paint a painting, millionaire buys it, hangs it on the wall of his corporate headquarters.

In the old days, man, rich people used to get lions' heads and tigers' heads, hang 'em on the wall—made 'em feel powerful, made 'em feel safe.

The system collects artists' *minds*, man. It sleeps better at night knowing the best and the brightest are dead from the neck up.

That's why I don't give 'em the satisfaction. I keep my mind inside my head where they can't get at it. Everything becomes part of the system, man. The only way to escape the system is not to do anything.

That's what I do. I want to paint a painting, I want to write something. I do it in my head, where they can't see it.

If they ever knew what I was thinking, man . . . I'd be dead.

FROM "NOTES FROM UNDERGROUND"

(1993)

51

APRIL 14

I really feel great today. I feel like I'm breaking through something. I took a bus out to the suburbs. Somewhere in New Jersey. And then I walked through these lovely neighborhoods with sidewalks and bicycles in the front yards and shiny Mercedeses. People cutting their grass. Lots of mowed grass.

I found this split-level house. White. It had a picnic table and a swing set in the backyard.

So I went into the backyard and sat at the picnic table. It was quite lovely. I had my portable radio with me and I listened to the news.

The people came home and you should have seen the look on their faces when they saw me sitting at their picnic table.

They kept looking out the window at me.

Then the man came home. The Dad.

He opened the back door and he said in this really gruff voice: "Can I help you with something?"

I said: "No, I'm fine."

He said: "Well, if you don't mind, you're in my backyard."

I said: "I don't mind."

He said: "If I can't do anything for you, you better get going."

I said: "Can I use your bathroom?"

He thought about that one for a few minutes. I could see him asking his wife.

Of course I was wearing my suit and tie. So the man had to give me the benefit of the doubt.

Then he said: "You can use the bathroom. But make it quick and then you have to get going."

I walked into his house and I looked him in the eye and I could see that he was scared.

I went into the bathroom.

He didn't say what I could do in his bathroom. So I thought, This would be a good time to take a bath.

The man came pounding on the door after fifteen minutes went by. He unlocked the door and I was in the bathtub. He saw me naked and ran out again, I guess to call the police. He said he was going to.

I sang my song in the bathtub. I got out, dried myself off. Then I took an aspirin and brushed my teeth with the man's toothbrush. The biggest one, of course. I cleaned my hair out of the drain.

The police didn't come. The police are only people. They don't have any real power to change anything. What can they do?

I splashed some of the man's cologne on me. I got dressed and left.

When I came out of the bathroom, the whole family ran into another room and I could hear the door lock. That was funny.

I found some car keys on the kitchen table and borrowed their Volvo station wagon. I drove around, then I found a shopping mall. I left the car in the parking lot with the keys in the ignition. Let some car thief get it.

I went shopping. I bought a very sharp carbon steel kitchen knife. They are sharp, those things. And expensive. Fifteen seventy-five.

I went to a movie in the mall. I think Goldie Hawn was in it. I'm not sure because I fell asleep and woke up and the movie was over and I was all covered with popcorn bits.

I called a cab and went back to the bus station.

A great day. Exciting, invigorating. It's nice to do something constructive for a change.

52

MAY 18

I didn't write yesterday because I had a wonderful experience. I got up early, drank some carrot juice, did my exercises, got dressed in my suit and tie and went to Fifth Avenue. I walked around, did a little window shopping. I got in a long discussion with a clerk about whether a Patek Philippe or a Rolex is the best investment. Went to Tiffany's, picked out a thirty-five-thousand-dollar diamond and had them set it in a ring. I told them that I had left my wallet in my suite at the Carlyle and would call them later with the deposit. Hah. That was a funny one. They were shaking my hand all the way to the door.

I had walked out of Tiffany's and was thinking about lunch, and found myself in front of the Museum of Modern Art. A woman walked by me wearing a long black coat and black boots. And for some reason I followed her in and she checked her coat and I could see what she was wearing: some faded jeans, a sort of tight sweater, and a little scarf around her neck.

She looked over at me and I smiled. She sort of smiled back and then she went into the museum.

I figured it was worth the investment and I followed her in. I thought: Isn't this exciting? It's like being in a movie! Everywhere she went, I went. I would stare at a painting really intently and then glance at her out of the side of my eye.

If she saw me looking, I would look away.

Then one time while I was looking away she must have walked into another room, because I lost her. I tried not to seem too anxious about it, but it was a terrible loss.

All of a sudden there was a tap on my shoulder. I thought it was a guard telling me to stop following the woman around. But it wasn't a guard. It was her! My heart started to pound, my mouth became dry.

She said: "Where is Picasso's *Guernica*? Do you know?" And I said, "It's not here?" And she said, "No." And I said, "I think it's gone." She said, "Oh, that's right! I forgot!" And she smiled at me and looked into my eyes. And I looked into her eyes.

Then she said, "You're so knowledgeable about art. Do you come to the museum often?" And I said, "Only when I'm in New York. I'm staying at the Carlyle, so it's convenient." And she smiled some more. I said, "Do you come to the museum often?" And she said, "Once in a while, when I'm down." I asked her what she was down about, and she said, "Nothing." I looked at my watch and said it was lunchtime, would she have lunch with me, and she said she'd love to. So we went to the lunchroom in the museum.

It was very pleasant. We talked about the Carlyle, about her job (she's a designer at an ad agency), about exercise, about my job at CBS News and my friendship with Dan Rather.

The whole time we were talking, I realized I could look at her all I wanted. She was pretty in an over-thirty way. Her eyes seemed a little tired, but bright still. She had a little hair on her upper lip, but that was compensated by the large size of her breasts.

Her hair had some kind of bleach or lightener in it, and she was wearing a pin that looked like a salamander all covered with diamonds. Her fingertips were perfectly manicured.

Along with lunch, she had a white wine. And after lunch, she smoked a cigarette. I could tell by the way she sucked on the cigarette that she was very horny. Why else would she be in the museum in the first place?

We laughed small laughs, and when the check came I pretended to have forgotten my wallet. She seemed a little flustered, but paid the check anyway.

When we left, I asked her if she'd ever seen the Carlyle. She said no, and we took a walk up Madison Avenue to see it.

Outside the building, I insisted on paying her back for the meal. I said my wallet was right up in my room, let's go up.

When we got there, we just walked in, went to the elevator, and told the elevator man we wanted to go to the eleventh floor. He took us right up there and I found a room with a maid fixing it up.

I told the maid she didn't have to vacuum and we walked in and closed the door.

I broke the seal and opened the little refrigerator and gave her a beer. She took off her jacket and sat down on the couch.

She said, "You must do this all the time."

I said, "This is the first time."

I walked over to her and pulled her up to me. Our faces were very close and I could see the tiny hairs on her lip, her lipstick stain, the mascara on her eyelashes. She looked at me expectantly.

I looked into her eyes and told her to go into the bedroom. I said I had to call my office and I would be right in.

She went into the bedroom. I watched her as she started to undress. She seemed uncertain. I smiled at her and she kept going. I closed the door.

I called the front desk and told them to send up the repairman because my television set wasn't working. I told them I had to go out for an hour and wanted it fixed by the time I got back.

I left.

I went home and made a really hot bath. I thought about the woman and the TV repairman coming in. I got out a can of shave cream and covered my whole body with cream.

Then I jumped into the hot tub of water and fell asleep.

Life is good if you're willing to work at it.

FROM "POUNDING NAILS IN THE FLOOR WITH MY FOREHEAD"

(1994)

53

AMERICA

A silhouette against the back wall of the theater reveals a man speaking into a microphone. We hear a basso profundo radio voice à la Rush Limbaugh.

I was shaving this morning. Shaving with a disposable razor and suddenly I thought of my *dad*. I wondered, What would I be doing right now, if it were forty years ago? If it wasn't 1994, but 1954 and I'm my own dad? And I imagined myself going downstairs, and there's my wife and she's not racing to meet the *car pool, no,* she's making me *breakfast*. She's got a gingham apron on, she's making me bacon and eggs . . . which I consume with tremendous pleasure because I've never even *heard* of cholesterol before.

And here are my children sitting at my 1954 breakfast table and they're well-behaved and well-dressed. In fact, my son is wearing a *necktie. I'm* wearing a necktie. I pick up the morning newspaper—all the news is *good:* we've won the war in Korea, they've found a cure for polio, employment's up, housing's up, everybody's *happy.*

I own my own home, I own my own car (which I wash every single Saturday), I love my wife, I like baseball, I believe in the

president, and I pray to God in a place called *church*. No drugs.
No drugs *anywhere*. Only people doing drugs in 1954 are William
Burroughs and Allen Ginsberg!

No one's *complaining*. We're not hearing about women's
rights and homosexual *rights* and minorities' rights and immi-
grants' rights. No *victims*. No sexual *harassment*. No worries about
the environment. The environment is just fine, thank you. No
therapists. No twelve-step groups. No marches on Washington.
No homeless people. No *AIDS*. Just good old-fashioned values
like honesty and hard work and bravery and fidelity. And that's *it*.
It's America forty years ago. Everybody's working. Everybody's
straight. Everybody's happy. And I thought to myself, What a
wonderful world that must have been, a world without problems.
I would love to be there right *now*.

And then I remembered a *terrible* nightmare I'd had last
night. Now lemme tell you about this nightmare: It's the middle
of the night, I'm in bed, of course. Who shows up in my bedroom but *Bill Clinton*. As I said, it's a nightmare. He takes my hand
and he says, "Come with me." And we float out the window and
into the night air, and down to the street and we drop into this
open manhole. And we're walking around in the sewers, Bill and
I. I'm thinking, I never trusted this guy, where's he taking me? We
walk and we walk and we come to this big cave and in this cave
there are all these people lying around on mattresses, smoking
things: pot, crack, hashish, opium. Whatever these people smoke.
And through the haze, I see all these familiar faces! Oh, there's
Whoopi Goldberg reading the *Communist Manifesto*. And there's
Ralph Nader bitching about something. And Susan Sarandon and
Tim Robbins leading a peace rally. And Roseanne Arnold having
sex with Madonna. And Ice T and Ice Cube and Vanilla Ice and
all the other pieces of ice and all the other *troublemakers* and *com-
mies* and *lefties* and people with green hair and tattoos and goatees
and rings through their noses and rings through their nipples and
rings through their penises.

And some of them are marching around protesting something
. . . there's another bunch of them counting their food stamps and
welfare checks. Right in front of me a bunch of idiots are watching
Beavis and Butt-Head on MTV.

And I'm horrified. And I turned to Bill and I said, "Bill, where are we? I'm frightened." And he said, "Don't you know?" And I said, "No. Hell?" And he laughed and he said, "No, of course not! This isn't Hell. Look around you. Don't you recognize the place? This is America, 1994! Better get used to it."

Let's go to a commercial.

54

MOLECULES

A man emerges from darkness, coughing, scratching his crotch and ranting.

Good afternoon, ladies and gentlemens, homeboys and homeless, welcome to the soul train. We be making all local stops including fear, insanity, incarceration and death. Cigar, cigarette smoking is not permitted on my train, but if you got your stems, "BEAM ME UP, SCOTTY!" HAHHHHHHH!

I'm coming to Brooklyn, I'm coming to Queens, I'm coming to Manhattan!

(Stares at the audience) I am your *worst nightmare*! I got shit in my pants, I got fleas in my beard, I got so much syf-liss and gonorrhea pouring outta my penis, you can turn it on and off like a *faucet*.

(Arms flailing) I am an exploding SUPERNOVA of negative energy. I am a cosmic comet moving through space, spewing my essence wherever I goes!

(To a subway rider) Hey, sister. How you doing today? How you doing? This is my train, you know this is my subway train? It is! I'm the captain of this train. *(Addresses another rider)* Where

you going? You going to work? That's good. Nothing wrong with work, baby, get your ass on to work . . . See that strap you hanging from, baby? I *sneezed* all over that strap jus' this morning. I did. You too, have a nice day. *(To another)* Yo, homeboy! How you doing today? Watch out for that door you leaning against. Watch out! I threw up all over that door jus' last week. I did. Chicken pot pie. Was good. You dig around in those cracks and the crevices, you welcome to all the peas and carrots you can find.

See this seat here? This is my seat. This is my favorite seat in the whole train. Right in the middle so I can see both ends. I's sitting in this seat jus' yesterday. Jus' yesterday. Got all nice and comferble. I got so nice and comferble, I wet my pants. That pee went running down through my curly hairs, down through my crusty underwears, made a little puddle. Made kind of a soup out of myself. Hah! Got all the ingredients right there, stuck on me. Smear of dog food left over from breakfast. Some rat blood from some rat I stomped. Some Chinaman's snot, they don't give you no respect, you're lying on the ground, *(Mimes blowing nose)* hit you when you're trying to get some *rest*. All that stuff boils together, make a soup. I sat in that soup for a while then it got all cold. Then I wasn't comferble no more. So I got up, went down the other end of the train.

It's all right, it's all right. *(Indicates seat)* It dries. It dries. All's left on the seat were some molecules. Can't even see 'em. Know you can't see 'em, 'cause a guy came on the train, Frank—Frank, the businessman in his camel's hair coat and his briefcase—came on the train, sat right down in those molecules, didn't bother him in the least. He was rushing home, had to rush home 'cause he's got to see the evening *news*, find out what's going on in the world. He can't see with his own eyes, he's gotta see it on the TV set.

Go home to his condominium. Walked in the door, threw his camel's hair coat on the couch and said, "HONEY, I'M HOME!" That's what they say those suburbs people, gots to let everyone know where they are at. "Honey, I'm home." "Honey, I'm going out for five minutes." "Honey, I'm back!" Who gives a shit where he is?

Frank sat down, ate his dinner. Yum! And then Frank stood up and said, "Honey! That was delicious! That was the best roast duck I had all week. Hey, honey! Guess what I did at work today? I fired a hundred and fifty motherfuckers! My dick is ten feet long, I'm feeling sexy, let's fuck!"

And then he grabbed his wife (who has a beautiful body 'cause she's on the StairMaster three hours a day) and drug her into the living room and threw her right on the couch. And they proceeded to have some really really good sex. That's 'cause they got this video called "How to Have Really Really Good Sex." And they did it every which way, up and down all around. The one-legged position. Doggie style. Handstands. And they be bouncing up and down on that couch. And the camel's hair coat be bouncing up and down on that couch. And all my *molecules* they be bouncing up and down, right along with 'em.

And then Frank decided to do something he hadn't done in a long time. He took his wife's legs and he spread 'em—like this—and he took the tip of his tongue—he's gonna put that tongue right on his wife's vagino, don't ask me why—but just as the tip of his tongue was going to touch those wet curly hairs, just as it was going to touch—shwoop—one a my molecules went right down his throat!

He didn't feel it. Didn't feel a thing. *But he will.* 'Cause my shit's strong. And those molecules gonna bubble and boil, gonna mutate and grow down there deep inside of Frank. Gonna make a change in Frank. Gonna change his *lifestyle*. Those molecules, they gonna start spinning inside Frank's brain. He's gonna start doing shit he never done before. He's gonna get himself some bulletproof underwear. He's gonna start sterilizing his water. Get his wife checked for HIV, his kids checked for HIV, his granma checked for HIV. He's gonna start looking over his shoulder when he walks down the street. He's gonna put radar on his roof. He's gonna put extra alarms on his car, extra locks on his doors. He's not gonna let his kids out to play. He's not gonna answer his phone. He's not gonna get the mail. He's gonna get himself some dark glasses, stay inside the house, never go out. And then he's gonna get himself a gun. And then he's gonna wait. First person knocks on his door—BOOM—he's gonna shoot him.

See, 'cause Frank's been infected. He's infected with the disease. The disease of *fear*. And that fear's gonna eat him right up from asshole to brain. And those molecules—when they done with Frank—gonna jump off to the next guy. *(Pointing around the audience)* To the next guy, the next guy, the next guy, the next guy.

'Cause we all infected see? 'Cause we all on the *same train*. And nobody gets off this train. Nobody gets off this train. And I'm the captain of this train. I'M THE CAPTAIN OF THIS TRAIN!

I say: Fasten your seat belts, ladies and gentlemen, hang on to your straps. 'Cause, like it or not, me and my molecules are about to take everybody here for a nice long ride!

55

INTRO

After "Molecules," the audience has applauded weakly or not at all. The man picks up a hand mike and addresses the audience:

Thank you.

(Some people clap, if none clapped before.)

No, no, it's too late. But thank you. I'm very happy you could all make it tonight. It really means a lot to me. Means a lot to all of us, I'm sure. Or maybe not, maybe it doesn't mean anything, I don't know.

But thanks anyway. It's great that you're all, uh, sitting out there and I'm standing up here, and you're all, uh, you know, looking at me. I like to be looked at so, uh, thank you. You're doing just what I want you to do. Just sit back, relax, put on your glasses, get out your binoculars, focus your telescopes 'cause here I am.

And I want to thank you for this opportunity to reveal myself. Expose myself. Strip naked, so to speak. Take it off. Take it all off. Really show you everything I can be. Which isn't much, I know. I mean, if you're disappointed, I understand. I've never really been a likable person. In fact I'm kind of an unlikable person. And, you know, maybe you're a *likable* person, so maybe you feel *superior* to me because you're easy to get along with and I'm not.

I don't really care what you think.

But, so, uh, is everybody ready to have a good time? Just went out and had something to eat in the neighborhood? Maybe a little nouvelle cuisine before the show? *(Addresses someone in the front row)* Maybe a little wilted radicchio salad with a honey-mustard vinaigrette? Would you like some fresh pepper with that, sir? We have a very nice chardonnay. A very *nice* chardonnay. Would you like to hear today's specials? . . . No. How 'bout the balcony? Something ethnic before you came by tonight? Something third world? A little couscous, maybe, tandoori, fajita, burrito? Nothing like a nice hot ethnic dish before you go to see that semi-expensive, semi-meaningful Off-Broadway show. Nothing like a nice hot dish from a country where no one can actually *afford* to eat the very thing you're stuffing your face with. Waiter probably had rickets when he was a kid. "Here you go, sir . . . oh, thank you, a penny tip! I'm so happy now!"

Did you have some nice third-world beer with your burritos? Maybe some DOS EQUIS? Six-pack of Dos Equis? Down front here, a couple of bottles of chardonnay. Couple of hits of acid in the back row?

I don't care what you do with your free time. You come in here and you're just so comfortable and so easygoing and likable and you're just such a nice person. And you come in here and you've got this *attitude*. No, no. I know the attitude. You don't even clap when I kill myself on the first bit. You judge me. You sit there and you *judge* me. Don't act like I can't see you, I can see you.

(He mimics an audience member whispering to her neighbor) "What is this? Why did you bring me to this? . . . No, there are no nails up there, Sid, he's not going to pound anything, I'm telling you! Phyllis came last week. She says all he does is play *assholes*. I have enough assholes in my life already, who needs one more?"

Well you know what? Who needs *you*? You're just taking up a seat. You don't think I'm so great? I don't think you're so great either. So we're even. I mean, you come in here, you make no effort at all. I'm supposed to jump all over the place, like some kind of puppet on a string, *entertain* you! Hey, let's get something straight, in case you don't know what you just paid thirty-five bucks to see, this is what I do. This is my work. This is my life up here. OK? This isn't *Ace Ventura, Pet Armenian*!

(He hits the floor with his fist.)

You don't like it, fine with me. Fine with fucking me.

(He storms offstage.)

(From off) It's OK, it's OK, I'm not angry. "He's angry! He's got an angry social message. He's the cutting edge of the black hole of the American psyche! I read about it in the *Village Voice*!"

(He returns.)

Fuck that shit! I'm not angry, OK? I'm happy. Because I know that being unhappy and angry and pessimistic is a big turn-off. You didn't come here tonight to hear a lot of pessimistic, negative stuff. You came here tonight to be entertained, to be uplifted, to build up an appetite for the decaf cappuccino after the show.

And I *want* you to like me, I want to have a warm loving relationship with this audience, I don't want to have a dysfunctional relationship to this audience. I want to bond with this audience. By the end of the night I want us to be as one, like a giant school of fish swimming shoulder to shoulder with hundreds of thousands of compadres. And we'll move together as one to make a greater dream possible! A world where love and harmony will rule, and everyone is happy and well-fed and disease-free and PART OF. I want to stand up here tonight and say: "I AM ONE AMONG MANY." I don't want to rock the boat, I want to help *row*!

That's what I want, and I know that's what you want, too.

You know we've all been through a lot of therapy over the past ten years, and I'm very proud of where my therapy has taken me. I learned some things. And the cornerstone of what I've learned can be said in three little words: "People are special."

You know I was in my apartment last week when that big snowstorm hit and I could see the first few snowflakes falling. And I didn't get all negative. I didn't think: Oh shit another snowstorm. No. I watched those snowflakes falling. What was I watching, a hundred thousand, two hundred thousand snowflakes? And you know what I thought? I thought: Every one of those snowflakes is different. Unique. But you know what else? They're all the same, because they're all snow.

And that's what we are. Every one of us. Every person here tonight is unique, special . . . but every person here is exactly the same. Every person here has a skull in their head, blood in their veins. Take a straight razor, run it across your wrist, every person here bleeds.

We just have our particular loves and hates, likes and dislikes. That's what makes each of us different.

(Looks at an audience member) You. You like Mariah Carey. Now, I, I hate Mariah Carey. So in that way, we're different. *(To another audience member)* You think Phil Collins is a genius? Phil Collins makes me puke. *(To the balcony)* Up in the balcony: You love Pearl Jam. Every time I listen to them I think: What the fuck does "Pearl Jam" mean? What does it mean???!!!

You want to know what I like? I like the sound of a jackhammer ripping concrete at six o'clock in the morning outside my bedroom window. I like the sound of a dentist's drill. I like the sound of the dial tone, real loud. I like the sound of two cats fucking. I like the sound of an eighty-year-old grandmother taking out her dentures at night. I like the announcements they make in the subways. *(Garbled gibberish sound)*

What do you like? Do you like it a lot? Have you given it a lot of thought? I hope so. I really hope so. Because I'll tell you something right now, you take everybody in this room and strip all of you naked and shave your heads, stick you in a tiny little cell, feed you one watery bowl of gruel a day and you know what? IT WOULDN'T MAKE A FLYING FUCK'S DIFFERENCE WHAT YOU LIKE!

So thank you . . . thanks a lot for coming . . . thank you. I hope you like the show.

56

INNER BABY

A man strides out onto the stage, arms outstretched, to applause. In a mild Southern accent:

Thank you! Thank you so much! I am so *happy* to see so many happy, smiling faces in this audience here tonight. I am *turned on* by the potential for change I feel in this room. I can feel it coming up out of the audience, into my legs, my body, my head. I am *exploding* with the power of change in this room tonight!

You know, I go all over this great country of ours, talking to audiences just like you, about change, about human potential. And everywhere I go, people ask me the same question, they say, "Phil . . . what is the secret of happiness? What is the secret of joy? Of ecstasy?"

And everywhere I go, I tell people the same story. I tell them a story about a little boy who went into a candy store and all he had was a nickel. He went into that store and he picked out the candy bar he wanted more than any other. And he said to the man behind the counter, "Sir, I would like that candy bar right there. Here is my nickel."

And the man looked down at the little boy and the little boy's nickel and he said, "Son, that is a ten-cent candy bar. I'm sorry, I can't sell it to you." And the boy was disappointed by this news. But he thought and he thought and he thought and he came up with an *idea*. He said, "Why don't we *compromise*? I'll give you my nickel. We can take that candy bar, cut it in half. I'll have half, you have half for yourself. How 'bout that?"

And the man said to the little boy, "Son, that is a ten-cent candy bar. Get your skinny ass out of my store. Get yourself another nickel and I will sell it to you." And with that the man turned his back on the little boy.

And the little boy felt terribly rejected and cut off and abandoned. And he looked up at the man's broad back, and he looked at the nickel in his hand, and then he looked at the candy bar he wanted *so much*. And he reached out and *touched* the candy bar. And then he reached out and he *held* the candy bar. And then he ran out the store with the candy bar.

And as he was running down the street, he realized something: He still had his nickel in his hand! And in his other hand he had a *whole* candy bar! And he was suddenly filled with a tremendous feeling of *happiness* and *joy* and *ecstasy*.

Now let me ask you something: When was the last time you felt that good? I bet you can't even remember.

You wanna know something? I feel that good every day. I feel that good every day because I am in touch with something deep inside of me. And I'm going to show you how to get in touch with the same thing deep inside of you.

You see, a few years ago, I was in a very bad place in my life. Like most of you here tonight I was severely depressed, I was virtually suicidal. And I had to do some serious soul-searching.

One day, I was searching around in my soul, and I heard a little voice behind me. It said: "Hi, Phil, remember me?" And I turned around (I was in my soul of course), and there on the floor of my soul was a *little tiny baby*. I had discovered my *inner baby within*!

You see, I have a baby inside of me and that baby needs to be picked up. That baby needs to be coddled. That baby needs to have things go its own way once in a while. It needs to cry. It needs to piss on people, it has to throw up on people. That's my inner baby within.

And the miracle is, every single one of us here has a little tiny inner baby inside of him or her. I don't care how old or ugly, perverse or disturbed you might be, you were once a sweet, little, adorable, happy little baby. That baby is inside you right now. That baby is talking to you, but you're not listening. Let's listen to our babies for a moment. Let's listen to my baby. What's my baby saying? "Mommy." Hear that? "Daddy." "Barney." My baby wants to get out, watch some TV!

Come on now, I want everybody to reach down and pick up his or her little baby. Go ahead, don't be afraid! Put your baby on your lap. And I want you to think about little babies.

Ever watch a happy baby playing? They don't worry about tomorrow, they don't worry about yesterday. They don't worry about hurting other people's feelings. They don't worry about being responsible on the job or driving too fast or smoking too much. They don't read the newspaper, they don't watch the news, and they don't obey the law. Babies are in the NOW, they are connected to their centers. Babies are rude, they are crude, they are selfish, and they are *happy*.

And what do we do to these perfect little happy human beings? We take them and we make them into adults, don't we?

(Mimes building a wall around a baby) We build a wall around our inner baby, made of fear and anxiety and negativity and responsibility and hatred. Brick by brick, we build that wall: jealousy and guilt and ambition. Shame, lots of shame, let's get that shame up there. Brick by brick we wall them in around and around until our inner baby is trapped *(Miming being trapped)* like a miniature Marcel Marceau!

I'm telling you to tear down that wall and let that baby out! Come on now and let your baby go!

Get rid of that negativity. Stop worrying about tomorrow, stop worrying about yesterday! Stop worrying about what everybody else thinks about you all the time, what people think about you is none of your business! Stop worrying all the time. It's not helping anything! Sure there are people who are miserable all over the world, but hell, being all pissy and negative isn't going to do them much good, now is it? Sure the world is a complicated place. Trying to understand it isn't going to make it any less complicated! Let me tell you something, the world has existed for twenty million years without your help, and it's gonna keep on going with or without you. Stop worrying about the whales and the elephants. They don't need you, your *baby* needs you!

I want you to take your baby's hand, go ahead, take it, it's not very big. And let that baby lead you to a new life of happiness, joy, and *healthy selfishness!*

From this day onward you're gonna get up every morning and look into the mirror . . . you're gonna look into the mirror, you're gonna say to yourself: What . . . about . . . *ME?* When's it gonna be my turn? What about my *baby?*

You get in late for work. You're fifteen minutes late, the boss is pissed off. TOO BAD! FUCK YOU! My baby needed the sleep. You forgot to send your mom a Mother's Day card? She'll just have to wait till next year. Sorry, Mom. I'm busy being the mother you never were! Driving around for half an hour trying to find someplace to park. Only parking spot is one of those handicapped parking spaces. You *park* there, your inner baby is handicapped! It's midnight, you're watching Letterman on TV, halfway through that pint of Häagen-Dazs, you finish it up, your baby needs that *nurturing.* Have another one! Chase it with a couple of Slim Jims. Your baby needs your love!

You're gonna take care of your inner baby and this isn't going to be some part-time thing! You're going to be thinking about your inner baby incessantly. You're gonna be going to inner baby groups, talking to other inner babies on the phone. You're gonna buy videotapes, you're gonna buy my audiotapes, you're gonna read my books. I'm gonna sell you a little yellow sign, you put it in the window of your car, it's gonna say: CAUTION, INNER BABY WITHIN!

You're gonna make your inner baby happy and when you do, you make yourself happy. And when you're happy there will be one more happy person in the world. And you know what? . . . You will have made the world a better place.

OK, we're gonna break up into groups now and I'm gonna come around and talk to each of your inner babies, individually.

57

THE GLASS

Picks up a glass of water, drinks, puts the glass down and addresses the audience:

You know what they say: "The glass is half empty or the glass is half full." That's pretty much my philosophy of life. You're born, you live, you die. And somewhere along the line, glass is going to be empty or glass is gonna be full. Empty, full, empty, full, empty, full, empty, full.

I remember when *I* was a little baby, glass was definitely on the empty side. I didn't have much going for me when I was born. I was only about this big, very small, only weighed about seven pounds. Naked. Crying. Bald. Life was full of challenges: Learn to walk, learn to talk, use a spoon, tie my shoe, wipe my ass. *One thing after the next thing after the next after the next thing after the next!*

I mean I'm just this little baby and they cut me *no* slack. Then it's: "Get out of the house." Kindergarten, high school, college. I mean it's the same for everybody, right? Learn to drive, get a job, find a place to live, find a love. It's exhausting.

And basically what happens is one day you find yourself in a store buying a TV set and you realize you've arrived, you're all grown up. You're an adult now. Glass is finally half full. Here's your TV, go home and watch it.

And then you have to make it in this world and if you have any luck at all, you have some modicum of success and then you get to do all these adult things. You get to have a credit card: "Here's your credit card." Get to go on vacation packages, have a barbecue now and then and um . . . what else? A bigger TV with a remote control, give you a little power in your life.

Get to be condescending to people younger than you. Get to enter the Publishers Clearing House contests, subscribe to lots and lots of stuff you don't really need, trying to put some hope in your life. But all you end up with is stacks of glossy magazines all over your house with little perfume inserts in them that you peel apart so you can sniff the sweet smell of success and remain completely frustrated.

And you do this. You do this for about twenty-five or thirty years and then one day you look in the mirror and you realize your hair's getting a little thin and your stomach's not as flat as it used to be and your dick isn't as hard as it used to be. And from that day on all you can think about is how your hair is falling, your stomach's drooping, your dick is limping.

And basically it just gets worse and worse and worse until you're incontinent, mindless and drooling, stuck in a wheelchair in some firetrap senior citizens' home next to an interstate highway. And your big thrill of the day is when they're serving strained peaches. You're sitting in your wheelchair, strapped in so you don't fall over, you're listening to the sound of the traffic whizzing by out on the highway. Maybe you're counting the cars: "Two thousand one, two thousand two, two thousand three." And the attendant brings lunch, which you don't really like, but you like the strained peaches.

And there's this moment, just as that fragment of peach runs down over your old cracked tongue, and for that one moment, for that two or three seconds, everything is good again. Hope is in the air, the glass is half full once more.

But then you start coughing and gagging 'cause you don't have any teeth, you're not that good at swallowing anymore, and the attendant is shouting in your one good ear, "Come on! Come on! You can do better than that! That's no attitude to take!" as you shit your pants for the fourth time that day. And think to yourself, if you're capable of thinking anything at all: DOES DOCTOR KEVORKIAN WORK IN THIS PLACE? I WANT DOCTOR KEVORKIAN!!!

But that's all kind of in the future for me. I'm pretty happy, things are good. It can be a beautiful day like today and I can step out into the day and I can think to myself: This is good. But even if it *is* a perfect day and the birds are singing and the sky is blue and I'm holding my four year old's hand and everything is perfect, in a way it isn't, because *somewhere*, and I am reminded of this constantly on the evening news, somebody is suffering like you would not *fucking believe!*

I mean right now as I say these words, somewhere in Africa, there is a vast sea of human beings slowly starving to death! A sea of human skeletons *dying*. They're standing under the same blue sky, the same sun, they're holding their children's hands, too. What can they be thinking as they look down at their kids' bony heads and ribby ribcages and bulging bellies and big brown eyes full of death flies? What can they possibly be thinking? *(African voice)* "Oh well, the glass is half empty or the glass is half full?" Yeah. *Right.*

STARVING AFRICANS, STARVING AFRICANS, STARVING AFRICANS, STARVING AFRICANS, STARV-ING AFRICANS! They spoil everything!

I mean, wait a second. I'd love to help them. And I try. I send them money. But I can't *fix* them. I don't even really know where they are. Where are they? Does anybody here know where they are? You don't know where they are. *I* know where they are. They're on my TV set, every night, six-thirty P.M., Channel 2.

It all gets very confusing and depressing. And when I get confused and depressed, what I do? I get in my car, I go to the supermarket, I grab a cart and push it around. I don't know, some-thing about the supermarket makes me feel better. The environ-ment is so clean and orderly—air-conditioned. I mean the name says it all: SUPERMARKET. It's like where Superman goes to shop. And that's the way I feel, as I push my cart around, my cape flying behind me, grabbing that bottled water from a melted glacier, ("Oh, only five dollars a quart! That's reasonable!") the mesquite charcoal chips, double-A alkaline batteries for the kids' toys. Blue Jamaican coffee beans from some blue Jamaican! "Oh! Strained peaches on sale! Never know when I might need some of those!"

I keep going until I fill up my cart, then I know I'm finished. I push my cart to the check-out counter, I am reaffirmed in my right to exist in this environment, because I have the *cash*. This stuff costs a lot of money and I've got it. Makes me feel good. And as I pass the cash over to the check-out girl, it's almost a sexual thing. It's like I am inseminating her with my worth. I want to say to her: "See, I can pay for it! I got it up! Now, check it out!"

And as I carry my bags of groceries out to my freshly waxed and detailed automobile sitting in the middle of the parking lot, I'm not confused and depressed anymore. It all makes sense now. I'm serene again . . . because, because I feel deep down, I deserve this good life. I work so hard. I work hard at my job, I work hard at my marriage, I work out hard at the gym, I work hard at raising my kids. I MAKE AN EFFORT. I wear sunblock when it's sunny out. I floss my teeth every day. I recycle!

I'm a team player and I play by the rules: Pay the charge cards on time, change my oil every three thousand miles, don't drink when driving. No binging, no drug-taking, no wife-swapping, no four-in-the-morning-one-more-shot-of-vodka drinking, no speeding, no yelling, no spitting, no cursing, no dancing, no running. Just say, "No." That's my life: "Just say no."

You're either on the bus or you're off the bus. But you gotta know the rules: Don't black out, don't shoot up, don't go down on strange pussy. Wear a condom on everything: dick, tongue, eyes, nose, fingers, rectum and brain. Remember your social security number and don't disappear. Don't go to India for a year, don't hitchhike down Highway 61, don't walk on the wild side, don't leave your job or you may find the bus has left without you.

And in exchange for all this good behavior I get a brand-new car and a cell phone. And I can drive my car and talk on the phone and it feels good. I feel like I really belong.

I can come to a stop sign and be blabbing on the phone and there's a guy picking bottles out of a trash can for a nickel apiece and it's OK. It's OK. 'Cause I'm doing the best I can, and I know he's doing the best *he* can.

I want to roll down the window of the car and throw that guy a buck and say: "I'm there for you, man, I'm there for you. When the revolution comes, I am on *your* side." Because I am on his side. I'm one of the good guys! I give money to every charity, I wear my red ribbon, I lick stamps for the benefit committee. I have the T-shirts and the tote bags and the coffee mugs to prove my commitment. I read the morning paper every day, I watch the evening news every night. Lot of painful stories on that news. And I am there for those people. I am there for their pain: "SHOW ME YOUR PAIN, I AM THERE FOR YOU!"

And because I know that I care, I know that I am concerned, my glass isn't just half full, it's overflowing! Because I love. Love is in my life. I love my wife and kids, I love all of you here tonight, I love every single person in the whole world—every single person in Africa, in Asia, in South America. I wish they were all here right now so I could give them a great big hug!

My glass is overflowing because the glass is the glass of life and it is filled with love. And I am drinking with relish from my glass of life. And that love is going down my throat, into my body and it fills my soul. And I drink and I drink, and after a while I drink so much my bladder gets kind of full and I have to pee. And I pee love. I'm drinking, I'm peeing. I'm drinking and peeing love at the same time.

And, oh, here comes that guy from the trash can with his bottle and he needs some love, too! Well I've got plenty of love to spare. Bring that bottle over here, dude. Let's fill that right up. And here comes somebody from Zaire with a little tin can and that guy pisses into the Zaire guy's can. And here's somebody from Haiti, and somebody from the slums of Rio! We're all drinking and pissing and drinking and pissing and everybody is giving love to everybody else and that's the way the world goes round.

I'm doing the best I can.

Look, a hundred years from now I will just be some bones in a box and so will you and so will that guy picking out the bottles. So what I did in this puny little life of mine will not have made much difference.

But I will tell you one thing. While I was on this earth, I lived and I loved . . . and I was *concerned*. And that's what's important.

I am concerned therefore I am.

58

RED

A man holding a beer bottle shouts offstage in a gruff voice:

Come on up, man, come on up. Don't worry, dogs won't bite ya, they won't bite ya, 'less I tell 'em to. Just come up the stairs. HAR-LEY! DAVIDSON! Sit! Come on in, man. Sit down, sit down. You wanna beer?

(Shouts off) RAINBOW! RAINBOW! Get my friend a beer here, please! *(To man)* What's your name again? Richard. *(Off, to Rainbow)* GET RICHARD A BEER! THANK YOU.

(Reaches into his T-shirt pocket) Here, man, check this out. Hawaiian sensimilla. Seven fifty for the quarter ounce. Excellent, excellent weed. Two tokes of this, you forget how to jerk off.

(Off, to Rainbow) Rainbow! Come on! Help me out here, I'm working. I don't want to leave this guy alone with the dogs! *(To man)* She's a stripper so she thinks she's better than other people . . . What do you do, man? Wait, lemme guess, I'm good at this . . . a . . . federal narcotics agent! Hah-hah. No, no, wait a second—Armani suit, Rolex watch, shifty eyes. You're a stockbro-ker. Right? . . . I always get it, 'cause I deal to a lot a people make a lot a money. You'd be surprised who I deal to. Nothing wrong

with making money, nothing wrong with money, as long as you know how to spend it.

I know some people, they make all this money, they waste it on like expensive cars, expensive boats, houses. They waste it on their kids. Kids' college education. What's the point of making all this money if you're not going to enjoy it, if you're not going to use it to either get fucked up or get fucked, you know what I mean?

I know this one guy, stockbroker like you, he's into skiing. Flies all around the world, skis in all these weird places. Spends like fifty thousand a year on skiing. Takes helicopters to the top of mountains so he can, you know, ski where nobody ever skied before.

Hey, I been skiing, man, skiing's cool. You go up the hill, you come down the hill, you go up the hill, you come down the hill, you go up the hill, you get cold, you come down the hill, you break your leg. It's a *goof*.

But, like, how can you compare that with like getting together with your old lady on a Saturday night, rolling up some fat doobies of some fine Jamaican shit, get nicely toasted, put some mellow music on the stereo, ZZ Top, Motörhead, whatever. You start dancing around, screwing around. You're licking each other, you're sucking each other, next thing you know, you're humping like a couple of happy puppies. All of a sudden—BOOM—you spill your load. You're lying on the bed and you feel fucking amazing. You feel like Jesus Christ resurrected.

. . . Why? Why do you feel so good? Because . . . you're *stoned* and you just had an *orgasm*, right? Simple arithmetic. It's like the pinnacle of human experience. You know what I'm saying, man? I mean, isn't that the best feeling in the whole world? Don't you love that feeling? I love that feeling. You're lying on the bed, the two of yas, you're all spaced out. All sweaty and smelly, you smell like a couple of camels at the zoo. You got stuff all stuck all over ya. Your hair's all pushed over to one side. She's lying there, she's got a big puddle a come on her belly. And you're like writing your name in the come. And then you start fooling with her honey pot. And she's like, "OHHHHHH!" And then she reaches and starts yanking on your joystick and the two of you are like, "OOOOOHHHH!! AAAHHHHHH!" Next thing you know: "Oh, look who's back in action, the little soldier!" So you get ready to do it again, because the second time's always the best, you know what I mean? Always the best. And you get ready to stick it in . . .

But what do you gotta do before you stick it in? What do you *always* have ta do?

Get out the hash pipe, right? One hit on the hash pipe. Toss some coke on her tits, lick it up. And then you slide it in nice and slow. You stick her toes in your ears, she sticks her thumb up your asshole. You grab her ass, she grabs your butt. She's screaming, you're barking, "OH OH OH OH OH!" BOOOOOOOM!—and you come so hard you feel like you're gonna be brain-damaged for the rest of your life. And you fall back onto the bed but, just before your head hits the pillow, you grab that bottle of tequila, take one last snort, and your brain does a slow-dive into a black hole of complete and utter *satisfaction.*

(Tokes, thinks.)

I mean, how can you compare that with skiing, man? You know?

Good pot, huh, man? You got some drool hanging down off your lip there, better wipe it off.

Here try this coke. It just came in, haven't put a cut on it yet. No charge, no charge. Come on, man, *party* with me. You only live once! Here lemme cut you a line.

(Cuts a long line on the table. Pause.)

Actually, I'll do that one. *(Snorts up the line. Shouts)* ROCK AND ROLL! People just don't know how to relax anymore!

I was watching TV last night and this commercial comes on . . . Go ahead, man, knock yourself out, I got three keys in the back you finish that . . . This commercial comes on, these two people are drinking cups of coffee, and they're going like, "Oh, I love to relax with a cup of coffee." Who the hell relaxes with coffee? Serial killers, that's who. I hear Ted Bundy was a big coffee drinker . . . I mean what's with this coffee thing? Cappuccino, expresso! Everywhere I go now there's these little places where people are sitting around sucking down this black shit! Get themselves all wired up then they hook themselves up to their cell phones and their beepers and their fax machines and they're like, "AAAAAAHHHHH!" . . . I mean why does everybody need a cell phone all of a sudden? I remember when the only guys who had car phones were cops. Like for emergencies. What's the big emergency, everyone has to have a car phone? *(Picks up imaginary phone)* "DON'T FORGET TO PICK UP THE COFFEE ON YOUR WAY HOME!!!"

(Off, to Rainbow) RAINBOW BABY, COME ON BRING OUT THOSE BEERS! THIS GUY'S GRINDING HIS TEETH SO HARD I'M GETTING A HEADACHE!

She's great, wait till you meet her, man. She's very talented. We should go see her show. You like nipples, labia? She's got all that stuff, man. We'll go see her, you and me.

See, you're normal, man, you're a normal human being. The people out there, man, they're so psycho, I'm afraid to go out of the house.

I go down the 7-Eleven last night to like pick up a little night-cap before I go to bed, right? So I'm walking out of the store with my three six-packs, right? Minding my own business. And there's this guy sitting in his Mercedes, talking on his car phone. And he's like checking me out. So I check him out. So he checks me out again. So I check him out again. So he locks all the doors of his car. I'm like, "Hey." You know? Walk up to his car. Pulled out my lizard, whizzed all over his hood ornament. Then I snapped it off and I ate it. *(Laughing)* Not really. Break ya teeth if you do that.

So anyway, I'm in this weird mood, so I get in my pickup, pop a cold one, turn on the radio. And my favorite song in the whole world is playing: "Give Peace a Chance." So I'm like rolling down the road, singing. You know? All of a sudden this negative deejay comes on starts going on and on about the "tragedy of John Lennon." Bumming me completely out. And I'm thinking, What the fuck is the tragedy of John Lennon? I mean I know who John Lennon was, right? Guy was rich, he was famous, people thought he was God, he was a Beatle for crying out loud . . . Went around the world about nine hundred times, had sex with everybody he wanted to have sex with, did more drugs than you can carry in an aircraft carrier—he did it all! One night, he's coming home from work and some asshole is waiting for him with a .38—BOOM, BOOM, BOOM, BOOM, BOOM!! Like flipping off a light switch. That's it, finished. That's the way I want to go, man: bullet straight to the heart, no warning. I mean we all go, right? Or did I make that up?

Shit, I left friends back in the 'Nam, they were still twitching the last time I saw 'em. Half his age. I got buddies in the AIDS ward, shooters, dying that long slow painful death. Fuck that shit.

Tragedy of John Lennon! My life should be half as tragic as that dude's. I could use some of that tragedy in *my* life.

You wanna know about tragedy? I'll tell you about tragedy. My best friend in the whole world, Kenny, man. Now that's a tragic story. Most righteous, courageous motherfucker I ever knew. Me and him were like this, man. *(Crosses fingers)* Used to deal drugs together. Washington Square Park, 1971. Used to deal to the hippies. Just soft drugs: pot, mescaline, psilocybin, acid. We used to get this acid, man, pure liquid LSD. Absolutely pure. You fill a syringe with this shit, stick it in your neck, you're tripping in five seconds. You'd love it, man, I know you'd love it . . . We used to deal drugs all day long. And then at night, anything we didn't sell, we did it. It was like bungee jumping without the cord. Whoaaa!

Me and Kenny, we used to ride around on these big Harley hogs. And one day, we were stopped at this stop light and both had these two knapsacks full of psilocybin mushrooms strapped to our backs. We just looked at each other, didn't even say a word. At the exact same moment, we reached into our knapsacks, pulled out a handful of 'shrooms, ate 'em, took off down the highway. Did not come back for three *years*, man.

Ended up in Loveland, Colorado. Ever been to Loveland, man? Nice in Loveland. Mountains and trees and shit. We used to just hang out in the mountains, tripping. Check 'em out. Try and figure out how much the mountains *weighed.*

Most righteous man I ever met in my life. Amazing human being. He's gone, man. Gone. Know where Kenny is today? He sold out. Manages a Starbucks in Nashua, New Hampshire. Fuck that shit. Not me, man. Never. I will never sell out.

(Thrusts his arm forward) Check out this scar, man, a hundred and fifty-seven stitches. You know how I got that scar? I put my fist through a plate glass window. You know why I put my fist through that plate glass window? 'Cause it was *there*.

Check it out, man, *(Thumps his chest)* forty-five years old. You wanna know why I look so good? 'Cause I get fucked up every fucking day. I'M FREE. LIVE FREE OR DIE. DON'T TREAD ON ME. I'M AN OUTLAW, MAN, DON'T EVER FUCK-ING FORGET IT.

(He calms down.)

It's OK, man . . . I'm not pissed off at you. You're an outlaw, too. It's like you're an inside outlaw and I'm an outside outlaw.

I like you, man, you like me, man? *(Beat)* Good.

(Beat.)

I love you, man, you love me, man?

You know, she's never gonna bring that beer. Fuck this pot and coke shit, you and me we should do something. We're getting solid. I can't let you go back to that rat wheel where you work.

You know what? I got a great idea, man! I still got some of that liquid LSD in the freezer. No, don't worry about it. You don't have to pay. You and me, man, let's go out and look over the edge, man. No. No. Listen, this is a great idea. Just sit there, man, I'll go get the syringes. Just sit there, don't move. You don't move, the dogs won't bite ya. I'll be right back. *(Runs off)*

59

THE FAN

Hey, man, man, excuse me, man, I just want to tell you, man, uh, I just saw the show and it was . . . it was really intense. And I wondered if I could ask you a question? I've been taking this course on performance from Willem Dafoe, well actually from this woman who used to work with Willem Dafoe and, uh, she's been teaching us about breathing and honesty in breathing, and I was watching you tonight, man, and uh, you breathe so honestly, man . . . And I was wondering uh, could I buy you a cup of coffee, man, we could just hang out and rap for an hour or two?

Oh, yeah, of course, cool, cool. I understand. No, you're busy, that's cool . . . I just want to tell you, man, that I think your shit's great. And, uh, I think like you and Gary Oldman and Steven Seagal are doing like the only interesting shit out there right now. I mean it, I think you're a genius.

Me? I make performances like you. I mean, not like *you*. But, uh, like you. It's funny, like some of the shit you do out there, man, it's like you've been to one of my shows and you're like stealing my shit. I mean I know you're not . . .

But I wish you could come see what I do, man. I like perform and I have this friend who does this music while I'm performing because you know you have to have music with your shit for like marketing purposes and stuff, you know? They won't put you on MTV if you don't have music. I mean, you don't have to worry about that shit, you're old and everything . . .

But I wish you could see it. I know you'd dig it.

I do this one thing, where I take this human skull and I cover it all with cheese food until it looks like a real head and I stick it on this stick and stick the stick on like this spring on my back and like when I'm jumping around the head is like bouncing around and I'm like, "Whoa! A *head*!" And I grab it and I bite it and all the skin's like falling off and the audience gets totally grossed out . . . and . . .

Oh! And last week, man, you would have loved this . . . We went down to the meat market and we got all these pigs' guts and blood and shit, and we filled up these Ziploc bags with 'em, stuck 'em under our clothes. The audience didn't even know they were there. And we're like jumping around and doing our show and like all of a sudden we pull out these straight razors and sliced our stomachs right open and all the guts and blood are like falling out and chicks are screaming and I'm slipping on the blood. Fell down, took three stitches over my eye, man. See?

Like art imitating life.

Yeah. Yeah. That's what everybody says. My shit's intense. But it's kind of frustrating too 'cause we play all the time in these like small places and we try to get like agents and managers and critics to come see it and they don't, it's pretty frustrating, you know?

It must be great to play a huge place like this, huh? You must have had to really hustle somebody to get in here, huh? Like did you have an agent who set this up? . . . Yeah? Who's your agent? . . . William Morris, cool.

That's what I want to do, man, I want to be with William Morris and do what you did: *Use* the system to *destroy* the system. Like you, like Johnny Depp.

It's funny you should mention your agent, man, because I happen to have this video with me of my stuff . . .

Well, wait a minute, man, I'm talking to you, man. Don't walk away from me like that. It's like I'm some kind of jerk or something. I'm just trying to honestly tell you how I feel, I mean isn't that what your work's about, or are you some kind of hypocrite or something?

Yeah, I understand you have someplace to go, man, I have someplace to go, too, but I'm taking the time out to talk to you. The least you could do . . . Oh, wait a minute, what's that look, man? What's that look? OH! I forgot, you're more important than me! Oh, I'm *sorry*!!! You're a big deal and I'm not.

Hey, man, lemme tell you something, just because you get your name in the paper and you get to play all these big places, doesn't mean that you're like better than me, man. OK? My shit is just as important as your shit, OK? I don't need to get my name in the paper for my shit to be important.

That's what I'm saying. That's what I'm saying. Right. So basically our shit is equal. So why don't you give your agent the tape? I mean didn't anybody ever give you a helping hand when you were starting out?

(Pause. He accepts a business card.)

Oh, no, oh, that would be cool. So this is like your agent? This is his name? Thanks, man. So I just drop off the tape and he'll like look at it and maybe like have a meeting with me and shit. Great.

Hey, hey, listen, man, thank you so much and uh, listen, it would mean so much to me if you would come by one night and see my show. You know what, we're playing this week. I'll put your name on the guest list . . . plus one. Come on by, you know, bring your agent if you want to. It's going to be a really great gig. I ran into Harvey Keitel on the street the other day and, uh, you know, he might be coming. And I sent a letter to Christian Slater. He hasn't written me back, but he'll probably be there, too. You never know, you might meet those guys there, be a good career move for you.

Oh, OK. I gotta get going now, too, I'm busy, too . . . But listen, I'll give my number to your agent and you know if you ever need to talk to me about anything, you need advice or anything, just gimme a call. I have voicemail.

(Backing away) OK, man, OK. OK. Good luck, man. See you at the gig.

60

RASH

Man walks toward the audience, gesticulating with a long stainless-steel cooking fork.

So what we did, we put a chain-link fence around the whole fifteen acres. Barbed wire on top. For security, for security. 'Cause you know, Charlie, we're here all summer, the kids are running around in the yard. I sleep better at night just knowing it's out there.

Oh, yeah, we're here all summer. I go down the city maybe two, three times a month. But you know it's hot down there and we got everything we need up here. The pool. Sonia's got her tennis court, I got my griller. I just stay here all summer and grill. I put everything on this thing: steaks, chops, chicken. Last Sunday, I did some lobsters. Came out beautiful. Once they stop moving, they're a snap to cook.

Did you look at my grill, Charlie? Look at my grill. Brand-new, I just got it. It's beautiful. See, right here where the steaks are, this is the grilling part. Then over here I got two stovetops, you wanna boil some peas, carrots. Underneath, oven. You can bake a cake, cookies, whatever you want. Up here, microwave oven. Ice chest on the side, 'frigerator on the back. Three phone lines.

Very reasonable, around three grand. Got it from the Hammacher Schlemmer catalog. I love it. I just stand here all summer and grill. Very relaxing, I just stay here by the pool, they swim, I grill. Makes me very mellow. Like meditating.

(Shouts off) WHAT?!! NAH, WE DON'T WANT ANY! . . . *(To Charlie)* You want any goat cheese? *(Off, to house)* CHARLIE DOESN'T WANT ANY EITHER! I DON'T CARE WHAT YOU DID TO IT, WE HATE GOAT CHEESE. LISTEN, HONEY . . . HONEY? WE'RE STARVING TO DEATH OUT HERE, SEND OUT SOME DORITOS OR SOMETHING . . . THEN, IF YOU'RE TOO BUSY, GIVE 'EM TO JEREMY. HE CAN DO IT. GIVE 'EM TO JEREMY!

(To the pool) Jeremy, honey, go up to Mommy on the porch, get Daddy and Uncle Charlie some Doritos.

(Off, to house) HE CAN DO IT, SONIA, JUST GIVE HIM THE DORITOS. GIVE HIM THE DORITOS! DON'T GIVE HIM THE GOAT CHEESE! *(To Charlie)* Why would anybody eat goat cheese? We went to a farm one time. You see what goats eat? Who knows what's in that stuff?

Oh yeah, he loves it. He's in there all day. Like a fish. No. No. No. No. There's no chlorine in that pool, Charlie. They use chlorine in the *cheap* pools. This filter, this is the best you can get. Fourteen layers of charcoal, three layers of sand. Then there's a machine, you can't see it, under the tennis courts, boils the water into steam, sterilizes it drop by drop. Comes back to the pool, completely pure. Completely pure. You can't get water like that in *nature* . . . 'Cause I figure we got people coming over every weekend. Somebody's gonna come over, do a couple of laps. Guy's got herpes, next thing I know everybody in the house has herpes. What do you do with a six year old with herpes? I figure spend the money, get the filter. Why waste the aggravation?

'Cause you know, Charlie, I'm at that time in my life, I don't want to spend the money on the crazy stuff anymore. Remember, I used to have that car, that Porsche? What did it cost me? Hundred grand, plus a grand a month for insurance, parking? I never drove the damn thing. Sat in the garage . . . No, well, I don't drive a stick.

Now, I spend the money on the good things in my life: my family, the house. Spend it on the garden, the pool, the kids. You know that's what's important. I want to enjoy the kids while they're still young.

Of course, I got the other kids from the other marriages. Uh . . . Bobby just turned twenty-five. Finally graduated college. And Nancy, she's a sophomore. She's shacked up someplace with her boyfriend for the summer. And little Frank, baby Frank, from the other marriage, he's fourteen now. Can you believe it?

But you know, those kids, I want to say to those kids: "GO AWAY!" You know? "Your *mother* hates me, *you* hate me, so leave me alone. Here's a check, get lost!"

I mean, Sonia and I have a good thing now—since the therapy. Little Jeremy, you saw him, he's a good kid. And little, uh, Genevieve, you see her running around in her bathing suit, so cute.

I got a good life. I never want to leave the house. I had to go to the city last week, visit a client, it was *torture*. It was like going off to war. I mean you go down there now, it's like the black hole of Calcutta. You been down there lately? It's depressing. They're lying on the streets, begging, on drugs. With the babies, now they're begging. I feel so bad for those poor people, 'cause it's not their fault.

But what can you say? Life isn't fair. It's the roll of the dice, they're *fucked*. I didn't make up the rules. I just say thank God he loves us.

(Fiddling with his steaks) I'm stopped at a stoplight, down Houston Street, and this character is washing my windshield and I'm looking up at him through the glass. I can see his face and I start fantasizing. We had this stuff in Vietnam, napalm. You know what napalm is? Jellied gasoline. I have this fantasy, I'm in a helicopter, just flying down the Bowery, I spray 'em, drop a match, put 'em all outta their misery. They wouldn't even know what hit 'em. I'm not saying it's a solution. I mean it's a solution, it's not *the* solution. You wouldn't actually do it.

You like roast peppers? *(Stabs downward, then holds the fork up)* Look at this pepper, isn't it beautiful? Balducci's, five bucks each, the best you can get. I'll have one, too. See, I keep 'em on ice over here in the ice chest, anytime I want peppers, I— WHAT? YES! PUT THE CORN ON *NOW*. PUT THE CORN ON NOW, SONIA! THE STEAK'S GONNA BE READY IN FIVE MINUTES. YOU WANT COLD STEAK? I'M ASKING, YOU WANT COLD STEAK? THEN PUT THE CORN ON NOW!

Did I tell you about last spring when we went on vacation? No, I know you know we went on vacation, but let me tell you . . . About three weeks before we go away, I'm working in midtown around Forty-eighth Street. And every day, I go out to lunch, stretch my legs. And every day there's this guy in front of the building with one of those signs: WILL WORK FOR FOOD. Begging. So every day, I pass this guy, I give him a quarter, I figure, I can afford it.

The guy gets used to seeing me. Every day at lunch, sees me coming, kinda gets all perky when he sees me. Gets up on his hind legs.

So about a week before we're gonna go on vacation, I go out to lunch, I see the guy, guy sees me, I reach into my pocket, I don't have any change! He's looking at me. So I figure, what the hell, who's it gonna kill? Give the guy a buck. I throw a buck at the guy. Turns out, it's not a buck, it's a twenty-dollar bill. Don't ask me how it happened. Guy jumps up, starts shaking my hand, blessing me, telling me God loves me, Jesus loves me. Shaking my hand in the middle of the sidewalk. And I never really looked at this guy up close before. He's got all these sores all over his face, no teeth, his breath could peel paint. And I'm thinking, you know: I gave you the money, now go back and sit down!

Anyway, I forget about the guy; three days later, me and Sonia go down to St. Barth's . . . Very nice hotel by the beach, they give you a brochure about the food and how there's these dolphins and you lie on the beach and watch the dolphins. Seven hundred dollars a night . . . We get down there, I'm a little tense, I want to relax, so we go down the beach. I'm lying there, looking for the dolphins, no dolphins. I'm getting a strain in my neck. Turns out, there's no dolphins in the Caribbean. I'm in litigation with the hotel as we speak . . . Anyway, we're lying there, Sonia says,

"What's that?" She's pointing to my hand. There's this rash on the back of my hand. I say, "I don't know, poison ivy from the country house." Forget about it.

Charlie, by the end of the week, this rash is halfway up my arm. We come back to the city, I go straight to my doctor's. He says, "Good thing you came to see me. If you hadn't come to see me, that would have gone right up your arm, up your neck, into your eyes. You'd be *blind*!" Turns out—RIGHT! THAT'S RIGHT! The *guy*. Turns out, it's some kind of disease they give each other in the men's shelter. Some kind of *bum disease*.

All I'm saying, Charlie, all I'm saying is: I give the guy money, he gives me a disease!

(Looks up) Jeremy, what are you doing? No, honey, don't throw Doritos in the pool. Get away from the pool. YOU'RE GONNA CLOG UP THE FILTER—IT'S GONNA COST ME FIFTY THOUSAND DOLLARS, NOW GET AWAY FROM THE POOL. JUST GO SOMEWHERE.

(Back to Charlie) I ever tell you about my friend, George, down on Wall Street? Now, here's a guy, about three years ago, makes a killing. Shorts some stock, makes fifteen million dollars on one deal. Says to himself: That's it, I win. Gets off the street. Goes down to the South Pacific, buys an island. They're not that expensive, about two million bucks. Moves his whole family down the island.

I'm talking to him on the phone yesterday, says it's great down there. Beautiful weather every day. Inexpensive. He's got a satellite dish, gets a hundred and fifty stations. Gets it all: *Seinfeld*, the Knicks. No problems with parking, car hijacking, drugs . . . It's his own island, he's the king of the island. And I know how he feels . . .

I mean, look, I'm the world's biggest liberal. But you know I'm watching that CNN, I'm watching those riots in L.A., and I'm thinking to myself: What if they start doing that around here? What if they start running around like that around here?

I mean, look at this house, Charlie. You can't see this house from the road. We're vulnerable up here. What happens, we're up here one Sunday, we're hanging out: reading the paper, eating bagels, grinding coffee beans. I pick up the phone to call my mother: "Oh, the phone is dead!" I look up, a couple of black guys are at the back door. Breaking down the back door. They don't even have to be black guys, could be anybody. Then what do I do? What do I do then? "Oh, come on in, would you like a cup of coffee? Maybe you'd like to rape my wife, kill my kids, burn my house down?" What do I do then, Charlie? What do I do then?

That's why I have the gun. *(Fiddles with the steak)* I would, I would shoot them, for the kids I would shoot. Even if they were from the phone company, I would still shoot them . . . Anyways, these are ready.

(Calls off) Jeremy, honey, come out of the bushes, Daddy's not angry anymore. Come on out, we'll discuss it later. We're gonna have din-din now. No, no hot dogs, we've got fifteen-dollar-a-pound prime sirloin from Dean & DeLuca, now come out of the bush. COME ON! COME IN THE HOUSE!

61

THE RECOVERING MALE

Man seated in a folding chair raises his hand.

Me? Oh . . . thank you. Hello, my name is Eric and I'm a recovering male.

And I just want to share that I agree with what Tim was just saying about feeling shame for his penis. I think a lot of my masculinity issues are very shame-based. In fact it's funny, when Tim was sharing just now, I was thinking of all the times I've been in the shower in the morning and I'll look down at my penis and it will remind me of what a bad person I've been.

But I'm glad Tim brought this up, because this is something I've been trying to get in touch with. *(Laughs to himself)* Not my penis, of course. Although that has been an issue for me in the past. Well, when I was very small, my, uh, mother would whip me with a phone cord whenever I, uh, touched myself down there and, uh, it's only been recently that I've stopped getting erections whenever the phone rang.

But I want to talk about where I'm at today. I'm in a good place today. I just completed a course at the New School: "Your Self, Your Shame, Your Orgasm." Yes, it was very good, you should try it. Because you know, I used to just worry about my own orgasm, and now I worry about everyone's orgasm.

But I feel so stuck sometimes.

Like on my way here tonight. This beautiful girl walks by me on the street and she's got this really tight sweater on, you know. Kind of large breasts. Jiggling. And I can't help myself, I have to check out her breasts. *(Mimes the move)* Like some kind of Pavlovian dog! And then once she's walked past me I have to check out her butt! Like I've never seen a butt before!

It's depressing. I feel like a human being trapped in a man's body!

So anyway, about two weeks ago, this friend of mine gets these tickets to go see this woman he knows do this concert at Carnegie Hall. So he asks me to go along. This woman is a pee-nist . . . *pi-ah*-nist. And I don't really know anything about classical music, but I go and it's great. She's playing all this stuff—Bach, Chopin—and I'm blown away.

So afterwards there's this reception for her at this apartment, so I tag along with my friend. And I'm just hanging out, next thing I know, he's bringing her over to introduce her to me. So I'm shaking her hand and she's got these beautiful brown eyes and beautiful smile and she's got this evening gown on and she smells great and she's just done this fabulous concert and I'm shaking her hand and all I can think about is: "I would love to have sex with this woman." SO INAPPROPRIATE! I mean, where does that shit come from?

I was so ashamed. I was ashamed of my shame. I ran out of the room, locked myself in the bathroom in this apartment. People are pounding on the door. I'm crying . . . I'm trying to cry. Fortunately I had my portable John Bradshaw with me.

Anyway I was sharing this with my therapist last week and she suggested that I write a letter to one of the women I fantasize about when I, uh, masturbate. Not send it, just write it. So I did and she said it was good and then she said I should read it to my group.

So here's this letter.

(Pulls letter out of his pocket and reads it:)

Dear Michelle,

First of all I don't know if your name is Michelle or not, but that is what I call you. Maybe we will meet some day and I will be able to learn your real name.

Maybe I will see you walking down the street, or in a subway, or maybe I will sit down in a movie theater and you will be sitting next to me. I hope it will happen, because then I will be able to apologize to you for all the harm I've done.

You are probably thinking: How could you have done me any harm? I don't even know you.

And I know that that's true. Probably hundreds of thousands of men fantasize about you every week. So in that way, I know I'm not special.

But I have to apologize.

Every Sunday I tear through the magazine supplements looking for you. Where is she? Where is Michelle? I look for you in the lingerie ads, the health club ads, the Club Med ads. I get frantic and then, finally, every week I find you. Yes! In a string bikini, in a matching bra and girdle combo, maybe reclining in a steamy bathtub full of bubbles, almost revealing a nipple!

And then you are mine, all mine.

I hate to tell you what I do, but you belong to me, and I have you in every way I can think of . . . I consume you. I turn you inside out. You are my willing love slave and I am your love master.

I relish your burn. I adore your boobs. I idolize your succulent . . . uh . . . vagina! I am in heaven.

Sometimes it lasts a long time, sometimes it's only a few seconds, but I have you and let me tell you, you are *wonderful*.

And then, as always, I *debase* you. At the very moment of sheer joy, I can't hold back, and my life-force splashes onto the very thing I love: your image, your picture. You are lost once more, covered in the product of my sticky love.

I'm sorry, I really am. But I love you just the same. I'm just a man with a penis. And for that I'm sorry.

(He stands, puts the letter away) And that's it, thanks for letting me share. I don't want anyone to share back to me. Thank you.

62

MEDICINE

Calling off:

David come on in, sit down. Sit down.

(Gets a chair for himself, picks up a prescription pad and a pen.)

We got the results back from the lab and they're good, they're good, lots of positive indicators. I'll let you take them home with you when you leave, you can look at them in your free time.

(He sits.)

Sit down, David, sit down. Now, David, just to be on the safe side, I'd like to start you on some medication. I can't say it's going to do anything but, on the other hand, it can't hurt either. *(Scribbles on pad)* Now, this is a very common prescription item. I've prescribed it many times before. Just take this down to the pharmacy and you should have no trouble getting it filled. There are *some* side effects. Just want you to know what they are, in case anything comes up, you don't get overly concerned. OK? *(Scribbles)*

Now, David, let me ask you this, do you drink milk? . . . Well, in your coffee in the morning, or on your cereal, any baked goods with milk in them? Stay away from milk, OK? No milk and no eggs . . . Well, because there are amino acids present in milk and eggs that can react negatively with certain proteins in the medication and, on occasion, cause *convulsions*, *seizures*. And we don't want that do we? We want you feeling better, not worse . . . I'll write that down: "No milk and no eggs."

Now after you're on the medication for two or three days, you will notice some blurring of vision. Just means the medicine is working. You'll also notice a diminishment of your sex drive . . . Well, to a great extent, to a great extent. I'd be surprised if you have any sex drive at all after a couple of weeks on this stuff. Also, when you get up in the morning you may experience some dizziness. Don't worry about that. What you might find worrisome is that when you're taking a shower you're going to be losing some *hair*. Clumps of hair. You might get some bald spots. If this is a problem for you I would prescribe . . . I would prescribe a hat.

Itching is very common. You'll get some itching on your arms and on your legs, palms of the hands, soles of the feet. You might even get what we call an "epidermal sebaceous trauma" which is just a fancy term for large bleeding scabs on your arms and on your legs. If this is a problem, just call Heidi at the front desk and she'll give you a prescription for some hydrocortisone cream, clear that right up. I won't charge you for the visit . . . Also numbness in your fingers, your toes, your ears, your nose, all your extremities.

And, how shall I say this? You may experience some temporary *blindness*. It's only temporary. You'll get up in the morning, you won't be able to see for a while. Has no medical significance, lasts about fifteen, twenty minutes. If you wake up and you can't see, just sit on the edge of the bed, wait it out, thirty, forty-five minutes. If it doesn't clear up by that time, be sure to call me.

Also in the morning it's common to experience nausea, vomiting, incontinence. If you have trouble holding your bowels, just give Heidi a call and she'll give you something that will clear that right up . . . And I tell all my patients taking this drug: Make sure to keep your meals *small* because you will be throwing up quite a bit . . . Bleeding from the nose can be unexpected.

(Leaning back) Actually there's a funny story: I have a patient who's been on this drug for, oh, must be four years now, and they were throwing this birthday party for him at this ritzy restaurant. You know these places, they take forever to bring the food. He's waiting, waiting. Finally, they bring the food. He looks down at his entrée, *drops of blood* start falling from his nose!!! *(Laughing, then stopping himself)* They brought him another entrée, of course!

Just have a handkerchief with you at all times. And if your nose starts to bleed, just dab lightly, do not blow, just dab, and it should clear up in . . . about fifteen minutes.

(Signs the prescription) And that's it. We'll do some more tests in about three months, see what kind of results we're getting. If we don't like what we see, we'll put you on something stronger. OK?

(He stands.)

Oh, don't thank me, David, it's just the miracle of modern medicine. Thank you . . . Yes, got a little tan. Just got back from St. Barth's. You look good, too, David, you look very good.

(Snaps his fingers) Oh, David, I almost forgot! The insurance company sent the claim back. Yes, they're not going to pay. No. So could you stop by Heidi on your way out and drop off a check today? Uh-huh, for the whole amount, the whole five thousand would be good.

OK, David, all right. OK. You, too. Take care.

63

THE MESSENGER

With quiet intensity:

Excuse me, you look confused. Did you know that there's a path out of your confusion? There is. It's your ego that causes your confusion. You are *not* the center of the universe. You are not God. You have to realize that you are nothing. Just as I have accepted that I am nothing.

I finally realized that I am nothing more than an ant crawling on a leaf on a vine in the middle of the Amazon jungle. I am one pebble on the beach. I am just shit on God's shoe. But even though I am nothing, I am part of a bigger plan. And so are you.

See, like you, I used to get confused. I'd watch TV and I'd see all those rich famous people and I'd think to myself: Why do they have everything and I have nothing? . . . I'd get angry. But maybe those people are being rewarded for being good? If I look at them I can see they have such nice smiles, such nice teeth. They are so beautiful, so good. No wonder good things are happening for them. They deserve it.

You see, God gives you what you deserve.

I'll be walking down the street and I'll see a person lying on the ground, in pain, and I'll think to myself: Why is that person in pain? Why is that person suffering? . . . But I don't know why God put that person in my path. Maybe God is trying to teach me something? Or maybe that person did something? Maybe that person is a murderer? I don't know. Maybe, probably, probably did *something*, otherwise why is God making that person suffer?

You know there's a lot of terrible things that happen to people in the world. A lot of things we can't understand. But that's the way it has to be. If everybody just did what they wanted all the time and had it easy all the time and nothing bad ever happened, we'd just be like a bunch of children having fun, and that wouldn't be any good, would it?

So don't be confused. And don't worry. Because you are part of a bigger plan. You can't understand it and you can't change it.

Have a nice day.

64

BLOW ME

Man pacing the stage. Into a microphone, loud:

I woke up this morning and I had a big fucking headache, man!
You know why I had a big fucking headache? 'Cause I got fucked
up last night, that's why!

So you know what I did when I got up this morning, man?
I got fucked up again, man! You wanna know why? 'Cause I hate
the *taste* of fresh-squeezed orange juice, *man*, I hate the *smell* of
fresh-ground coffee, I hate the *sound* of Bryant Gumbel's voice!
I hate driving to work, I hate standing up, I hate breathing, I hate
waiting to die!

Why should I work a job, man? So some ASSHOLE who has
nothing better to do can get off by telling *me* what to do, so that
maybe, JUST MAYBE, I can take home a check for a hundred and
forty-eight dollars and twenty-seven cents after they take fucking
taxes out, so that a bunch of lying, cheating, POLA-FUCKIN'-
TICIANS can get their free *limos* and their free *haircuts* and their
free *postage stamps* and their free *blow jobs*????

BLOW . . . ME!

Blow me. Blow me, Bill Clinton. Blow me, Hillary Rodham Clinton. Blow me, Al Gore. Blow me, Tipper Gore.

Why should I work a job? So maybe I can get some *fringe benefits*? So maybe I can get some *health insurance*, so that if anything really goes wrong with me, I can call up the insurance company and they'll say: "I'm sorry, sir, your coverage doesn't cover stomach cancer. I'm sorry, sir, your coverage doesn't cover massive brain tumors. I'm sorry, sir, your coverage doesn't cover secret incurable CIA-sponsored diseases." Blow me. Blow . . . me.

I have the same dream every night when I'm not blacked out. It's World War III and the bombs are falling onto New York and L.A. and there's this huge ultra-megaton bomb, slowly falling onto Washington, DC. And all the politicians, the congressmen and the Supreme Court judges and the president and the vice president are all scurrying down these secret passageways to these secret bunkers underground that they think are bombproof. But what they don't realize is that me and my friends have already stuck a whole bunch of other nuclear bombs down there in those bunkers and once they're stuck inside, we padlock all the doors and me and Lee Marvin and Charles Bronson and Trini Lopez and the rest of the Dirty Dozen go running down throwing these hand grenades down their air tubes and blow their fat asses away on golf carts to hell.

Yeah, yeah, yeah, yeah, yeah, I have a death fantasy. This is my death fantasy: I'm driving down the highway doing about ninety miles an hour, and I have a head-on collision with a bus filled with those singing nuns from that movie *Sister Act*. But just before I hit, I want to be shooting up heroin between my toes, and jerking off to a copy of *Hustler* magazine and listening to Howard Stern on the radio. So when I'm in the fireball burning up I'll be laughing and coming at the same time. At least I won't be bored, at least I won't be bored with all the *stimulation*:

"Oh I wonder what's on TV tonight? Maybe SOMETHING GOOD is on!"

"Did you see the latest issue of *VANITY FAIR*? Did you see what it said about WOODY FUCKING ALLEN? Did you see what it said about DEMI FUCKING MOORE? It was so FUCKING INTERESTING!"

"Don't my triceps look great, I've been working out."

"I just waxed my car! I just waxed my skis. I just waxed my legs. I just waxed my brain."

"I LOVE MOVIES WITH EMMA THOMPSON. THEY'RE SO . . . MOVING."

"OH, I'M GOING TO GET AN EARRING AND PUT IT IN MY NOSE!"

"OH, I'M GONNA GET A BASEBALL HAT AND TURN IT AROUND BACKWARDS."

"OH, I'M GONNA GET A TATTOO!"

I'm gonna get a *tattoo*, man, I'm gonna tattoo my *eyelids*. It's gonna say: BLOW ME . . . so everybody knows how I feel about 'em.

OH I'M SO WORRIED ABOUT THE RECESSION!

OH I'M SO WORRIED ABOUT STARVING AFRICAN CHILDREN!

OH I'M SO WORRIED ABOUT THE PLAYOFFS!

OH I'M SO WORRIED ABOUT LYME DISEASE!

OH I'M SO WORRIED ABOUT THAT STAIN ON THE RUG!

OH, THANK GOD I'M NOT POOR!

OH, THANK GOD I'M NOT BLIND!

OH, THANK GOD I DON'T HAVE AIDS!

THANK GOD I'M NOT A FAGGOT!

THANK GOD I'M NOT A NIGGER!

Blow me. Blow me. Blow me.

I'm gonna find the biggest ugliest pig, all covered with mud, and I'm gonna take that pig and lift up its curly tail and I'm gonna grease up its asshole with Vaseline. And then I'm going to get a huge hard-on and shove it in. And while that pig is squealing with joy, I'm gonna be smoking crack in a giant crack pipe while Sally Field stands behind me in a leather bondage outfit with a strap-on dildo, fucks me up the ass while she bangs me over the head with a giant wooden mallet.

It will be a lot more interesting than driving my Honda Accord in the fifty-five-mile-per-hour zone. A lot more interesting than grinding my amaretto-flavored coffee beans. A lot more interesting than setting my alarm clock to 6:15 A.M. A lot more interesting than reading *Time* magazine's analysis of Ronald

Reagan's colon polyps. A lot more interesting than listening to Michael Bolton sing songs of LOVE.

Hey, you know what I'm descended from, man? Animals, man. Animals are put on earth to do four things: eat, sleep, fuck and bite each other. That's it. That is what I'm genetically designed to do. Eat, sleep, fuck and bite. All the rest is extra. All the rest is some shit some little dogs made up to get in my way. Hey, if you can't run with the big dogs, stay under the porch.

I was going down the highway the other day, minding my own business and a state trooper pulls me over. He comes up to the car and he said, "Son, do you realize how fast you were driving?" I said, "Why don't you tell me—while you BLOW ME!"

I went down to the unemployment office and there's this lady sitting behind the counter, she's *eating* from this giant bag of potato chips, she's got a can of chip dip on her desk, she's dipping the chips in the chip dip. She's eating while she's talking to me. She goes, "You're not fit for employment." I said, "YOU'RE NOT FIT TO BLOW ME."

I'm standing in line for two hours to see this movie they should pay *me* to see, and this security guard in a uniform with a nightstick comes by and goes, "Get in line. Get in line. Get in line." I said, "GET IN LINE TO BLOW ME!"

This guy comes up to me and says, "Have you heard the good news? God loves you." I said, "Look, I met God, and he's a five-foot-tall Chinese transvestite with AIDS and he told me to tell you to BLOW ME!"

I'm going through a change of lifestyle, I'm going to change my lifestyle.

I'm going to stop bathing, stop brushing my teeth, stop wiping my ass. I'm going to smell so bad people are going to smell me before they *see* me. They're gonna run away when they smell me coming. I'm going to overeat. I'm going to eat ten Sara Lee cakes every day, all covered with whipped cream and melted butter. Four or five a day. I'm gonna get so fat that when fat people see me, I'm gonna *cheer them up*. I'm going to be a junkie, take every drug: crack, Prozac, Advil, Children's Tylenol. I'm gonna be so bad, strung-out junkies are gonna see me and go, "There but for the grace of God go I." I'm going to hang out in shopping malls and become a serial killer. Have a freezer in my basement full of body parts. I'm gonna bring them up piece by piece, put 'em in the microwave, cook 'em and eat 'em while I watch tapes of the last episode of *FRIENDS*!

(Falls to his knees) I want you to shave my hair off, peel my skin off, wrap me up in rusty razor wire and whip my feet so that maybe I can feel something real for just two or three seconds. So that maybe, just maybe, I can CLEAR MY HEAD OF ALL THE NOISE! *(Pounds his head on the floor)*

FROM "31 EJACULATIONS"

(1996)

65

NUMBER 19

So I'm walking around the apartment nude, my erection waving in front of me like a divining rod. It was sure to stay rock-hard for a while, since I had about fourteen rubber bands wrapped tightly around its base. I could see the shaft was turning purple. Only problem was—now I needed something to shove up my a-hole. And finding the right item was mildly embarrassing, since I had to search all over the bungalow, and I don't keep any curtains on my windows. I know the woman across the way sits in the darkness and watches me. She works for an executive at a movie studio down in Culver City, so keeping an eye on me is probably the most fun she has all day. I should send her a bill.

I was on a mission. Find something longer than it was wide. Door handle, no good. Bicycle pump, too painful. Small vase, too wide. And then I remembered: old faithful . . . vegetation! I mean you really have to wonder why God made all these vegetables in the form they take. And indeed, I was in luck, a bag of organic carrots was nestled behind a six-pack of soy milk on the bottom of the fridge. I selected a nice thick one and I was all set. A little Vaseline daubed on for comfort and—Uhhhhhh!—rock-and-roll!

Now I was in fine shape, looking good! Rubber bands strangling my dick, clothespins on my nipples, a freshly shaved head and a carrot up my ass. Time to get busy. A little Oil of Olay on the old helmet—buff, buff, buff—bring it up to speed. Oh yeah. Feeling fresh. Get out that hash pipe packed with Maui bud. Umhmmm, here we go. Like a mallet beating a xylophone, that THC strokes up the cocaine percolating through my bloodstream. I'd try another hit right now, but shooting up with a carrot in your ass can be dangerous. (Sit down too fast you could rupture something.) So I take a sip of a Starbucks triple espresso. Gone cold, but I'm beyond temperature. Time to fly! Polish, polish, polish . . . oh yeah . . . memories coming up, dimly, faster, stronger: playing doctor behind the shed, getting pissed on for the first time . . . and now . . . oh yeah . . . Where am I? Living room, get into the bathroom—quick! Oh yeah, oh yeah, there it is, the noose, my lover, over the door. The noose, the noose. Just get my smooth head in there. Quick, the train's coming into the station!!! Oh yeah, and nudge that carrot. Uh-huh. Here we go, coming, gonna come, get it tight around the neck, now DROP . . .

66

THE PROMISE

Garrulous, menacing, shouting into a mike directly at the audience:

LET'S GET ONE THING STRAIGHT. THERE ARE THOSE THAT RULE AND THERE ARE THOSE THAT ARE RULED. THE FUCKERS AND THE FUCKEES. THE MASTERS AND THE SLAVES. THAT'S THE WAY THE WORLD WORKS. THE WINNERS, THE LOSERS, THE KILLERS AND THE DEAD. AND I AM THE TOP DOG. AND DOG SPELT BACKWARDS IS GOD.

THOSE WHO WANT TO FUCK WITH ME, I GOT ONE WORD FOR YOU: *PAIN*. YOU DON'T LIKE PAIN, DON'T GET IN THE RING WITH ME, 'CAUSE I'LL BREAK EVERY BONE IN YOUR BODY. JUST TROT DOWN TO THE LOCKER ROOM AND HAVE A TEAR-FUL LITTLE SHOWER.

IF YOU DO LIKE PAIN, YOU KNOW WHERE TO FIND ME . . . 'CAUSE I'M THE DOG ON TOP!

(Slams down the mike stand. Pause. Then gently into the mike:)

Thank you.

67

INTRO

Lights up. The man slips on a black sports jacket and walks toward the audience.

Thank you, thank you. Thanks so much for coming by. I really appreciate it.

Tonight we're going on a journey. This theater is our ship and I'm your captain. Hopefully, you're going to see things from a slightly different perspective, gain a little insight, renew your empathy . . . And we're going to have some fun too. I'm gonna give you that Lenny Bruce–esque experience that transforms tragedy into comedy. That turns it all upside down and cuts through the bullshit and the hypocrisy . . . Because that's what theater is all about, isn't it? Insight into human nature. And with that insight comes understanding; with understanding—action; and from action, change and a better world.

Sure, I'm just one guy up here. And let's face it, you're pretty much a room full of strangers. But tonight, tonight we become as one. Tonight we're not just separate individuals, islands, lonely and adrift. Tonight we are like snowflakes in a storm, swirling together, each one of us unique, but also part of something much larger, each one of us a frozen droplet of potential . . . As we swirl together tonight, who knows where we might end up? We are limited only by our imagination! Perhaps as a snowdrift high upon a mountain peak! Perhaps the highest mountain—Mount Everest! Why not? . . . We fall gently, one upon the other, one flake upon his fellow flake, immobile, caught in the frozen silence of the Himalayas.

Until one day, the sun warms us and we melt. We become a trickle, the trickle becomes a stream, the stream a river, as we reunite with all the other little drops and become a mighty torrent. Powerful, roaring, cascading—we are the *Ganges*—yes! Immense, pouring down into the valley. Full of life and energy and *fish*! People are swimming in us! Bathing in us! Laughing, joking!!! . . . Elephants squirt arcing sprays from their trunks! Shamans baptize their followers in our sacred waters! Dark-eyed women scrub their washing on the rocks, pounding their dhotis and saris with sticks, the water droplets splashing joyously up into the air! Even the dead are brought to us upon their fiery funeral pyres, as they say their final good-bye to this transient life. People chant! They sing! They celebrate! We are the river, we are life itself! We are HOLY!

(Pause.)

Wow. All that right here in this theater, tonight.

And so, hopefully, if my humble little show touches you in any way, if I do manage to reach out and communicate to just a few of you, an incremental change may come over you, and you might walk out of this theater a slightly different person . . . You'll walk out of here and who knows what you might do? Maybe you'll write that letter to your mother your therapist has been telling you to write. Break up with that boyfriend who's been vegetating on the couch for the last six months. Lose ten pounds. Throw away those cigarettes for good. Give someone a hug . . . Or write a novel. A play. A screenplay!

Inspired, you just might invent something, some great new invention—penicillin! Well, they've already invented penicillin, but something *like* penicillin. Something that changes the lives of millions. That changes the course of *history!*

Or not.

Maybe *none* of that will happen. Maybe you'll just walk out of this theater, and enjoy nothing more than a pathetic wordless ride home, you realizing that, despite my every effort up here on your behalf, *nothing* has changed, there has been no progress in your life whatsoever. And indeed you will go home and set the alarm clock one more time, knowing full well that you're going to get up tomorrow morning, same as every morning, and go back to that same godforsaken job you hate with every molecule of your being. And everyone of those misfits you've endured for the past five, ten, fifteen years, will be there tomorrow, same as yesterday, same as today and there's *nothing* you can do about it.

You are locked in an endless cycle of conformity, a grinding featureless routine, punctuated by only the most lame and insipid diversions, of which *this* is obviously one.

And I want to tell you, I relate. I identify. I do. I feel your pain. And it hurts. It hurts a lot. And I want to help. But I can't help. There's not much I can do about it from this vantage point.

I don't have any answers. I don't have any "message." I can't make you *think* unless you were already thinking before you came by the theater. Which is a fifty-fifty proposition. All I can do up here is distract you for about seventy-five minutes. Make you *numb*, sedate you. Make painless this unending trail of shit we call a life. This tar pit of stupidity, this vat of spiritual oatmeal, this slimy snail track of frustration, this pointless, stupid, mosh pit of fuckwits and hypocrites and pinheads with whom we must *cohabit* like ants on an anthill, like crabs in a bottle, like bacterium in a dirty drop of water, endlessly fighting and competing, fighting and competing, fighting and competing, consuming and shitting. Like food tubes with absolutely *no* purpose whatsoever.

Let's be honest. You'll sit here tonight, watch the show, leave, shove an ice-cream cone down your throat . . . And come tomorrow morning, this show, like that ice cream, will be nothing more than a vague memory, flushed away and forgotten.

I don't know why I waste my breath. Because everybody knows, everybody knows what I'm saying, but everybody pretends not to know. It's mass delusional self-hypnosis. It's meaningless. Really. C'mon! Communication? Inspiration? Insight? Bullshit.

If I had any guts at all, I'd walk off this stage right now. *(Walks offstage. From off)* I'd walk off and I wouldn't come back. *(Returns)* But I don't have any guts. And I need the check.

OK. OK. OK. You want insight into human nature? OK, here's some insight into human nature. Let's play a little game, we'll call it: "The Insight into Human Nature Game"! . . . No, that's a lousy name for a game. Here's a much better name. We'll call it: "Who Wants to Be a Millionaire?" But we won't play the TV version, that's bull. Let's play it the way it's really played in the real world. "Who Wants to Be a Millionaire?"

(He jumps over to the mike, and speaks in an announcer voice) OK, contestants! You know the rules! There's a little button in front of each one of you. Push the button and one million dollars tax-free is instantly deposited in a Swiss bank account in your name. But don't forget when you push that button, millions of people will also be instantly thrown out of work and spend the rest of their lives in abject poverty and misery.

Question: How long do you *wait* before you push the button?

Or let's bring it right here, right now: There's a button in front of each one of you. You push the button and I go up in a big ball of flames. And I die, writhing in agony, right before your eyes. Question: Do you push the button, or do you just wait for the person sitting next to you to push the button?

(Youthful voice) Yeah we went to this show, man, and it was kind of interesting. There was this guy onstage talking about something, I'm not sure what, and then he just went—whoosh—and went up in a ball of fire! Turned all black and wrinkled-up and crusty like a piece of chicken you leave on the barbecue for too long. It was awesome! *(Catches himself)* I mean it was disturbing, too, you know. It really made me think.

(Switches back to normal voice) C'mon, admit it. Wouldn't you love it if I just dropped dead up here right now? Wouldn't that be a unique experience? Right? You don't really know me, why should you care? You could dine out on that one for the next six

months: "I was there, man." You could email your best friend: "Went to this show, guy died onstage. It was . . . it was disturbing. Really made me think."

If you think there's any level of compassion or empathy or civilization whatsoever being shared out there by anybody, I got news for you, there is none. Wake up and smell the coffee, it's anarchy. It's chaos barely being held together by pious hypocrisy and gross sentimentality. The blind leading the blind.

No, that's not right, it's the *retarded* leading the blind. *(Forrest Gump voice)* "Life is like a box of chocolates. You never know what you're going to get." Great moments in Western civilization! I have to write that one down. Never thought of things that way before: "You never know what you're going to get"! Deep! A hero for our times. *(Voice of Karl from* Sling Blade*)* "SOME CALL IT A SLING BLADE." Great retard, Billy Bob. Will somebody please give that man an Oscar? "Some call it a sling blade." *(Dustin Hoffman* Rain Man *voice and posture)* "Eighty-two, eighty-two, eighty-two. Two hundred and forty-*six*, two hundred and forty-six toothpicks in the box, Raymond."

(Drops to his knees, pleading to the audience) WE'RE DOWN HERE LOOKING UP AT THE MENTALLY HANDI-CAPPED. WHERE DOES THAT PUT US???? RIGHT IN THE ESPRESSO BAR WITH A TATTOO AND A CELL PHONE, THAT'S WHERE!

(Jumps back into Forrest Gump) "Life is like a box of chocolates, you never know what you're going to—" I KNOW WHAT I'M GOING TO GET, I KNOW WHAT I'M GOING TO GET: I'M GONNA GET *FUCKED*. THAT'S WHAT I'M GOING TO GET!

68

VOICE IN THE WILDERNESS

Audience member, seated, fanning herself with her Playbill. *Disgruntled:*

What's this show about anyway? What is this? What are you *talking* about up there? What happened to the journey down the river? I was looking forward to that part. You came out, you were saying life is beautiful and how theater was about insight and communication and I thought, Well, it won't be *Venus in Furs*, but at least I'll be moved. I want to be moved! I want *catharsis* when I go to the theater!

Instead you start swearing and became very negative. *Very* negative. I spent the whole afternoon at the yoga center getting rid of all my stress. I come by here to see a nice piece of theater and now my neck hurts…just by listening to you for five minutes. What are you saying, we should all just *kill* ourselves? Is that what you're saying? All these unlikable people! Why? Why can't you be more positive? Why can't you make a show about *nice* people for a change? Why all this negativity? What's the point? I need *you* to tell me that life is suffering? I know, I know!

I was a subscriber at this theater which I will not name at this point in time, and I want to tell you, they decided to do all these

Greek plays. *Ancient* Greek plays. Oh my God! These people were eating their own children! They were having sex with their mothers! Chopping up barnyard animals! Why? Can you explain that to me? I can't think of a good reason. And look at Greece today! Look where all that negativity got them! Nowhere!

I'm confused. And to tell you the truth, it's the theater that's confusing me! I live in a nice world filled with nice people. My house is clean. My children are doing very well, thank you. Neither myself nor my husband is an alcoholic or a drug addict. So how come every time the lights go down I feel dirty? I feel like I'm at a peep show for perverts? Seriously, is that all the world is? Depressing negativity? Why? Will you please explain that to me? Please?

(Rummaging around in her handbag) I know I have a piece of hard candy here somewhere, where is it? *(Finds a hard candy, unwraps it and sticks it into her mouth)* You know what your problem is? You're too negative. You know why you're so negative? You're full of *fear*. My therapist told me that, cost me a hundred and fifty bucks. I'll give it to you gratis. You're full of *fear*. Because you have no spirituality. You don't believe in anything. You need to have more *faith*!

And what's the deal with your hair? Is that your real hair or do you have that done?

(She fans herself with her Playbill.*)*

FAITH

Leaps out of the chair, addresses the "theatergoer" in the chair:

"FAITH"? You mean "faith" like faith in my government?

(Swivels around and mimes firing two handguns at an invisible assailant.)

WATCH OUT! HE'S GOT A GUN! *(Mimes shooting)* BOOM, BOOM, BOOM, BOOM!!! *(Trots forward)* I THINK HE'S GOT A GUN! *(Mimes shooting)* BOOM, BOOM, BOOM, BOOM!!! *(Stands over the "fallen target")* I'M PRETTY SURE HE'S GOT A GUN! *(Mimes shooting at "prone figure")* BOOM, BOOM, BOOM, BOOM!!! *(Stands over the "body," kicks something out of the way. Looks up, distracted)* Never mind!

(Addresses "theatergoer" in chair again:)

Or maybe you mean "faith" in the goodness of mankind? I'll have to take a trip over to Chechnya or Bosnia or Rwanda and refresh my memory of how wonderful people can be to their fellow man. I'll pick up a femur, keep it on my mantelpiece to remind myself of human nature.

No, you don't mean any of that, do you? You must mean "faith" in *God*! Right? Is that what you mean? Faith in a "higher power" as we say these days.

(Turns away from chair and addresses the audience:)

Well, let me tell you something: *my* God—I believe in God—*my* God is a capricious little fucker. Or should I say "big fucker"? I mean, here's a guy—we're all clear here on who God is, right? The most powerful being in the universe! Has to be, if He weren't, if there were some other being more powerful than Him, well then . . . that guy would be God wouldn't he?

My God is all powerful. He can do anything. My God could feed every hungry person on the planet Earth—like that *(Snaps fingers)* —tomorrow! He could rid the world of disease—like that. *(Snaps fingers)* All those little bald children on the Cancer Channel? Gone, healthy, in great shape! *(Snaps fingers)* God could do that.

He could give us an extra hour of sunshine every day. Create a few more parking spaces. But noooooo! That would be too easy. He doesn't want to do *that*! No, my God doesn't like to do the easy stuff, it's boring to Him. He doesn't want to do what everybody wants Him to do. Kind of like Lou Reed, He does what He wants to do. He's got integrity. He's not going to sell out.

So, anyway, my God is hanging around Heaven one day, two thousand years ago, getting a little antsy, and decides to take a trip down to Palestine, starts hanging out with this Jewish chick named Mary. Right? Kind of a weird name for a Jewish girl. But anyway, they get busy and the next thing you know, she's knocked-up, pregnant. Nobody's even sure how He did it. Kind of a theological question: Does God have a dick? If He does, how *big* is it? How many angels can dance on the head of it? We don't have to answer that question tonight.

And they have this kid, baby Jesus. Not just any kid, God's *only* son. God isn't like some kind of NBA player that has a kid in every town. This is God's *only* son, the only son of God. (By the way, I'm not making any of this up, it's all in the Bible, you can read it when you get home.)

So what does God do with His *only* son? Does He take him

to a ball game? Teach him how to fish? Read him the Sunday comics? No, He has him tortured to *death*. Takes this poor guy. This meek, little, skinny Jewish carpenter. Nice guy, sweet guy, looks just like Willem Dafoe. With the little *Home Improvement* carpenter belt, little hammer and everything. Has these Roman soldiers march this poor little guy all over town in his underwear, whipping him, sticking things in his side, the sponge with vinegar (which I never got), giving him a hard time, crown of thorns on his head, the whole nine yards. Terrible. Dragging this huge piece of lumber on his back. How ironic, he's a *carpenter*.

They drag him up on top of this hill, nail his hands to the wood. Can you imagine what that felt like! You ever get a paper cut? How much *that* hurts? *NAILS!* I mean, who thinks this stuff up? *Daddy*, that's who! *(God voice)* "Just use one nail on the feet, I'm building a shed behind Heaven, I don't want to waste the hardware."

(He strikes a crucifixion pose: arms out, head tilted, looking upward.)

And Jesus's hanging there in the sun, cooking, blood dripping. His abandonment issues are kicking up. His inner child feels like shit. He's got some issues with his father. So he looks up to Heaven and says, *(In a California surfer voice)* "Like, Dad? Yo, can I ask you a question?" *(Contemplates one nailed hand, then the other)* "Are you pissed off at me about something? Because I've been really good, you know? I've done everything you asked me to. Did all the weddings and the bar mitzvahs. Hung out with those twelve deadbeats. And they never pick up a check, Dad, *never*. Walked on water. And then you wanted me to go out in the desert and I did it. Said don't eat anything and I didn't. Don't drink and, Dad, you can get real thirsty in the desert. And then Satan came and tried to tempt me with like chicks and money and he even said he could get my film into Sundance and I said, 'NO! Get thee behind me, Satan-dude. Uh-uh, not inter-ested, because I'm with the Big Guy.'" *(Points upward, pulling at his nail)* "Owww! 'I'm with the guy upstairs, I'm with *DADDY*!'"

(Jumps off "cross"; preaches in a Holy Roller voice, very animated:)

BECAUSE HE *BELIEVED*! HE BELIEVED THAT THE GOOD LORD WOULD *PROTECT* HIM. HE BELIEVED THE ALMIGHTY LORD WOULD TAKE HIM INTO HIS ALL-POWERFUL ARMS AND SHELTER HIM. HE BELIEVED THAT THE GOOD LORD WOULD TAKE CARE OF HIS LITTLE SHEEP! HE HAD *FAITH, FAITH, FAITH*!!!

(Switches back to normal voice:)

So, what happens? The old man in the sky, *Daddy*, took little Jesus, His son, nailed his skinny butt to a piece of wood in the middle of the desert so a bunch of jerk-offs could check him out like some kind of rotisserie chicken at the Safeway.

Now the only reason I bring all this up, and this is kind of the long way around to make a point, but dig, this is what God does to His *own kid*. You really think He's going to get all bent out of shape worrying about *your* anonymous ass? I doubt it. I doubt it *sincerely*.

You want me to have "faith"? I have faith. I have faith that *shit happens*. Really, really bad . . .

70

ARABS

His face changes expression as if witnessing some horrible event on the horizon over the audience's heads. Redneck voice:

OH MY GOD, NO! THEY JUST BLEW THAT BUILDING UP IN OKLAHOMA CITY! THAT'S THE WORST THING I EVER SEEN IN MY LIFE! HUNDREDS OF PEOPLE KILLED! LITTLE CHILDREN! WHO COULD A DONE SOMETHIN' LIKE THAT? *(Realizing)* MUST A BEEN ONE OF THOSE ARAB TERRORISTS! SURE IT WAS! ONE OF THOSE A-RABS. LOTS OF A-RABS OUT HERE IN OKLA-HOMA CITY! YEAH IT WAS ONE OF THEM ARABS ALL RIGHT. ONE OF THEM BUSHY-HAIRED, BEADY-EYED, BIG-NOSED, BLACK-BEARDED, TOWEL-HEADED, OILY-SKINNED, SMELLY, GOAT-FUCKING, MOHAMMED-LOVING A-AS-IN-ASSHOLE-ARABS. *(Gesticulating, miming)* WHY WHEN WE GET A HOLD THAT SAND NIGGER, WE'RE GONNA SHOVE A POSEIDON MISSILE RIGHT UP HIS CRACK, TEACH HIM *YOU DON'T FUCK WITH THE U.S. OF A*!!!!

(Cocks his head) Wait! What's that? Not an Arab? Blond hair? Blue eyes? Loves Kenny G? Shit, well, he must be misguided then. We have to learn to understand and forgive. But you're right, right! He killed all those little kids, and many of whom were white. We're gonna have ta lynch him! Come 'ere you Timothy McVeigh! Quick where's a rope? Where's a tree? Where are the TV cameras? This is America—can't do this without a TV camera. Where's an anchorman, where's that Bernard Shaw guy?

(Bursts into operatic voice à la My Fair Lady*:)*

> The rain in Spain
> Falls mainly on the plain . . .
> La-la-la-la-la!!!

(Switches back to redneck voice:)

NO, NOT THAT ONE, YOU DICK! THE CNN ONE! WHERE IS HE? IN KOSOVO? WHERE THE HELL IS KOSOVO? WELL, WE NEED AN ANCHORMAN! YOU, YOU'RE AN ANCHORMAN, GET UP THERE, LET'S GET THIS SHOW ON THE ROAD! *(Counts down with his fingers, facing the upstage mike on its stand)* FIVE, FOUR, THREE, TWO, ONE! YOU'RE ON!

(Runs over and gets behind the mike, switches to anchorman voice, speaking calmly and directly to the audience:)

A dark day dawns on this American city this morning. A city in mourning . . . this morning. What forces seek to disrupt our cherished American beliefs of love, peace and justice? A tragedy. Children were killed. Why? Who knows? Some lunatic got "pissed off." A veteran? Perhaps. Let's not think about that too much—it hurts to think. Let's think instead of our president's words just this morning.

(Switches to hoarse Bill Clinton voice, almost cheerful, eyes twinkling:)

This is a terrible thing. We are so sad today. We will find the motherfucker who did this and we will kill him as slowly and painfully as possible.

(Anchorman voice:)

Today, as we feel this tragedy, let's feel all the tragedies. Let's think about crack babies and homeless people and starving Africans. And let's cry. Let's all have a good cry. For them and even more so, for ourselves. Because we feel their pain, because we know their pain, because we want their pain to go away so we don't have to hear about it anymore. Thank you, good night. And remember that tonight's Oklahoma City bombing coverage will preempt the previously scheduled documentary: "Hiroshima: The Little Nips Got What They Deserved," or "Hiroshima: If They're Not White, It's Not Terrorism," or "Hiroshima: Thirty Thousand Is Not Really That Many People When You Consider the Alternative," or . . . And now a word from our sponsor:

71

THE OFFER

Easygoing, sipping from a mug of coffee.

Do you feel like life is passing you by? Do you get up in the morning and ask yourself, "What's it all about anyway?" And what's your answer? Prozac? Viagra? Suicide? Hi, I'm Satan and I'm here to tell you there's a much better solution.

What do you want out of life? Money, power, sex? How about guns? Drugs? Fireworks? You can have it all. But why stop there? People come in and say, "I want to have sex with my secretary." Come on! Use your imagination! How about sex with your *grandmother*? Sex with your neighbor's *dog*? Sex with your own *kids*? The sky's the limit. What have you got to lose? Your *soul*? Hell, when was the last time you even knew you had one?

Time to stop *denying* yourself. Time to start doing *all* those things you *always* wanted to do! And I'm not just talking about smoking crack and chowing down on Krispy Kreme doughnuts. I've got clients out there today, doing really creative things like fire-bombing helpless villages, stockpiling anthrax, rigging election ballots. Why should the big boys have all the fun?

So many millions of miserable people are out there not over-eating, not smoking, not drinking, not masturbating! No wonder you're all so depressed. And why? To be good? Because "God's watching you"? I got a little secret I'll let you in on: God's got better things to do than watch you play with your pee-pee.

You know, I was checking out that plane that crashed in the Rocky Mountains last week. Three hundred people dead. Boom! Like that. Body parts all over the snow. It was awesome. And all I could think was, I wonder how many of them were on a diet? How many were trying to stop smoking? Hey, they're smokin' now, baby!

Only one thing I can't get you and that's *peace of mind*. It's not my thing. I honestly think it's overrated. All these people trying to chill out and calm down and be serene. You'll have plenty of time to be serene when you're six feet under in a box. You want serenity, you gotta go to those other guys, Jesus and Buddha. See what that gets you. A REALLY BORING LIFE. But what do I know, I've only been in business for over five thousand years! Fuck me.

So come on down and sign on the dotted line, you *know* you want to. We're here for you, twenty-four-seven/three-sixty-five. Especially Christmas and Easter. Time to start living!

72

THE AIRPORT

Addresses the audience:

So I'm in the airport the other day. It's a special experience going to an airport these days. It's pretty much a paradigm for life as we know it today. There are only two modes: running and waiting. You know the drill, you've all been to the airport. Hundreds, thousands of people. Running, waiting. Or some variation thereof: running to wait, waiting to run. Standing in ticket lines, sitting in the departure lounge, crowded around the baggage carousel, watching the luggage coming out as if awaiting the birth of your first child: "Oooooh! Look, look! Here it comes!" Washing and flushing in the smelly restrooms. They never stop cleaning the bathrooms at the airport. Trying to take a leak while some guy mops around your feet. *(Miming harried pisser)* "Just a sec, just a sec!!!" *(Hops from one foot to the next, still holding on to his dick)* "How's that?"

Drinking in the bar area, sitting on those ugly bent chrome-and-naugahyde stools, watching the drop-down color TV, watching live coverage of plane crashes from around the world. Snacking in the snack area, being served by the sullen Mexicans and

Pakistanis shoveling out the tacos and nachos and hot dogs and doughnuts and pizza. Chewing furiously like rodents before dragging their dirty little spoiled children from Cleveland to Orlando to Denver to Philly to L.A.

(Starts running in circles, illustrating:)

Running to wait. Waiting to run. Faster and faster. Hot decaf lattes sloshing out of the cups scalding their hands. Beepers beeping. Overweight garment bags ripping the muscle and sinew from their shoulder bones. John Grisham novel tucked safely under their arm. Cell phones to their ears.

(Removes a cell phone from his jacket pocket and puts it to his ear as he finds a spot in line:)

73

GOLD CARD

Talking into his cell phone, harried, nasal businessman:

Jerry, yeah, hey it's me. I'm at the airport. Oh, they delayed my flight and they're gonna stick us on another plane. No, no problem, I've got the gold card. Just a sec, Jerry, someone's asking me something. *(Turning, putting the phone to his chest)* This is the gold card line, do you have a gold card? *(Reveals gold card from his pocket)* One of these? You don't have a gold card? See that long line runs all the way down through the terminal? That's your line. No, I don't know where you get one. Sorry. Good luck! Have a nice flight! *(Returns to call)* Jerry? Yeah, so, no, things are very mellow. I've been taking this meditation course. It's great, only takes thirty seconds a day, and the best part is, you can be doing something else at the same time! And me and the fam just got back from vacation, man! Oh, yeah, kind of a *working vacation.* Pittsburgh! In the morning I'd see clients and then in the afternoon we went sightseeing, visited coal mines. *(Checks his watch)* So listen, Jerry, I just wanted to call to say they're keeping me out in L.A. through the weekend, so gonna have to scratch the golf date. Yeah. So how's next week? No? Uh, week after that's no good for me. And next month I've got the convention in Chicago. Then I hit Detroit, Osaka, Tampa, Vancouver, Mexico City and Ulaanbaatar. Then after that is my busy period . . . Well, hey look, we'll get together sooner or later. We're best friends, aren't we? Look, Jerry, why don't I call you, say, in two months, how's that sound? And hey it was great getting together with you last year. Sorry I had to leave a little early, I had a client in town. OK! Yeah, me too, I gotta go, too. Yeah. Cool. OK. Say hi to Janey. Judy, Judy, right.

(Starts to dial again, then notices someone cutting ahead in the line.)

Excuse me? Sir? Excuse me! This is a line here. We're standing in line. *(Pause)* I know you have a gold card, we *all* have gold cards in this line. This isn't some new-age party game, it's a line. *(Pause)* Oh, OK, no problem, an honest mistake. *(His eyes follow the interloper making his way to the back of the line, past him)* I'm curious though, you came in here, you saw all these people standing in line and you thought—what?—Oh, look at all those people standing in line. I'll just cut in front of them, fuck them.

Hey, you know what? *FUCK YOU! (Pause)* Watch my language? Watch my language? You walk in here, treat me like shit on your shoe and you want me to watch my language? You know what you are, pal? You're the kind of person when they have those soccer games in Europe a riot breaks out and everybody's rushing for the gates, you're the one who steps on some baby's windpipe.

No, no. You know who you are? You're the kind of person who, when a plane crashes in the Andes and the survivors are freezing and starving to death, you're the guy who starts chewing on someone's leg!

But why should you care what I have to say? You're never going to see me again. I'm nothing to you. Just one more anonymous human being in your way. I could drop dead at your feet right now, and you'd just step right over me: "Oh lucky day, an extra space in line!"

(Dials the phone again, but then can't help himself; he turns.)

You know what you are? You're everything that's wrong with the world today. Nobody respects anybody else anymore. Nobody wants to participate in civilization. That's what this is. This line, this line of ten people standing here is civilization. And *you* are the Dark Ages, pal. You are the barbaric hordes coming *down*. That's what you are. You are the Mongols, the Huns, the Visigoths, the Turks. Why don't you just get a sword and chop us all to pieces? Then there'd be no one ahead of you. You could stick our heads on poles. Maybe send us to a camp someplace. Yeah, just go stand in that line! That's not the gold card line.

(*Into phone*) Sonia? Hello, honey? Oh, honey, it's Daddy. Jeremy, is Mommy there? Get Mommy . . . Daddy. Daddy. DADDY! The guy who lives in your house. Listen, can you get Mommy. I'm at the airport, and it's an emergency and I have to talk to Mommy right now. (*Impatient, but talking in a slight babyish tone*) Yes. That's right. Daddy's going to fly in a big airplane. No, no, I don't think so. It's not going to go "BOOM" and crash. That wouldn't be nice, now would it? Get Mommy please. Huh? Of course I'm gonna get you something. Don't I always get you something? I don't know, something. Yes, it'll be worth at least twenty dollars, yes. Please get Mommy. Get Mommy now.

(*Pause.*)

Hello? Hello? Sonia! Why are you letting him pick up the phone? What if it were an emergency—the plane was about to crash and I want to tell you how much I love you—and I'm explaining the meaning of life to a six year old? (*Speaking more and more rapidly*) Well, I don't know, they canceled the flight and they're moving me from line to line and the battery on the laptop went down and I'm fibrillating from all the cappuccinos I've been drinking. Well, I don't know what they did before laptops, I'm just saying . . . Oh, you'll never guess who just came into the lounge. Here! Here! (*Covers the cell phone not to be overheard, whispering*) Calista Flockhart! I can't say it any louder than that. (*Again covers the phone, almost unintelligible*) Calista Flockhart! (*Out loud, figuring it out, in awe*) We must be on the same flight! We'll be breathing the same air molecules all the way to Los Angeles!!! Wow. Do you think she'd think I'm an asshole if I asked her for her autograph? Wait, what's the name of her TV show? Come on, Sonia, this is important! Listen, call my sister in Buffalo, ask her what's the name of the show that *(Whispering)* Calista Flockhart *(Normal)* is on—she knows these things. Put it on my voicemail, I'll check in later from the plane. Just do it, OK? For Jeremy, please?

Oh shit, they're calling me for the flight. So listen, the reason I called is I'm not coming home tomorrow, they're gonna hold me out there until Monday for meetings. I know. I know it's our anniversary but . . . Of course, I don't have to. I can come home right now if I want. Do you want me to come home? You want me to come home? I'll come home right now. I won't have a *job*, but I can come home. I don't need this job. I'll just stay home, we'll make tie-dye T-shirts, candles, macramé.

Honey, honey, don't say that. We have lots of quality time together. Of course we do. What about Pittsburgh? You got to wear that neat hat with the little light in the front. Oh, now you're crying, come on!

Honey, listen, I promise when I get back, we'll take the frequent flyer miles and we'll go somewhere really nice. Someplace expensive. With a spa, yes. With massages, yes, facials. I don't know if they'll have liposuction, I don't have the brochure with me.

Listen, honey, let me get on the plane. I'll call you from the plane. *(Starts to move toward the gate)* Listen . . . Sonia, the next time you feel bad about us always being apart, just imagine this: You and me, together all the time, working a double-shift at a McDonald's . . . I gotta go. OK, all right. OK, all right. I love you, too.

74

UPGRADE

Perky and patronizing:

Here you go, sir, you're all set. You have a seat on this flight, it's leaving in ten minutes so you better hurry up! Yes, sir, that's right, it's a coach seat. Yes, I know you had a fully-paid-for-first-class ticket, sir, but this seat is coach. Well, let me see what I can do, OK? *(Types into keyboard)* All right, I'm looking at a first-class seat on a 3:30 A.M. departure with a six-hour layover in St. Louis. How's that sound?

Yes, 3:30 in the morning, sir, that's correct. I understand that, sir. Yes, I can see that you have a gold card. All the people behind you have gold cards, sir. Well, sir, sir, sir, why don't we do this: Step aside for a sec here, let me get everyone on board, get them seated, let the flight leave and then we can see what we can do, OK? *(Signals to next person)* Next in line?

I'm not trying to get rid of you, sir. Our gold card passengers are our first priority. Would you like a voucher for a complimentary cup of Starbucks coffee while you wait? Sir! Sir! Sir! There's no reason to use that language. May I remind you, sir, that we are being videotaped as we speak, and this videotape is admissible as evidence in any court proceedings that may arise from our conversation on this date.

Well, I'm sorry you feel that way. Yes, you may file a complaint. Just get in touch with our operations manager. He's not in right now, but if you'd like to drop by tomorrow morning around seven A.M., I'm sure he'd love to see you.

You can't, sir, no. No, you can't sue us, sir. Well if you read the notice on the back of your ticket you will see that it says that when you fly with us you agree to abide by all the rules and regulations of this airline and any disagreements you have with the rules and regulations of this airline are subject to arbitration by an independent arbitrator. OK?

You *can* win, sir. You can win. You just can't win *today*. Have a nice flight!

Next!

75

HARMONIOUS

A man speaks in a British/Indian accent, deep and resonant with a slight lisp:

Thank you so much for joining me tonight on this journey of spiritual recovery. Let me remind each and every one of you in this room that you are full of energy. With this energy, each of us can change our lives. Together we can change the world.

The first thing you must understand in order to harness this energy is that *you are nothing*. You do not exist. There is no "you." You are only a temporary vessel for the use of the universe to make manifest this moment and this time. You are merely one stitch in the vast carpet of the cosmos. You are no more than one grain of sand in the endless Sahara of the universe. You are one hair on the butt of the hairy gorilla.

The second thing you must understand is that we exist in two states. We are either in sync with the universe or we are out of sync with the universe. When we are in sync with the universe, we call this being *harmonious*. When we are out of sync with the universe, we call this being *alienated*.

We are either in sync or out of sync, harmonious or alien-ated. How do we know which state we are in? *(Pause, smiles, shrugs shoulders)* We just know!

So let us now clear our minds and still our centers. And let us contemplate these two states of being—harmony and alienation:

I am warm, I am happy, I am harmonious.
I am cold, I am angry, I am alienated.
I am swimming in my heated swimming pool. I am
    harmonious.
I am doing my taxes. I am alienated.
I am buying a brand-new Lexus with all-leather interior.
    I am harmonious.
I am working three jobs to pay for health insurance. I am
    alienated.
I am flying first class to St. Barth's. I am harmonious.
I am going to jail for food stamp fraud. I am alienated.

If we carefully meditate upon these two states of being, we find a deep and abiding spiritual principle becomes obvious: Alienation is simply a lack of *money.*

And, of course, the corollary: Money brings deep and abiding harmony.

When we have money, our days are full of sunshine, the air is fresh and clean. We love everyone we meet. And everyone loves us.

When we lack money, we become empty and angry. We listen to overly loud music. And we are frequently constipated.

And so each and every one of us is on a path and must answer the eternal question: "How do I get more money?" This is the path that I am on. That is why you are here tonight.

The paradox of life is . . . paradoxical. In order to breathe in, we must first breathe out. In order to grasp, we must first let go. In order for the sun to rise, it must first set. In order to take what I have to give you, you must first give me two thousand dollars in four easy installments.

Life surrounds us with an endless bounty. An overflowing cornucopia of goods and services. They are all there for our tak-ing. We only have to pay for them. Thank you. *(He puts hands together in prayer and bows silently)*

76

BREAKTHROUGH

A man sits talking to an unseen listener.

I had a pretty good week this week. Constructive. Constructive. I've been thinking about what you were saying last week about, you know, putting things on the shelf and how I've got to learn how to love myself today, because if I don't, who will? Like you say, "I'm not a human being trying to be spiritual, I'm a spiritual being trying to be human."

I saw my ex . . . Picking up the kids.

Total pain in the ass. As usual. Oh yeah. Oh yeah. You know she still blames me for the breakup. It was all my fault everything got fucked up. Hey, if she had kept a better eye on things and not let me stay out every night till four in the morning but, no, that had nothing to do with *her*. When I was there getting arrested and wrecking the car, did she ever think, Maybe this is a cry for help? You know, I'd be in the kitchen, seven A.M., puking my brains out, and she'd be getting the kids ready for school and she'd act like I wasn't even there. Completely ignore me. Did she ever stop to think, Poor guy. Why is he doing this to himself? How can I help him? No, she's a completely self-obsessed human being, out of touch with her feelings. I had to live with that all those years.

Well, I took the boys to the ball game. Oh yeah, it was fun. They're so great. Acting up, throwin' Cracker Jacks at each other. Yelling, screaming. And I'm like, "Hey! Hey! Hey! Quiet the fuck DOWN! RIGHT NOW!" I'm so good with those guys, you know? Oh! Oh! And this busybody behind me is like, "Stop yelling at your kids, I'm trying to hear the game." And I'm dealing with boundary issues today, like we've been working on, so I'm like, "Are these *your* kids? Or are these *my* kids?" Right? "You don't hear me telling you to stick a sack over your wife's head 'cause she's so fuckin' ugly." And from this, the guy gets an attitude. You know? All indignant. Gets in my face. Now I'm in a fight. How did this happen? And I can walk away, I can walk away. But I have my needs today. And I've learned to respect my needs. And my need was to punch him in the face, so I did.

So yeah, we got thrown out of the stadium. But you know, shit happens, I understand that today. I take life on life's terms. They give you lemons, you make lemonade.

The kids don't always understand. The little one was like, "Why were there only four innings in the game, Daddy?" (*Laughs*) They're so cute. And they want the pennants and the key chains and the baseball caps. And I'm honest with them, you know? "Sorry guys, Daddy doesn't have any money. OK? Daddy doesn't have a job, OK? It's not Daddy's fault he has a dickhead boss who can't take a little honest criticism."

And the little one's like, "I want a Derek Jeter autographed baseball, I want a Derek Jeter autographed baseball." Like a broken record. And I'm like, "You want a Derek Jeter autographed baseball? Go ask Derek Jeter! He's probably got baseballs lying all over his house."

So now *he's* crying. And I'm guilty. I want to kill myself, right there. I even said to them, "You know what? You kids piss me off so much, I'm going to jump in front of that subway train, right? Get sliced right in half. Then you'll be happy. Just like your mother!" Of course I didn't. I can't win!

I drop the kids back at my ex's. And she's all pissed at me for giving 'em Cracker Jacks for dinner. You know what? I *love* my kids. They want Cracker Jacks for dinner, they can have Cracker Jacks for dinner. I was denied that love as a child when I was their age. And I'm not gonna do that to my own flesh and blood.

So she gets on the phone to her best friend, complaining about how I'm not nurturing, blah-blah-blah. Right in front of the kids. Emasculating me. Fortunately, I know what to do today. I calmly walked over to where she was standing, grabbed the phone, and pulled it off the wall. I did not throw it. I did not throw it.

And she goes berserk. Screaming and crying. Nuts. I'm like, "HEY GET OFF THE CROSS, WE NEED THE WOOD!" And I can't be around all that insanity today. It's too much for me.

But it's OK. You know, one thing I've learned here is that in every couple, there's two people. The lunatic and the sane one. And we know which one I am. I know when I'm not wanted, so I split.

So finally I get home. Fortunately Terry is there for me. Thank God for Terry, my only friend. She knows how to be there for me. She never takes my inventory, never judges me. Never yells at me. I mean, she barks at me every now and then when she wants to go out for a walk. But that's the thing about dogs— they're there for you. They're centered. I mean, Terry's got her shit figured out. I look into her eyes and she's so centered . . . "spiritual." Unqualified love. That's the only word for it.

Sometimes I think that's the only time I'm really at peace, when I'm sitting there with her watching TV. By the way, she loves all the same shows I do. It's like, "Why can't things always be like this?" You know? But I know why. Because the world is full of assholes, that's why.

And then *Oprah* comes on TV. She's got this guy, this doctor, and he says . . .

Right, shit! *(Checks his watch)* OK, well, next Wednesday sounds good. Sure. And don't let me forget, I still owe you that seventy-five bucks from last month. You know, I really feel great coming here. I'm a completely different person now. I feel a breakthrough coming, don't you?

77

THE AUDITION

A man approaches "two people" and shakes hands. His first handshake is warm and friendly; the second is respectful, slightly awed.

Oh, hey, how you doin'? You look great. Oh . . . Hi, hi, sir, it's an honor to meet you. Yeah.

(*Steps back*) Uh, just got back from L.A., actually. Pilot season, you know. (*Pause*) What was the last thing you would have seen me in? Uh, did you see *The Matrix*? I was in that, yeah. Did you see it? You know when Keanu was pushing through all those crowds of people on the sidewalk? I was one of those people on the sidewalk. Oh yeah, working with Keanu was great. He's a great guy.

(*Pulls pages of a script out of his back pocket.*)

Yeah, she did . . . She said I should read pages twenty-five through thirty-five? Just twenty-five, OK. And my agent said it should be "intense but funny." (*Listens*) "Funny but intense." Right.

OK.

(*Turns to an invisible video camera, starts to read from the script:*)

"Hey, man, listen, it's not the end of the world. Linda isn't . . ."

Wait, I'm sorry. Could I start again? I'm a little nervous.

(Settles, exhales, turns around, faces upstage, shakes hands out, chants "om." Returns.)

"Hey, man, listen, it's not the end of the world. Linda isn't the only woman in existence. Hey, I got an idea, my cousin Sharon is coming . . . uh . . ." *(Changes inflection)* "Hey, I got an idea, my cousin Sharon is coming to town next week and why don't we all go out? Do something." *(Pause)* "Of course she's good-looking! Hey, man, would I lie about this to my own best buddy?"

And listen, could I please also do page thirty-five? I worked pretty hard on it last night with my coach. Only take a sec . . .

"Hey, man, listen, it's not the end of the world. I know, I know, I'd be pissed off, too . . . but how could I know she was a *lesbian?*" *(Chuckles)*

What a great script. You know why this script is so great? It's *intelligent.*

So do you want me to try it a little more intense? A little funnier? . . . It was perfect? Oh thanks, coming from you that means a lot to me.

So. OK! Uh, that's my new head shot. My new number is on the bottom. Or if you need to reach me this afternoon, I can give you my beeper number? . . . You don't? Oh, OK. Well, I want to say thanks for, you know, asking me to come in. And I didn't want to say this before, but . . . uh, you're pretty much my favorite director. I see all your movies and I think you're a genius and really admire your work. *(Looks over at the casting agent)* OK . . . I know, I've got to get going, too, we're all busy, OK . . . thanks . . . *(Again to the director)* Thank you. But before I go, could I ask you a question? I've been writing this screenplay, and I was wondering if I wanted to get it to you, how would I do that? *(Again in response to the casting agent)* OK, OK, heh, heh. All right, I'll just drop it by the casting office. Yeah, I should go . . . but thank you again for having me . . . Right, I'll let you guys . . . I'm pretty busy, too . . . but thank you, thank you for having me . . . OK . . . Bye!

(He runs off.)

78

THE LADDER

As embarrassing as all this looks, this is what's called "auditioning." In fact, that was a verbatim transcript of an audition I was on just last month. Actually, I'm exaggerating, I was much more obsequious.

It's important that I audition because it reminds me of why I became an actor in the first place. For the *pain*.

Because pain is important. Some day, when I'm riding around in my stretch limousine gazing out the tinted windows at all the losers out there living their humdrum existence, that pain will come in handy. I'll be able to say to myself: "I deserve this. I earned this. I PAID MY DUES, MAN."

Because that's what it's all about when you think about it, about making a supreme effort and rising up to another level of existence. Another plateau. Another *world* where everyone knows my name and wants my autograph and smiles at me wherever I go, listens to my opinions even when I don't know what the hell I'm talking about. I'll go to a diner and the waitress will cut me an extra slice of pie. Go on a plane and the stewardess will flirt with me while she fluffs my pillow. I'll be walking down the street and someone will shout out the window: "HEY, ERIC!

ALL RIGHT, MAN!" And someone else will turn and say: "Is he somebody famous?" And a huge chorus will cry: "Don't you know who that *is*?"

I won't have to wait anymore. People will wait for *me*. No more lines at the bank, at the movie theater. No more, *(Secretary voice)* "Please hold, I'll see if he's in." No more, *(Maître d' voice)* "Yes, sir, we have your reservation right here. Your table will be ready in about forty-five minutes. Would you like to sit at the bar while you wait?" *(In response)* "*No!* I don't want to sit at the bar. If I wanted to sit at a bar, I would have made a reservation at a bar, wouldn't I???"

I'll be so rich and famous they'll throw people out of the restaurant just to make room for *me!* *(The patronizing maître d' rushes up to a table)* "I'm sorry, sir, someone more important than you has just arrived and we need the table. You have to go now. Please, hurry up. You can take your crème brûlée with you. You can eat it in the alley." *(His face lights up)* "Yes, Mr. Bogosian, right this way, so happy you could join us this evening. We have a lovely table for you. Is this table to your liking?" *(Pulling out a chair and fussing)* "Here's your napkin! Would you like ground pepper with that?" *(He backs away, twittering)* "Oh, Mr. Bogosian, Mr. Bogosian, Mr. Bogosian!!!" *(Bowing, scraping, licking the floor, etc.)*

(He returns to normal voice, but more histrionic; he addresses the audience:)

To be above the lines, above the crowds, above the norm! To be loved by millions, never again to be touched by *one!* Never again to be crushed in the fray, everyone would know me, but from afar! Real far!

People will watch me on TV. I'll go on talk shows and everyone will be riveted as I go on and on about my dog's *constipation*. People want to know that stuff. I'll complain about how the power window in my stretch limo got stuck on the way to the show. *(Voice of guest on talk show)* "I just kept pushing the button and nothing happened, Dave! Just pushed the button, pushed the button." *(Normal voice)* The audience hanging on every word. *(Audience member in wide-eyed wonderment)* "You pushed the button, yes, and then . . . ????" *(Normal voice)* And Dave, good ol' Dave, will clap and grin like an organ grinder's monkey, like I'm the smartest, funniest fuck he's ever met. And the audience will stand and cheer as I chatter on and on, because the tiniest moment in my life will be bigger than the biggest event in theirs.

See—there's another world and it's just like ours, but it's much much better. It floats above us. Call it Heaven, call it Valhalla, call it Mount Olympus! Whatever you call it, the gods are there. I'm down here on earth, but I can see them up there. I can see the gods. They're having such a great time, And I want to be up there, too. Where every seat is first class. Where every room is a deluxe suite. Where the love of millions shines like a sun that never sets!

Can you see them up there? Can you see the gods? Look at them. Aren't they beautiful? They're playing volleyball. There's Gwyneth passing off to Drew! Ooooh! Here comes Britney, and she's just been cut off by Mariah! GO GIRL!!! Oh, and there's Michael Bolton getting down with Kenny G and—oh my goodness—Sting! They're gonna jam. And there's J-Lo and Jay-Z and LL and Eminem and all the other letters of the alphabet. And there's Madonna giving birth! How *intimate!* And Robin Williams is the attending physician. Marilyn Manson is the nurse! How cool is that?

My life is good, but the gods' life is better—better parties, better clothes, better cars, better sex, better breath. And, see, I'm going to get there some day, because I'm paying my dues. I can take the pain, I'm not afraid. My nose is too big—chop it off. My hair is too curly—straighten it. And what kind of name is "Eric Bogosian" anyway? It should be . . . "Ricky"! "Ricky Hanks." Much better name!

I'll make any sacrifice, do what it takes. You want me to play a serial killer who grinds little children up and eats them for lunch? *No problemo.* I'm an actor. Get humiliated by Tom Cruise? Where's the script? He wants to kick the piss out of me too? All the better, that's what I'm here for. *(Mimes getting ass kicked across the stage)* Oh, Tom, you're so intense! *(Crashes into the proscenium, revives, brushes himself off)* The location's six months in the deserts of Tierra del Fuego? Where's my plane ticket? Sure I have a wife, I have kids. I might not see them again for another five, ten, fifteen years. But when I'm rich and famous, they'll be happy I was gone all that time because *they'll* be rich and famous, too.

And sure, maybe I'll have to step on a few people as I make my way to the top. But every head I step on will be just another rung in the ladder of fame and fortune. Because I'm honest with myself. Let's face it, we're all on a ladder, from the lowliest beggar in Calcutta all the way up to Steven Spielberg, we all have our place. And it takes guts, it takes willpower and vision to reach up to that next rung and drag myself up. And sure when I get to the top, maybe all my friends will hate me but by then I'll have new friends. Better friends. *Everyone* will be my friend!

People will line up just to hang out with me—even my parents! They'll be like Mary and Joseph standing by the manger when all the kings came by. Puffed-up with pride like blowfish. And I'll be like baby Jesus, a godlet, on the straw for all to admire!

And when my new friends come by to visit, we'll be happy. We'll be happy together because now we can do what we've always wanted to do: just hang out all day and think and talk about *ME!* Interviews with me! Photo calls with me! Me! Me! Me!

And when I get tired of my new friends, I'll say good night, climb into my king-sized four-poster bed, snuggle under the covers and pull out the remote control, and as my eyes slowly close, there I am again. On E! I'm on E! I'm on *Charlie Rose*. I'm on *Conan!* I'm on *Leno!* I'm a VH-1 veejay! I'm EVERYWHERE! I'm *ubiquitous!* *(Becomes transformed, rising to his full height, arms out, emanating power)* God-like, like the sun, my rays shining down on every surface of the earth! My tentacles entwined around every mind, every imagination! *(Playing a fan, fawning on his knees in awe)* "What is it like to be him?" *(Triumphant)* That's what they'll all want to know!

And *yes*, maybe some puny journalist will dare to question my talent. But I'll just say: "FUCK YOU! You're just a poor writer who lives in a tiny rental apartment who has to take the subway to work. I'm a big famous rich guy. I'll be around long after you're gone. Millions of people love me and no one gives a shit about you."

Even if I died tomorrow, it would make *headlines*. Because when the gods suffer, the world is *mesmerized*. Doesn't make any difference who they are: an ex-football-star crack-head wife-slaughterer; some reclusive high-pitched animal-loving child molester; a promiscuous "adult child of an alcoholic" leader of the free world!

They're famous, they're in pain, we're *sad.*

Some little baby girl in a crib starves to death in the ghetto—no one cares. Why should they? She's a nobody. It's hard to work up an emotion over a "nobody."

(Drops into a chair, a guy at home watching TV, holding remote control:)

Hey, honey, look at this! Some little girl starved to death in her crib in the South Bronx! Terrible. How do those things happen? *(Pause, his face drops)* Oh, look, oh NO! Did you hear about *this? (Almost in tears, listening to the bad news)* Kelsey Grammer has a *urinary tract infection!* Oh shit! Wow. Oh, wait a minute . . . Shhhhh!!! *(Listens)* It's OK, they're having a *benefit!* They're going to raise money to buy him a gold-plated catheter. Where's my checkbook? We gotta go to this thing. I don't want to miss it. I've always loved him. *(Looks the audience straight in the eyes, god-like:)* Some day they'll say that about *me!*

79

IN THE AIR

Seated, addresses the audience:

I'm in the air now, moving from one place to the next. Everything is taken care of. I'm strapped in and I have a purpose in life—arrive at LAX.

Things are good. My seat is comfy. I have a little white pillow and a little blue blanket. My John Grisham novel is compelling. And after dinner they'll be showing a movie, something with Tom Hanks in it. I like Tom Hanks because he's happy. I'm happy that he's happy.

They even give us dinner. Not the kind of stuff I normally eat, but they serve it, so I eat it. An amazingly white roll with butter, a salad and a salad dressing in a little plastic pouch, made with guar gum. And for the main course I had—it was good—I think it was either turkey or fish. And for dessert a little white rectangle with a red dot in the middle.

Now the stewardess comes by. She wants to know if I'm OK, would I like anything to drink? Normally, no one cares what I want, so this is very stimulating. Perhaps she really does want to know. She's smiling at me. She's very pretty. Maybe she likes me.

Maybe she's flirting with me? I know what this is about. I know how to do this. *(Transforms from mild-mannered speaker to self-assured passenger, addressing the stewardess)* I'll have a Diet Coke, no ice. And I'll keep the can. Thanks. *(Takes can, checks his watch)* Say, do you know if the flight is on time? Cool. Wow. You must fly this flight all the time, huh? . . . Just back and forth . . . What is that accent? Ohio? Really, where? Columbus? Yeah, that's a great town. Little movie theater downtown. So I'm curious, you fly into L.A. . . . *(Takes his drink)* Oh, thanks . . . And then just turn around and deadhead it back to New York? Oh, you stay overnight in Los Angeles? That sounds like fun. It isn't? It sucks? Yeah, I heard that airport hotel is pretty bad . . . Four Seasons. It's very comfortable. *(Getting more and more casual)* You know, it's funny that you should say you find L.A. boring. Do you know who Ricky Martin is? Well, his business manager's brother-in-law is good friends with my brother-in-law and he's got this sold-out concert tonight at the Hollywood Bowl . . . Oh, so you know about it, yeah, well anyway, they laid, like, two free tickets on me, front row center, and I don't really know anybody in L.A. to take. You know what? I've never done anything like this before, forget it. *(Mock surprise)* You would? Well, you'd really be doing me a favor. Yeah, yeah, well check, make your call. You know where to find me. OK. Bye. *(A twinkle in his eye)* See you in a while.

(Aside to the audience) I can see she's thinking about the free tickets to the Ricky Martin concert. If only she knew what I was thinking. I've been checking out her butt every time she turned around for the last hour and a half. Nice butt. Nice tight Columbus, Ohio, butt.

Yeah, we'll go to that Ricky Martin concert and then we'll go out to some trendy L.A. nightspot that only cool people like me know about. But we'll be above it all and leave once we get past the velvet ropes. And then . . . then we'll go for a ride . . . But they roll up the sidewalks at ten P.M. in L.A., so we'll have to go back to my room at the Four Seasons. And she'll be impressed by the four-star-edness of the whole thing—the cashews in the little mason jar, the free playing cards. We'll sit on the couch and talk about life for about three minutes, then we'll start kissing, tear each other's clothes off. And I'll get that tight little United

Airlines outfit off and that Wonderbra and that thong she doesn't think I notice underneath. And she'll be completely NUDE. Just like Mary Elizabeth when we were six playing doctor behind the elementary school. I'll be able to examine her all I want: toes, knees, belly button.

And then I'll say, "Why don't we take a shower?" That's always a good icebreaker. Girls like that. And we'll kiss under the flowing water, very erotic. And then I'll say, "Why don't I wash your back?" And I'll lather her up. I'll *cover* her with lather, I won't stop at her back. She'll be all white from all the lather and I won't wash her off . . . I'll just *(Mimes picking her up and carrying her)* carry her to the bed and she'll be this big slick white lathered-up stewardess. And I'll spread her legs, and the only thing I'll be able to see through all the soap bubbles is a little pink sideways smile looking up at me. And I'll lean over, and with my tongue, I'll very very gently place the tip of my tongue . . .

80

CAPTAIN

Jumps up and starts speaking into a mike on a stand; deep, resonant, good-ol'-boy captain's voice:

This is your captain speaking. We're currently cruising at an altitude of about thirty thousand feet with clear skies all the way in to LAX, making up a little time for that delayed departure. Which is the good news. *Bad* news is we got a little problem up here in the cockpit. Nothing to get too concerned about. Seems that when we were refueling back at JFK, the fuel gauge got stuck, and, thing is, we're not carrying a whole helluvalot of fuel this afternoon. In fact, we're pretty much bone dry.

Now you're probably asking yourself, What does that mean to me? Well, it means we're going to have to try a little landing here this afternoon. And as I just said, we are currently thirty thousand feet over the Colorado Rockies. Beautiful time of year. If you look out the right side of the cabin, you can see the aspens just turning golden there on the mountainsides. Those of you who are skiers are probably familiar with Vail or Beaver Creek. Me and the wife have a little time-share down around Eagle. We go down there for about three weeks every winter. Not that I'm much of a skier myself,

I prefer those bass-fishing shows on cable-TV. But I digress. We're going to be attempting a forty-five-degree descent this afternoon. So please check that your seatbelts are fastened securely about your middle, with your tray tables in their upright and locked position. And no moving about the cabin, please, as we make our descent. Now when we land, or I should say "scrape" into a landing, it's gonna feel kinda bumpy, kinda like we're crashing. But let me assure all of you onboard today that in the rare event we actually *do* crash, you . . . you won't feel a thing. You'll be knocked unconscious instantly, they'll be lucky if they can find our teeth when this is all over. So I'm gonna sign off now, try and concentrate on what I'm doing, instead of sounding like a damn jackass with one foot in the grave, let you get back to that movie you're watching. What is it, Billy? *Forrest Gump?* Love that flick: "You never know what you're going to get"! *(Puts his hand over the mike)* Billy, is the black box turned on? Give it a good thump with your fist. Thanks, bro. *(Full voice)* And let me remind all of you onboard this afternoon, we at United know you have a choice of airlines when you fly, and we appreciate your patronage. Have a nice day.

81

THE CRASH

In front of the mike, addressing the audience breathlessly while miming prayer:

And everyone on the plane has suddenly become deeply religious, praying silently—each and every one of them—to his or her own secret, benevolent and all-powerful God that He doesn't let the giant tin monster go swimming into some whacky air current and drag them sideways into the mountainside like one gigantic scraping aluminum fireball that millions of other middle-class Americans can watch on the evening news.

(Switches gears, surfer voice, another guy watching TV, holding a remote control:)

Oh wow, Heather, you should see this! No, it's not the new Limp Bizkit video, it's CNN, I turned it on by mistake. Whoa! A plane crashed in Colorado and they're showing it live. Wow! *(Pause)* 767! Rammed right into the health club at the Hyatt in Beaver Creek. Wow. Bodies all over the snow! Imagine what that must be like to be in that plane just before you hit. Like you know you're going to be completely flattened in about thirty seconds. Like you won't exist anymore. Every thought you ever had will disappear. All those phone numbers!

Or imagine you're in the health club working on your pecs, looking out the plate glass window checking out the mountains and . . . *(Imagines he sees the plane coming right at him)* . . . and you're like, "Oh shit," but you don't even have time to say, "shit," *(Mimes being blown backward)* and then you're covered with aviation fuel and you're jumping around frying alive in the snow . . . Oh, Heather, that reminds me did you order the crispy duck from Hunan Palace yet? I want my sauce on the side!

(Reverts to normal voice, speaks directly to audience:)

But, of course, if that actually happened . . . But then I'll be immortal. Which is what I've always wanted. I'll be up there with the gods. Nothing like a plane crash to confer immortality. Way better than a drug overdose. And you'd be happy because you would have seen one of my last performances. It would be historic. Historic and ironic. *(Audience member)* "Yeah, it was incredible: he kept talking about plane crashes and then he was *in* a plane crash!" *(Pause)* "Really makes you think!"

But then I'll be dead, which would be bad for me. No fun at all. *(Inspiration strikes)* I know, I'll *survive*. I'll be a survivor and I'll sell my story! Everyone will want to take a meeting with me. I will finally have arrived in L.A. *(Snaps fingers)*

82

THE MEETING

A nasal voice. Aging but energetic:

Eric, come on in. Siddown. Siddown. *(Points to chair)* So happy you could take the time from your busy schedule to come by. Siddown, siddown. You want anything to drink? We got it all, espresso, soy milk, guava juice, water from a melted glacier, whatever you need. Hold on a second. *(Calling off)* NAOMI! Would you come in here for a moment please? You met Naomi on your way in. She's your biggest fan, has pictures of the plane crash tacked up all over her desk. *(Introducing them to each other)* This is Naomi, my brilliant assistant. What would you like, Eric? . . . Just coffee? How do you take that? With milk? *(Walks around the chair, gestures toward Naomi)* You know, Eric, Naomi just graduated from the film school at Columbia University. Studied with *Milos Foreman*. How about that? She's writing a screenplay about the history of *feminism*. Isn't that something? *(Gazes at "Naomi" with admiration; then abruptly) Coffee*. With milk. Thank you. *(Following her out; brusque)* And, Naomi, did you call the guy at Range Rover? Did they get the stain off the seat? Follow up on that, please, Naomi. I got that Richard Gere benefit for the Dalai Lama tonight. *(Returning to Eric)* I can't show up at a Buddhist benefit in a dirty Range Rover, now can I?

A beautiful girl, isn't she? Not that I'm about to make a move. Not these days. Not these days. You know, Eric, in the old days everything was different. We were changing the world and we were having a great time doing it. Made movies about important stuff, we shook people up. Blew people's minds and then we got blown. Now everything's about money. Where's the fun anymore? What happened to the revolution? What's wrong with a couple of lines, a little reefer, some free love? No, go to rehab, go directly to rehab, do not pass go, do not collect two hundred thousand dollars! No more fooling around for me. All I do now is lie on the couch like an old dog and lick my balls.

You smoke cigars, Eric? Here, take one of these. I have a guy sends 'em up to me from Honduras. They're so hard to roll, the peasants go blind making 'em. Enjoy.

But, Eric, I want to tell you, we all watched it on the news! We were riveted! The burning plane, the ambulances, the helicopters, the bodies in the snow. It was almost dramatic. And I turned to my wife and I said, "Michelle, I have to make this movie." You understand? For me, for me. Not for the money. I don't need the money. I have all the money I need. I could have you killed right now if I wanted to, that's how much money I have.

For the humanitarian message, Eric. I want to get your story out there, Eric, because people have to hear it. Because people need a positive message in their lives, Eric.

They're tired of the negative stuff. Nobody ever changed the world with negativity, Eric. They know the world is fucked up—the ozone layer is kaput, there are terrorists around every corner, poor people in every nook and cranny—who the fuck wants to hear all that negative shit? Me, I don't even watch the news anymore. Sarajevo one year, Bosnia the next, Kosovo the next. Wrap it up already. Move on!

People don't want negativity, they want to be inspired, they want hope. They need your story. You know why? The audiences today, their lives suck. They're holding down two jobs, their kids are all on drugs, all they have to look forward to is a slow death by cancer. If it weren't for the inspiration they get from movies and TV, they'd jump off a cliff like a bunch of lemmings.

And that's what you gave 'em when they thought everyone on that plane was dead and you came walking out of the wreckage. Tears came to my eyes, I was so moved.

(Looks up suddenly) What? Naomi, bring it in. Don't just stand there. Bring it in and put it on the table! Did you bring him a napkin? Don't I always tell you, bring a napkin. Naomi, listen to me, NAP-KIN, N-A-P-K-I-N. Just put it down. It's OK, it's OK, get out.

It's mythic. Like something out of the Greek myths. Like the Phoenix rising out of the ashes. You know what the Phoenix was, Eric? It rose out of the ashes. And that's you! They thought everyone was dead, and out you came out of the burning wreck . . . with that stewardess in your arms. And then you gave her mouth-to-mouth resuscitation right there on the snow in front of fifty million people. That was incredible.

You survived. You saved that stewardess and you fell in love. I hear you're living together now. Getting married. What a heartwarming story. I mean, I'm very sorry about your divorce. How long were you married? Nineteen years. It happens, it happens. Kids? Yeah, that's always tough . . . But you know, they learn from it, Eric. It's good for them. That's what we're here for, to teach our kids. *Kids.* Mine are all grown. The oldest is just going through her own divorce, the middle one just got out of rehab, the baby's not even speaking to me.

But you know what I say to those kids? *(Flips the bird)* Fuck you! Because that's not what's important for people like us, Eric. Artists, like you and me, our work, our humanitarian message is what's important. The positive message we have to send, that's what it's all about. The humanitarian message of love.

83

SHEEP

Yeah, yeah, yeah, yeah, yeah, yeah. I'm so smart.

(Interrupts himself, picks up a chair and almost hurls it, sets it down again, and begins pacing the stage.)

In my black jeans and my righteous anger, ranting on and on about hypocrisy, pissing people off just enough to sell a few tickets. Always looking over my shoulder, making sure I don't lose my place in the big line. Desperately trying to preserve my modicum of success so that I can hold my head high in this giant pecking order of art and commerce and first-class plane tickets.

I'm a bullshit-slinger. That's all I am. One more bullshit-slinger from a long tradition of bullshit-slingers. A hypocrite. What do I do that's so *courageous* or *selfless* that gives me the right to say shit about shit?

And you, you come in here and get all fluffed up and expectant like a bunch of baby birds with your beaks wide open, waiting to be fed. But I've got bad news for you. I'm all out of worms today. Sorry! I'm empty. I'm a vacuum. I'm a black hole.

I'm just a mirror. I'm up here thinking about what you're thinking about what I'm thinking. Even right now, while I'm saying all this I'm hoping, They'll think this is really pushing it! *(Audience member)* "My God! Now he's gone too far!" But I haven't gone *anywhere*. I'm still here. And so are you. We're all here. We haven't moved an inch.

I'm just some skinny guy with curly hair and black jeans. My distinguishing characteristic is the brand of bottled water I drink. Which HBO TV show I prefer. The big choices in my life are between the *Star Wars* prequel or the *Austin Powers* sequel. The Big Mac or the Grilled Chicken. *(Scratches his chin, pondering)* "Tall" or "grandé." Yeah, those are the big decisions in *my* life.

I'm not fighting the system, I'm *part* of the system. *I toe the line*. And I do it for a very good reason: I'm a sheep. I am a gutless sheep.

So when they say, "Get in line," I get in line, you know? It isn't like I *want* to be in line. I *hate* getting in line. "I'm a rebel, man! I used to smoke pot! I marched in Washington against something once. I love to drive around in my four-wheel drive, blasting Rage Against the Machine with my seatbelt cinched tightly around my flabby middle! That's the kind of rebel I am.

Yeah, I'm a rebel, all right. But in the long run I have to get in line. I better fucking get in line. That's the deal. Because if I don't, then maybe nobody will, and if nobody gets in line, then what do you have? Chaos!

And if things get really chaotic, what's going to happen to *me*? I'm going to *lose*. Because I mean that's the whole point of civilization isn't it? To protect the weak against the strong! And when things get out of control, it's the bad guys who take over. And I'm no bad guy! I'm no Hun! I'm no Mongol! I'm no bad-ass. I'm no Hell's Angel.

(Jumps into gruff biker voice, "Red") You know when you just had sex . . . You're lying on the bed, the two of yas, you're all spaced-out. All sweaty and smelly, you smell like a couple of camels at the zoo. You got stuff all stuck all over ya. Your hair's all pushed over to one side. She's lying there, she's got a big puddle of come on her belly. And you're like writing your name in the come

on her belly. Then you go south. And then you start fooling with her honey pot. Stirring the honey, oh yeah.

And she's like, "OHHHHHH!" And then she reaches over and starts yanking on your joystick and the two of you are like, "OOOOOHHHH!! AAAHHHHHH!" Next thing you know: "Oh, look who's back in action, the little soldier! He's ready for another battle!"

So you get ready to do it again, because the second time's always the best, you know what I mean? Always more intense. And you get ready to stick it in . . . But what do you gotta do before you stick the little doggy in the doghouse? What do you always haveta do? Get out the hash pipe, right?

One hit on the hash pipe. Toss some coke on her tits, lick it up. And then you slide it in nice and slow. You stick her toes in your ears, she sticks her thumb up your asshole. You grab her ass, she grabs your butt. She's screaming, you're barking . . . *(Thrusting and shouting)* "OH, OH, OH, OH, OH!" BOOOOOOM—and you come so hard you feel like you're gonna be brain-damaged for the rest of your life, and you fall back onto the bed. But just before your head hits the pillow you grab that bottle of tequila, take one last hit as your brain does a slow-dive into a deep black hole of complete and utter *satisfaction*.

(Normal voice) Yeah, I can talk the talk, but I can't walk the walk. I'm weak and I'm scared. So I get in line. Like a sheep. Like a *cow*. So I stand in line like everybody else. Patiently waiting my turn to get to the head of the line so I can get conked on the head, a chain wrapped around my legs, get pulled upside down to have my throat slit. My blood drained and ground into hamburger. That's the kind of rebel *I* am. Just show me the line and I'll get in it. I need the line. The line is my friend.

And when the bad guys in the steel-tipped boots do show up and kick down my door in the middle of the night, I won't be a hero. No. I'll say, "I've completely rethought the revolution." *(Runs and hides behind the chair)* And I'll cower under my bed. I'll say, "I don't want to bother anybody, in fact I don't have any opinion about *anything* actually. I was just pretending to be a rebel. I'm just a little dog, see?" *(Barks a short, timid bark, gets up and starts running in large circles)* Like a little dog. Like a little dog.

I just want to be safe. I just want to hang out with all the other little dogs and run around and chase cars and sniff other doggies' butts and piss on trees. Just give me a bowl of water and pat my head and tell me I wrote a nice screenplay and I'll wag my tail and go sleep on the couch and not bother anybody.

(Curls up on the chair) I just want to be one of the pack, an ingredient, a component, a cog in the wheel. That's what I am, a cog! A cog dog. *(Stands on the chair)* Cog dog, cog dog, cog dog, cog. *(Barks three long howls)*

84

THE HIGHWAY

Effects of cars passing. Lights up reveal a man standing with his thumb out, hitching.

I hope we get a ride pretty soon, man, it's getting cold out here. *(Puts his hand up in refusal)* No coffee for me, man, it's not my thing anymore. You know? All those little starving peasant coffee farmers down in South America? I don't want to be responsible for all that, you know? Like you're either part of the problem or you're part of the solution. No coffee, no sugar, no meat, no Nikes. It's all connected man. It's all part of the big picture. If you don't believe that, then it's like we're living in a giant TV screen that isn't tuned to any station. Billions of dots, bouncing and frying around. Noise in a void. Snow. Dots. But there's always a big picture. Sometimes you can't see it, but it's there.

(Lights of a passing car.)

Last night I was hitching, and for a few minutes everything made sense. The stars were floatin' high in the sky. I could smell the grass. The crickets were cricketing. I was in harmony with the universe.

And then I heard this sound from far away: BEP!!!! BEP!!!! And then I saw it, this giant eighteen-wheeler blowin' down on me, doing ninety miles an hour. And I looked up through the windshield, I could see the driver. One of those bizarro zombies from our modern-day life. Big thick neck. Beard stubble. Circles under his eyes from all the porno videos he's been watchin'. Totally *insane!* Chowin' on this huge meatball sub as he drove.

And I thought, That pretty much sums it up. *Meatballs*, man. Like what's the karma in a meatball? Only humans make balls out of other animals. Like when you're in kindergarten and you're coloring in your coloring book: What does the doggy say? "Bow-wow!" What does the kitty say? "Meeoww!" What does the moo-cow say? "AARRGGGGHHHHHH!!!!!!"

Oh yeah, dude tried to run me over, man! And as I jumped out of the way and he blew past, he had his window down and he was swearing at me: "FUCK YOU, YOU LOSER SHIT FREAK FUCKIN' PIECE OF SHIT ASSHOLE SUCK MY DICK YOU FUCKHEAD FUCK FUCK FUCK!"

Spitting out these gobs of phlegm because he's filled with mucus from all the dairy products he consumes! And then reached up and—BLAAAAAAP! BLAAAAAAP! BLAAAAAAP!

Totally fucked me up, man. Couldn't hear the crickets for hours. Like what's an air horn, man, but the sound of the end of civilization?

See I can't be around all that toxic shit anymore, man. Cannot do it. That's why I hit the road, man. Oh yeah, I just went into the boss one day and said, "I'm outta here." . . . What? Oh, he didn't care, he's got people lined up around the block to make those lattes. He just looked at me and said, "What are you going to do for money?"

And I said, "I don't need money, man. Money's just to buy stuff. And I don't need stuff. I'm free. I mean, look around us, man, all these cars, always movin' out on the highway. They never stop. Like ants in an anthill. Ever watch ants, man? I love watchin' ants, man. Always busy doing something really important like moving a cookie crumb from here, (*Indicates*) all the way over to there. That's what all these cars are doin', just movin' stuff around. But instead of popsicle sticks and bits of chewed-up leaf, they're movin' DVDs and running shoes and frozen turkey burgers and microwave popcorn and flawless pieces of fruit with the little stickers on 'em that you can't get off . . . back to the anthill.

Oh, my boss? He said, "Yeah, well you'll be singing another song when you're old."

And I said, "When I'm old same thing'll happen to me that's going to happen to you. I'm gonna die. Except that *you're* gonna be so rich with your portfolios and mutual funds and IRAs and all that shit they won't *let* you die. They'll stick you in one of those old-age cells with adjustable beds that go up and down and a remote control for a TV set. Just hope you're not paralyzed or you'll be watchin' Home Shopping Network 'round the clock for the rest of your feeble life.

"Me, when I die, I'm just gonna curl up on a pile of leaves in the middle of the woods and croak. And, maybe if I'm lucky, an acorn will get lodged in my butt crack. And a giant oak tree will grow out of my ass and drop acorns all over my grave. And then a deer will come and munch on those acorns and my karma will go from those acorns into that deer. And then a mountain lion will come and eat the deer and my karma will go into that lion's sperm and when the lion makes it with his old lady I'll come back as a baby lion." *(Mimes the baby mountain lion padding about)* "Spend my next life in the woods, just boppin' around doin' that mountain lion thing."

Oh, he just gave this weird look, patted me on the back and said, "Good luck, dude."

And I said, "I don't need the luck, man, you're the one on the *Titanic*."

Alaska. The last real place in America. Alaska.

Just gonna take this highway as far as it goes, then find a road and take it as far as it goes, then find a path and walk it until there's no more path, until I'm completely surrounded by woods. And then I'm gonna step right into the wilderness. Just live on berries and shit. Not bother anybody. Not hurt anything.

Something I have to do, man. Because I'm a first-class passenger on the spaceship Earth. I've got a one-way ticket so I have to make the ride count, you know? And as far as I figure it, you can either take the service road or the scenic route. And, man, if I only have one ride, I want it to be beautiful.

And if nobody ever hears from me again, you know, it'll be OK. If nobody knows where I am, I won't mind, because I'll know where I am, and that's the most important thing.

(He jumps back as three cars pass in succession, followed by an enormous truck. He watches in stunned dismay as the truck passes, roaring into the night. Fade to black.)

FROM "THIS IS NOW!"

(2005)

85

THIS IS NOW

Ohhhhhmmmmmmm. Ohhhhhmmmmmmmm. Ohhhhhhmm-mmmm. NohhhhhhhhW. NohhhhhhhW. Now. This . . . this, This . . . this. *This.* THIS . . . is . . . this. This is . . . *(Softly)* now. *Now.* This is now. Right. No, wait . . . *This* is now. No . . . *this* is now. No. *This* is now. This is now. THIS IS NOW! This is now. This is now.

    (Anchorman voice) This is Now.

    (Easy-listening voice) This is now.

    (Stoner) This is now, dude.

    (TV ad voice) Right Now!

    THIS . . . this . . . THIS!

    This, *this*, this.

    (Bright and happy) This! *(Happier)* This!! *(Happier)* This!!! This is this. Is now.

    Now. Now. *(Almost angry)* NOW!

    (Insistent) Now. *(More insistent) Now!*

    Now? This? Now? Now? Now?!

    Is this now? Now? Now? This? This?

    How's this feel? Now? This? Now?

    This? This? This???

This is now. No, this is now. No, this is now.

Now. This. Now this. Now *this*!

Now. Now. Right now.

Check check test. Now? Now. Now? OK, *now*!

If not now, when? If not me, who?

Right now. Right this second. As we sit here. All over the world, brains encased in skulls, on top of *bodies*, moving, sleeping, eating, fucking. Each one has an imperative. It's own unique imperative. Because each one is "in the now," *but* the now is different for each one. So which one is "now"?

(Sotto voce à la Richard Foreman) You. Thinking. Breathing. Right now. Watching. Listening. Waiting . . . to hear something perhaps . . . Funny? Urgent? Interesting? Scary? Distracting? From your own now.

Take what you hear, take it in. Collect, take in and paste onto what's there already. Like a mental dung beetle. Rolling the giant ball of collected nows along the path toward the *next* now, which you will pick up and paste onto NOW.

Which will inevitably create the you inside of you. The collage composed of every movie and song, person and place, book and TV show you've ever experienced, all collectively providing you with a sense of you-ness. In the now-ness. In there, in a massive jumble of everything-ness. Until the bottom falls out of now and you start all over again.

(Slow) BUSH. WAR. BUSH. CUNT. BUSH. Push, push in the bush. Disco. Bee Gees. John Travolta. Stardom. Hollywood. Coolness. Non-coolness. Success. Failure. Death.

You're thinking, Hmmmmm. You're thinking, I don't buy this. You're thinking, What a load of shit. But behind that thought is another thought. You're thinking, Will she think I'm cool for bringing her to this self-indulgent performance thing? I'll cut my losses. I'll mock it when we leave. Joke around. We'll have some drinks. Laugh at the weirdos. Then maybe she'll fuck me.

Maybe she'll fuck me.

Maybe she'll fuck me.

Maybe she'll fuck me. Now.

Now?

(As in, "Yes!") Now.

She fucked me.

It was good.

But I wasn't good. I wasn't good at all. I was bad.

She fucked me up. Now I'm all fucked up. Now . . . she . . . fuck.

Now, she's pregnant.

Now, we're having a kid.

Now we have a kid. We have two kids. We have three kids.

Where can we live? How can we live?

I don't make enough money.

My career is just getting started. Now is not the time.

We have all these kids. Is that what it's all about?

I'm worried about the kids. Where are they? Right now? Where are my kids? Home with the sitter? But we don't know this sitter. The sitter is an unknown. She may be psychotic. She may be harmful to my children.

I may be psychotic. No, just anxious, fearful. Depressed. I suffer from depression and low self-esteem. Maybe I should take Prozac? Maybe I should control my urges? Maybe I should stop smoking?

86

SMOKING

Deep voice, calm, even:

I've tried to stop smoking.

I know it's important not to smoke. In fact, it's stupid to smoke. I smoke, but I try not to smoke. Every time I light a cigarette I think, I should *not* be doing this.

I want a better life. But it's an uphill battle, it *is* an uphill battle because I try to do the right thing, but I don't do the right thing. And . . . I smoke anyway.

Fuck it, I don't smoke that much. The chances that something really bad will happen to me as a consequence of my smoking habit are slim. In fact the chances that something *else* might happen to me for *other* reasons are far greater. Something will happen to me, though, sooner or later. That's guaranteed.

I could be immolated in a fiery plane crash. Or I could be infected with a fatal flu, or flesh-eating bacteria. Suffer a massive coronary. Slip on an icy sidewalk and lie there for hours slowly freezing to death. Choke on a chicken bone. Fall down an elevator shaft. I could be robbed at gunpoint and stupidly resist and get shot. Get hit by a speeding beer truck while crossing the street. Get dragged out in a riptide and get torn to pieces by sharks.

Fate has something to do with this. But there is no fate. There's just . . . happenstance versus my urge to control . . . my fate.

Still I try not to smoke because lung disease, specifically lung cancer which is the most prevalent form of cancer, is primarily caused by smoking tobacco, which furthermore is a product that has no constructive use and is farmed and marketed by massive evil impersonal corporations. If for no other motivation than political reasons, I should not smoke.

So I try not to smoke.

Plus if I ever *do* get sick from smoking, I will hate myself. I will hate myself while I am wracked in unbelievable pain, as I undergo chemotherapy and radiation and surgery. As my bank accounts are drained by massive uninsured health-care expenses, and as my wife and kids and everyone I know hate me for ruining their lives. Perhaps my last thought on earth will be, I was so fucking stupid to smoke!

But see the problem is, *(Beat)* I like to smoke. It gives me pleasure. I like to smoke because it makes me feel . . . different. When I smoke, I stop worrying for a moment or two. I stop worrying about all the things that might happen that are bad. I lose my fear. I feel happy. Even a little giddy.

Deep down the truth is I enjoy smoking because I'm not supposed to do it. And sometimes I want to do things that I'm not supposed to do. It's just a deal I have with myself. An attempt at . . . freedom.

Anyway, I'm sure if this were a bad habit that I knew for certain would cause incredible grief to myself and other people, like, for instance, being a serial killer, then of course, I would stop. *(Beat)* I think.

But stopping a habit simply because of a potential predicament in the future, well, that's asking a lot isn't it? Of human nature. Of *me*.

And besides, the problem with completely eradicating this bad habit from my life is that a vacuum will be left behind, a kind of hole. Something would be missing that was there before. Something that made my life complete.

The man on TV, the man who knows everything that's good for me, says: "*Fill* that *vacuum*! Fill that *hole*! Fill it right up. Now what are you going to fill that hole up with? How 'bout GOD? Have you thought about GOD? Just use GAAAWWWDDD like plaster. Spiritual plaster. And fill that hole up with Jesus or Buddha or Abraham or whoever you like. HIGHER POWER! Replace the bad thing with the new thing, the good thing!"

(Even more energy) Just fill it right up. And then I'll be fixed. I won't need to do the bad thing anymore.

Because God will be there instead. Right? God-plaster. It's logical, right? "God is love." Replace that cigarette with love, with unselfish behavior, right? That's spirituality, right? But what if I don't have *enough* love?

See, it's all a matter of relative degree. Because sooner or later, no matter what I do, I will do *something*. Something. And if that new something that I do isn't absolutely perfect behavior, then that new something that I do will become the *new* bad thing. The thing to be cast out. "If thine eye offend thee, cast it out!" Right? Makes sense. Sort of.

Not really. Because if I never did anything bad, then I'd be a fucking saint. And even the major saints weren't good all the time. They went through all this trouble of being a saint, and STILL, they were bad sometimes. Imperfect. Augustine and Saint Francis of Assisi and Thomas Aquinas, all those guys. Major league saints. Bunch of nut jobs giving themselves a hard time. Because, honestly, who wants to be like them? Those guys wore hair shirts and ate dirt and gave away all their worldly goods and all that, and I just think that's going too far. You know?

AND BY THE WAY—I'm a human being! Humans *are supposed* to be bad.

So Jesus came down out of Heaven! He came down because he thought he could get through to us. And the people checked him out! And they said, "Who the hell is this guy?" But Jesus, he was patient and he said, "Listen . . ." And they said, "Son, we can't listen, we're too hungry." So Jesus said, "OK, here's some loaves and fishes." And everybody ate till they were full and then he said, "Listen, if a mustard seed . . ." And they said, "Wait a minute, wait a minute, wait a minute, this *cat* over here is *blind*, what about that?" And Jesus said, "*No problemo*," and *(Sax beep)* gives the guy sight. Starts with the Good News routine again, "The fruit of the tree . . ." Blah-blah-blah. And they're like, "Fuck the fruit of the tree . . . check out, Lazarus over here, he's *dead*. Bet you can't do anything about that." But Jesus was like this codependent social worker, he won't quit. Brings Lazarus back to *life*! Everyone's like, "Wow!" . . . Jesus is like, "See?" And they're like, "NO! . . . DO IT AGAIN! DO IT AGAIN!" Eventually Jesus just got burnt out from trying to keep everybody happy. And when he ran out of tricks they got bored, so they nailed him up to a cross. Forgive them Father, they know not what they do!

See, all us self-improvement people, who spend all day obsessing about our own behavior, we're just this tiny little segment of the world's population. Not even a majority in the United States, just this thin, thin layer of humanity, this thin, thin, thin layer, like a layer of scum floating on top of a very big pond, who have either the time or the luxury of worrying whether we are eating too much cholesterol, or not getting enough fiber, or aren't recycling properly, or aren't getting enough miles to the gallon in our SUVs, whether we've booked our next pilates session or yoga class or tooth cleaning or colonoscopy. Most of the people in the world have no money.

None. Zero. No bank account. No pocket change. No jar of pennies on the dresser. Nada. All they have is the flip-flops on their feet and the chicken clucking in the yard. Spend all their live-long day searching for clean water and firewood, and hope they don't trip over a landmine while they're doing it. These people don't worry about sunblock, or flossing after meals, or whether there's bacteria on the sponge—they don't. They don't worry about any of it. And if they get a chance to smoke a cigarette, they smoke it. Whenever they can.

87

CHEESE

For Frank Z.

Say "Cheese!" . . . Cheese. Delicious melted cheese. Tangy, flavorful, mouth-watering. Now imagine that delicious cheese smothering your choice of all-white chicken meat, barbecue pork or shrimp. Then wrap that heavenly concoction in bacon, drench it in a buttery golden batter and deep-fry it to crisp perfection. What you've got is Dunkin' Donuts new "Say Cheese" breakfast celebration!! And we're not just talking about *one* kind of cheese, we're talking about *every* kind of cheese! Oh yeah! Swiss, parmesan, mozzarella, cheddar, gouda and *more*. All your favorites. Blended together in a tangy, multicultural mouth-watering jamboree! Can you imagine the flavor?

Cheese that melts in your mouth, meat that sticks to your teeth, and a crispy golden coating that screams, "I want more!" And you can *have* more. Because Dunkin' Donuts new "Say Cheese" breakfast celebration is an all-you-can-eat special breakfast for those times when you're hungry for as much as you can cram down your pie-hole! . . . And all you have to do is say, "Double Down," and we'll throw in your choice of fries, baked beans or tacos for free! . . . Can you imagine a better way to start your

American day? So whaddya say? Why don't you, "Say Cheese!" Get over to Dunkin' Donuts today and get yourself a great breakfast!

(New voice) Limited time only. Not available at all stores. Dunkin' Donuts reserves the right to make substitutions in cheese varieties. Not affiliated with any other offers. Not responsible for health consequences, which may include nausea, vomiting, flatulence, heartburn, acid reflux, diarrhea, constipation, incontinence, duodenal and peptic ulcers, arteriosclerosis, dementia, early onset Alzheimer's, cardiac arrest, stroke, Type-2 diabetes, obesity, gross obesity, depression and death.

88

CONFESSION

In the name of the Father, the Son and the Holy Ghost, Amen. Dear Lord . . . forgive me for I have sinned. I have done many bad things this past week. Things that I am almost afraid to confess . . . O Lord Jesus, have mercy on my poor soul. Please show me the love that you have shown for the vilest leper and the most wretched whore . . .

Jesus, I have sinned. I have been drunk twice this week. And while I was drunk, I smoked a lot of cigarettes and I swore. I told a story that mocked black people and that made fun of a woman's breasts . . .

Jesus, I have sinned. After I was drunk, I drove home and I broke the speed limit and tried to run over a dog. And I took your name in vain. Jesus, forgive me.

And Jesus, I have been gluttonous, too. On Thursday night, while I was watching TV, I ate an entire carton of ice cream, two bags of potato chips and eleven Slim Jims.

Also I have been lecherous, Lord. The same night, I watched the Mandrell sisters on television and imagined them naked and making lesbian love to one another . . .

And, Jesus, a man in my office was promoted over me, and I wished that I had the promotion instead. And I cursed him.

But, Lord, my worst sin is hard for me to say . . . I had a fantasy, Lord. I had a fantasy about that guy in the office. I had a fantasy that he and I were alone together after work. And when he turned his back to me, I grabbed a pencil from my desk and stabbed him in the neck. And when he fainted, Lord, I tied his feet and hands to the desk. Then I poured lighter fluid over him, Lord . . . and . . . and while he was burning I popped his eyes out with a letter opener. Then I broke the blade off the paper cutter and sawed off his arms and his legs while he screamed. Then I ground the pieces of his body up in a paper shredder and flushed them down the toilet. Then I took his still-screaming torso and compacted it in a trash compactor . . .

O Lord, forgive me, I have sinned . . .

89

THE QUIET MAN

A man speaks to the audience in a very sincere, direct and quiet manner:

This is my place. Welcome to my place. This is the place where people come to watch people. People love to watch people, don't you think? I know I do . . . There are so many, the variety is endless.

I can't imagine anything finer than a sunny Sunday afternoon in the park where I can just sit and watch the world go by. The young couples in love. The sturdy joggers. The pretty girls. And the children. I especially love to watch children playing . . . The way they sort of tumble along, singing and laughing in little voices . . . Everything is exciting and amusing, everything is new to them. Everyone's their friend.

"Little people." It's a miracle that hands could be so small and perfectly formed. Eyes so bright. Skin so fair. They haven't a care to wrinkle their small brows.

(Pause.)

Sometimes, one will come close by where I sit. Perhaps a little girl of nine years or so will come and quietly look at me. I can almost picture her now, the little rosebud of a mouth, the tummy thrust forward, the knobby knees peeking out from under a frilly dress. An angel come to visit.

How I memorize each feature as she stands before me; each gesture, each breath. If I sit very still, she might even speak to me. This is when I must be very gentle, careful not to scare her.

"Would you like to sit down?" I might ask.

She turns to see if Mother's watching, and then, like the little lady she is, she places her sweet bottom on the bench beside me. Then she asks me, "How old are you?" And I just smile . . .

She reaches out and touches my hand, curious, yet so cautious. If I am really lucky, she doesn't let go.

We hold hands and watch the world go by together . . . I look down at her shining hair, her barrette . . . the tiny, immaculate ear, the slender neck. So fragile . . .

What could be better than this? To be so close to pure hope . . .

(Pause.)

The mother calls. And my little friend, forewarned about the peril in our illicit love, runs off . . .

As I wave good-bye.

90

BEAT POEM

A man wearing sunglasses speaks into a microphone. His voice is resonant and hip.

I open my eyes
to the ragged skies
of another hot city morning.
The sirens scream
the hookers dream
a beggar shouts a warning.
I know this place
I've been here before
it hasn't changed in a hundred years
of tears and beers and cheers and leers and fears
in the asphalt-covered, blood-encrusted, copper-jacketed,
broken-glass-ornamented highways and byways of a
never-never land called:
"Take me out to the ball game, baby,"
honey-chile
suck my dick in the thick of the midnight fog
when the razors get sharpened

and the needles get filled
and the red flowers blossom
and the dragon's tail gets chased.
I know, I know
I know all about this place where the black leather buckles
and nooses go 'round and 'round and 'round
my arms and legs and necks and tongues
in the gray, gray cold dark beach sand morning
when the connection is closed and the Night Train's empty.
I know.
And I wake and I walk,
past hydrants gushing, cops reading, pigeons pecking,
bottle men digging,
past hustlers hustling and winos dying.
Past all that, past you, past me . . .
past the past and past the present.
I am the ancient insect trying to molt my skin and
find a new morning, but this morning . . .
"There's nothing happening, man!"
Like they say, like they say,
"To be or not to be—that *is* the question."
And then, and then . . .
A small piece of crumpled green paper on the ground.
Manna.
Specie.
Do-re-mi.
A portrait of a president if you will.
Who knows who lost it?
Maybe some nine-to-five, square-as-a-cornflakes-box
capitalist slave to the oppressive red, white and blue
Apache dance called America.
I don't know who lost the dough,
but I know who found it.
A member of the underclass
a member of the holy class
one of the knowing ones, one of the chosen ones
doomed to walk in the summer's heat
in search of powdered poppies.

Doomed to ride the white horse.
Sail the crystal ship.
Fly the magic carpet.
Me.
To be found, to be found, so that I am no longer lost!
And I find my man—
the heartless doctor who heals my soul, who gives me
my medicine.
And I take it and I
love it, cook it, smother it with my arms and
flesh and cells and blood.
Let it flow . . . let the tears of God flow into my arm.
Let the white mix with the red.
And then . . . and then . . .
This morning doesn't have to be broken glass and barnacles
sticking to the underside
of a long lost ghost ship of a life . . .
But a morning like any other . . .
full of coffee and cigarettes
and newspapers
and corn
muffins . . .
In the valley of the shadow of death . . .
my cup runneth over . . .
As the hydrants gush
as the sirens scream
as the hookers bop
as the junkie nods . . .
Forever
and forever
and forever . . .
Amen.

91

FOOD

A man stands at a counter, making selections.

Yes . . . Tell me something—are the dried tomato raviolis made
from dried tomatoes, or are they made with fresh tomatoes and
then the ravioli is dried? . . . Do you know? . . . Could you ask someone? . . . Well, because I'm allergic to fresh tomatoes, but I can eat
a dried tomato. Well, forget about that. The monkfish and arugula
ravioli—tell me, what sort of fish is the monkfish? Is it an oily fish?
. . . Well, like tuna or swordfish, as opposed to a whitefish like sole
or scrod. I can't eat an oily fish . . . You don't know that, either.

   You don't know much, do you? OK, well, just give me a dozen
of the smoked mozzarella and parma-prosciutto ravioli, a dozen
of the wild mushroom and Icelandic caviar and . . . um . . . the
lobster and pesto ravioli—the lobster, is it Maine lobster or is it
South African lobster? . . . Maine lobster has the claws, South
African lobster is just the tail . . . I can't eat South African lobster,
for obvious reasons . . . The lobster . . . the lobster they make the
ravioli out of . . . Oh, never mind. Forget the lobster—just give
me what I've ordered and . . . um . . . what's that? . . . Is it good?
How much a pound? . . . Twenty-seven dollars a pound?! Give me

three pounds . . . And um . . . tell me, how are the kalamata olives today? . . . Well, are they too salty? Sometimes they're too salty . . . Just give me a pound. And do you know if you carry those little goat cheese and Spanish avocado pies? . . . Well, no, they're not a quiche—they're more like a tart . . . um, they used to have them at Montrachet, and then the chef left and— . . . Um . . . no, they're not key lime pie . . . No, not chocolate—did I say chocolate? I said goat cheese! . . . I don't know! If I knew how to make them, I would make them myself, wouldn't I? Listen, all right, forget about the pies, it's OK, it's OK. Just, uh, give me the ravioli, the olives, the pâté, and, um . . . five pounds of the Royal Blue Jamaican coffee beans—don't grind them, please . . . *No, don't grind them!* Do you have trouble with your hearing? You should get it checked. Let me see . . . What else? What else do I need? That's it—just give me two heads of radicchio lettuce and a Dutch yellow pepper . . . What? I have to go over *there* to get the vegetables? But I'm here—there's a long line over there. Can't you get it for me? . . . I can see you're busy—you're busy waiting on *me*! And I really don't want to go stand in line over there—please go over and get my vegetables.

No, I don't want to speak to the manager, I will go over myself, but I want you to know that I purchase at least a hundred dollars' worth of groceries here every three or four days, and I should think that you would make some effort to assist a regular customer. But I guess that's asking too much, isn't it? You have more important things to do.

I'm not angry—there's nothing I'm saying that should make you think I'm angry. I'm simply pointing out that you should make more of an effort . . . I DON'T WANT TO GO OVER THERE! I DON'T HAVE THE TIME. I'M TOO BUSY—CAN'T YOU SEE THAT, YOU IDIOT? SOME OF US HAVE MORE IMPORTANT THINGS TO DO THAN HANG AROUND ALL DAY, BUT I GUESS YOU WOULDN'T KNOW WHAT I'M TALKING ABOUT, WOULD YOU? NO . . . I'm fine, it's fine—just give me the bag, and thank you . . . thank you for your help. Thank you very much. Thank you very much, you've been most helpful . . . I can't tell you what a great help you've been . . . Thank you. You, too. Merry Christmas to you, too . . .

92

LITTLE DOG

All I need is what I want! Park me in front of a TV set, give me something semi-meaningful to do, tell me I'm a good dog and I'll wag my tail. I'm not asking for too much. Give me some table scraps, a fresh bowl of water, throw me a bone, I'll be your friend forever.

I just don't want to be left behind. I see green lawns, I want green lawns! I know a dog who has a tennis racket—I want one too! I read about one dog who makes over a million dollars a year—me too, me too! Don't leave me behind. I just want to be able to run around, hold my head high and piss on things. That's all. Give me a Mercedes Benz, it doesn't have to be the *biggest* one. Send me stacks of catalogs in the mail. Give me a toll-free number and a gold American Express card. I just want to be one of the pack.

I know a dog, a very good friend of mine, his owner takes him for walks, lets him shit on the ground, and then the owner bends over and picks up his shit!!! I'm telling you the truth! I saw it with my own eyes! And I'm not asking for that! I have higher aspirations!

Give me art! I like art. Art is cool. Art gives meaning to my life. Through art I communicate with my fellow dogs. Through art I transcend my petty existence and am able to face another day of Alpo. Plus, art makes me rich and famous. Which I like a lot.

When I'm rich and famous I feel like a big and strong doggie. I get to bark at all the other dogs and be a bastard and hump all the bitches. Which I like a lot.

But I don't really want to be the BIGGEST dog. Then all the other dogs will try to assassinate me. And I don't want to be the smallest dog either, because then all the other dogs piss on me.

I just want to be a middle dog. I want to be one of the pack, a face in the crowd, a member of the gang, an ingredient, a component, a cog in the wheel. That's what I am, a cog!

I am a cog dog.

(Barks.)

Cog dog, cog dog, cog dog cog.

I just want to be able to run with the other guys and chase cars. Is that asking too much? No. I say, "No."

Look, it's a dog-eat-dog world out there. Life's unfair. Life's a bitch and then they put you to sleep. I didn't make the rules, I just try to live by them.

I was lying on the couch, watching TV the other day, engaged in some creative channel-surfing when this guy came on. He was on all the stations at the same time. He said: "My Fellow Americans, the only thing we have to fear is fear itself. Sure the country's in tough shape. Sure things are scary. But everything will turn out all right. It's not a question of *when* are things going to get better, or *how* are things going to get better, but *who*. Who will save us? And so we must ask ourselves, 'Who are we as a people?'"

And so I must ask myself, "Who am I?" And the answer, I think, is obvious, "Rowf! Rowf! Rowf!"

93

ART

OK, Stacey, now make love to the camera, make love to the camera ... now spread, spread, that's good, get into it, get into it, more tongue, arch your back, good, look at the camera, close your eyes, you're in ecstasy, more, more, more, more, more, more, more! That's it. Now spread the cheeks, spread the cheeks, stay in the light! Good! Excellent! Wait a minute—CUT! Where's makeup? Redo her lips, they're all wrong! No! Not those, you idiot! Yes, right, more pouting, more innocent. Thank you. And re-rouge the nipples, they're all smeared. Good, OK, is she wet enough? Where's Tony? TONY! Come on! More Vaseline, please! Do I have to do everything myself? Come on, hurry up, she's drier than the Grand Canyon! We need moisture here, I'm getting thirsty just looking at her! OK, good, Stacey? All right, all right, where was I? I'm getting confused here ... So now, Stacey, you're languid, you're erotic, you're languidly erotic ... Now you're turning over on your stomach, right, good, hugging your pillow, and now just sort of push your little buns up in the air, there ...

Your motivation? Your motivation is the hundreds of thousands of American men and women sitting in their homes who need you to take them by the hand and reveal to them the secrets of erotic salvation! Look into the camera lens, because they're out there with their TV sets and VCRs. Can you see them? They need you, Stacey, to lead them to ecstasy, so don't let them down. OK? Good!

Now, where's the guy? Bring in the guy. Where is he? Yeah, you, Hoss, come here, what's your name? Chuck? Chuck, you know what they call that in France? A "baguette." Just joking . . . could you make it a little harder please? OK, good, stop, that's enough. Jesus. Where'd they find you anyway? The Port Authority men's room? OK, now, bring it into the frame, bring it in. Is it in? Stacey, are you ready? OK ACTION!

OK, Chuck, go to work . . .

Come on, Stacey, let's . . . Yes . . . you want it, you want it, let's see the look on the face, the gratitude, the tears are running down the cheeks . . . You're in ecstasy, you've never had anybody as erotically incredible as, um, Chuck here before in your life . . . GREAT! That's it, now you've got it, wonderful! Wonderful!

Come on, Chuck, let's pump it! Make it count! Come on buddy, giddy up there, boy! You need anything? Some hay, a sugar cube? Come on! That's it, put the leg up over the . . . There we go, there we go! That's it, now we've got it! Are you getting all this? Get it, Johnny, come on, they're not going to do it all day! Come on, there we go. Don't run out of steam there, Chuck-O! This shot is gorgeous! Beautiful. Oh, this is wonderful. This is art! This is acting! A classic! Stacey, I've never seen you better. Great acting, great performing. Who needs Meryl Streep when I've got you, Stacey! Lovely, oh, I'm coming myself, I'm coming myself! Oh, oh, OH! Fantastic, great! Cut! Relax, you two, great work. Tony, hose 'em down. Did you get all that? How was it for you? You think so? OK . . . yeah . . . All right, Stacey? Chuck? That was a great take, really terrific . . . We're gonna try it once more like this, doggie-style, then we move on to the close-ups and the money shot. OK? Excellent!

94

THE DREAM

So I have to tell you about this dream I had last night. I'm fucking my grandmother, right? It's just a dream. OK? So, I'm fucking my grandmother and I'm like doing her solid, she's screaming, her toes are in my ears. One of those kind of dreams, OK? And all of a sudden I look up and there is Clarence Thomas, in all his Supreme Court Justice robes and things, looking down at me, drinking a can of Coke. Right? Except he's got this enormous hard-on thrusting out between the folds of his robes, right into his face. And he's saying, "You can't do that!" And I'm thinking, Aren't you supposed to be like in Washington, DC, helping to kick-start the Fourth Reich or something? I mean, I'll do what I want, it's my privacy. But I can't say any of this, because, you know, how in a dream, sometimes you can't talk? Well, I couldn't talk, but the reason I couldn't talk was because his dick was in my mouth, so I'm like . . . wah-wah-wah-wah-wah . . . Right? And I look down, and I'm not doing my grandmother anymore, now it's Madonna. In like this rubber thing with buckles and snaps and little holes all over the place. And you know, I'm thinking, Cool. I'll take Madonna over my grandmother any day. But now the door bursts open and it's Jesse Helms. But he's wearing like a Victoria's Secret lavender nightgown with like the nipples cut out and nipple rings and shit, and plus he's wearing these knee-high Nazi jackboots, right? And I'm thinking, This man has never had any taste whatsoever, I mean, a lavender nightgown with jackboots? And he's got a camcorder and he's jumping up and down shouting, "I got you now! I got you now, you secular humanist!" And just at that moment, the door bursts open again, and this time it's George Washington and Abraham Lincoln, who were both pretty tall guys, but now they look a lot taller because they're both naked and they have these incredible steroided muscle bodies, all oiled up, and each guy has a massive erection, and they just come over and start butt-fucking Jesse and Clarence with like no grease or lotion—nothing—not even spit. They were wearing condoms though. And then, I don't know, more and more people kept coming in: Leona Helmsley and Kurt Waldheim and Ricky Schroder and Ricky Nelson and Kim Basinger and Hayley Mills and Artie (this dog who got run over by the school bus when I was ten), and I don't know, a million people. Sally Field and Oliver Stone. Malcolm X. And just more and more people kept coming in, until like the whole room was shaking with the hot sex we were having, and then everyone had this gigantic simultaneous orgasm and I woke up. And I was in my bed in this cold sweat and I thought, Oh no, I'm a homo. And I went into a panic! I said, "I'm not prejudiced or anything but I don't want to be a homosexual! I . . . uh . . . my lifestyle wouldn't support it. I'm . . . I'm too busy. I don't have time for all the parades!"

95

REACH OUT

A guy briskly takes a seat for an interview. He takes a sip from a mug of coffee every now and then.

Hey, hey! Hi! Nice to be meet you. Thanks, man. Yeah, sure, a lot going on. The festival. The awards. Then, you know, number one at the box office. It's cool. Sure. Sure. Wow. Very exciting, you know. I feel like a big deal.

Well, we fought hard to get this movie made, because it was something we believe in. The corporate suits at the big studios basically said this was a movie that could never be made and, you know, nobody wanted to see a movie like this and, we, uh, proved them wrong so, uh, you know, it's nice to have them kissing our ass now, so to speak. Hah. Hah. Not that I'm bitter or anything.

And I don't want to take all the credit. Without Harry Horntoad at Bleeding Ulcer Films believing in us, it never would have been made. He believed in the cause, and he believed we could really reach a lot of people. And we did. You know, like they say, "If a tree falls in a forest and nobody hears it fall, does it make a sound?"

Well, maybe I'm getting a big head about myself here, but I think, maybe, *maybe* I changed things for the better just a little bit, just one little bit. If *one* homeless person can sleep indoors tonight because of what I've done, then I've done my job. I can say: "I told America—you have a homeless problem." And I did. And, you know, a portion of the receipts from the picture go directly to homeless relief. Which is cool. You know?

Yeah. It's nice. It's nice. I mean it isn't like I made a billion dollars on the thing. But yeah . . . Well, I did move out of my old place. I lived on Sunset for ten years, and as exciting as I find street junkies and male hookers to be, it was time to move on.

Last week? Last week, seven million. So far, we've grossed sixty-seven million, four hundred and thirty-five thousand. But who's counting, right?

No I don't have five Porsches!!! Shit, where does the media get this stuff? *Three* Porsches, man. Joking! Joking! Two. But, you know, man, I've always liked Porsches. They were just something I've always wanted. And it's like, why not? You know?

Yes, I did just sign a new deal with Bleeding Ulcer for two million a picture, but you have to understand that they won't pay me the money if I don't *make* them the money. I mean that's what it's all about. And the thing is that I really want to make movies that make money and reach people. Like Hitchcock. D. W. Griffith.

I really want to get my message across . . . Hmmmm? Well, it's just that we should all love one another and build a better world, and, um, that, uh, if we all work together and stop all this hate . . . I mean, I don't want to be radical about any of this. I think that people who take a radical point of view really cut themselves off from everybody else. I don't want to do that. I was at a show just a few days ago in New York, this Armenian comedian was at this place on the Lower East Side. Interesting stuff, the guy's talented. But *nasty*, you know? Like negative. And how many people come to his show? A hundred? No one hears his message. Millions of people hear my message, man.

The next movie? Well, talking with the executives at the studio, we felt that it would be good for me to sort of explore another subject the way we did the homeless. I mean, Gary was so great as Chuck, the homeless guy in my movie, we wanted to do something else with Gary. And so what he's doing in my next picture is he will be playing a retarded drug addict. I should say a "mentally handicapped" drug addict. Because I think, you know, uh, drugs are terrible. And I think, it's also pretty terrible to be, you know, retarded. And Gary's such a great actor. The next DeNiro. He's been hanging out with retarded people, talking to them and stuff. You should have seen him on the show. He's so fucking funny—oops!

Oh, OK. Yeah. Well, thank you. You really liked it? You did? Well, thanks. Thanks, man. It means a lot to me. It means a lot to me because I know you really care, and I care, and I care that you care.

Thank you. I hope so. Well come on up to the new place next weekend and I'll give you a ride in one of my Porsches. Thanks. Thanks a lot, g'night.

96

NO CRIME

A man walks around an empty chair, extra-large Starbucks coffee cup in his hand. Excited, he talks to the chair in a hip-hop voice:

Yo, dude, check it out. Guy getting handcuffed on TV! Dig it. I love this show, man—watch, watch they're going to search his vehicle, man! Looking for the ganja. Yeah, yeah, they found it. Oh, oh, time to go to jail, my friend. Uh-huh. You made a big fucking mistake, big fucking mistake, you got *caught*.

Like, I'm in the supermarket yesterday, and they've got this new thing, they give you a little card. And this card has all your personal shit on it and then every time you use the card, a data bank collects all the information about you. Like, yo: "Drinks Diet Coke, buys lots of Advil, doesn't eat meat." Like an alarm goes off somewhere if you DEVIATE.

'Cause that's the deal, man: They're looking for the dangerous deviates. That's why I made myself invisible, dude. They're not going to find me. No license, no credit cards, no shit. They want everybody to have an identity card. They puttin' those satellite locator chips in the cell phones. Oh yeah, that would make things easy when they start arresting everybody.

No crime. Gonna live in a no-crime world. Like the chickens they keep in those little cages with the food tray rolling by them. Happy fucking chickens. Cluck-cluck-cluck! Awwwkkkk!

It's just ant sugar, man. Just like bits of sugar they give us to trick us to eat the poison. The machine, man, knows what we want, better than we do. Sugar, fat, drugs, porno videos, popcorn in the microwave, Prozac and *People* magazine. DVDs, SUVs, MP3s, XTC. It feeds us and we—like leeches—suck, suck. Like velcro—the system is the hooks and we the loops.

Yo, yo, yo, yo, yo . . . check it out! Guy's walking his dog. See, he walks the dog, but all the time, the dog thinks he's walking the man . . . Are we walking the computers or are they walking us?

Check it out. Like the "revolution." Wow, man. "I am ANTI the establishment. I am alternative." Uh-huh. I'm into SONGS about guns and sex. Shit.

I remember the first time I got a tattoo, man. I was *expressing* myself. Just like those models in the ads, man. All those junkies in *Vogue* magazine.

Like I went into a bookstore and I bought a book. Was about revolution, real revolution. And what they do during a real revolution is, they kill people. Lots of people. That's history, man.

Human beings, they be killing each other and they make piles of stuff. Trash. Possessions. Bodies. No other animal makes piles. Or kills itself. The way we do, man. You know who Tamerlane was, man? He killed some folks. Made piles out of their *skulls*. Torquemada. Hannibal. Stalin. Hitler. All the great people in history that we remember killed shitloads of other people, threw 'em in piles. Lincoln, man, Abraham Lincoln. People died on his watch, big time.

I used to skydive. I used to see how far I could fall before pulling the cord. I'd look down at all the people and they were just like little ants. All these little ants whizzing as fast as they can in their carcinogenic gas-powered go-karts.

The system looks down at us from far above.

(Upper-crust voice) Look at the little ants, the foolish little ants, working all day and night. We will have them hurry and scurry for us, because they have no brain, they are only ants. We will convince them that they have caused their own unhappiness,

that if only they had more discipline, they would be happy. Fools! Hah-hah! Let's sell them some more self-help books!

(Back to hip-hop voice) See, a few years ago, I'd be hanging out with my friends. And it would be like, "What's on TV?" Nothing. "What's in the movies?" Nothing. "Wanna eat some shit?" No. "Wanna smoke a dube?" No. Nothing, man. It got so there was nothing. Heroin. Nothing. Pierce my dick. Nothing. Then what? After nothing?

You say: OK, here it comes, another day in my life. Let's see here, a little sex, a little exercise, a few cigarettes, maybe a frappuccino . . . now what? You know? NOW WHAT THE FUCK HAPPENS??

One time I was diving the sky over this shopping mall. And I thought, I just won't pull the cord. All these folks will be shopping and shit and—BOOM—I'll come through the ceiling right on their fat suburban asses.

But I didn't do it. I could have, but I didn't. 'Cause I'd realized while I was falling in the air down to the shopping center, What difference does it make? You know? I mean if I had been a Nazi at the Siege of Stalingrad I'd be just a frozen corpse chewing on some icy dirt. But if I were Barbra Streisand I'd be in a hot tub watching the sun set.

So I think, OK, get a gun. Blow some minds. I mean even Ed Gein was happy they put him in jail. It's like: OK, it's just one more thing. They got TV in jail, too, you dig?

Otherwise, it's just playing into the hands of the computers. Every year goes by, the computers think faster, figure out human desire better. We're running around watching videos, climbing all over each other like crabs in a bottle, while the sperm count goes down, down, down.

It's like this, something rocks the boat, make it a sin. The worse the sin, the better it feels. But don't do it. No fucking around. No taking drugs. No stealing. But all that shit's the stuff the big cats do all the time. *All* the time. They do everything bad. That's why they want to be big rich motherfuckers in the first place, so they can do the bad shit. Then, one day, when they're seventy-five years old, they wake up in the middle of the night and go, "Oh shit, I've been an *asshole* all this time. Sorry."

So I say, put a bullet in the chamber, lock and load, mother-fucker. You know? You know what I'm saying? Do you? Draw a line in the sand . . . pick a victim, it really don't make no diff who. Let's face it, just a bunch of ants. You ever step on ants? Sure you did.

97

VICTIM

A man, limping, shaking a cigarette out of a pack.

Just hold your horses here, all right? I'll tell you in a second, Terry. Wait a minute, my leg, my leg. *(Hobbles, fumbles with his cigarette)* Hold on, hold on, let me light my cigarette here. I'll tell ya, just shut up. All right? So I . . . so what happened was, wait a minute . . . *(Takes forever to light his cigarette)* . . . so I goes down to welfare, right? And I gets my check. And I pick up my methadone, right? So I say to myself, I'll snag a carton of Benson & Hedges, go home, drink my zombie juice, space, order up some chicken wings and shrimp fried rice—you know how I love my shrimp fried rice? Maybe take a bath, watch a little *Oprah* with Snowball. I deserve it. I deserve it. Been very stressed lately. What with Sondra calling me night and day. Oh yeah, she calls. She calls. Always bitchin' about the kid. You know he's in college now. Oh yeah. And she calls me wantin' money, you know? And I say to her, "Sondra, if I had the money I'd send the money. I love my kid, you know? I DON'T HAVE ANY FUCK-ING MONEY!" Wait a sec, I'll get to the leg, I'll get to the leg!

So I gets home, I'm waitin' for the Chink food to get delivered and I'm taking a minute to catch my breath, got Snowball on my lap and for two seconds—I'm happy. The phone rings. It's Sondra. Like she's got radar: "He's happy, I better call him and give him shit." And she starts with the money. And what can I say? I wish I had the money. I play Lotto every fucking day hoping I could get some money together to send to my kid. But the odds, Terry, the odds are stacked against me, always have been. So I hangs up on her and pull the phone outta the wall. That does it. Fuck the food. I'm doin' the methadone now. So I gets out the bottle and all of a sudden there's a knock on the door. Who is it? Carol, that satanic bitch. She just copped, she's lookin' for a place to fix, right? So she's gonna lay twenty bucks on me so she can sit on my couch and catch a nod, right? So I'm sittin' there, trying to stay calm, watchin' her tryin' to hit a vein, gettin' blood all over the place. Finally I say, "Here let me do that," and I find a spot in her neck—she got a great neck—hit her good. She's out so fast, I'm bootin' her 'cause you know if I take the spike out, she's gonna be pissed. Right?

And I'm gone to the races, Terry. What else could I do? I can taste the junk in the roof of my mouth. I mean I'm scopin' how she's nodding her face off like a wax dummy on a hot day, the cigarette burning her fingers, the needle in her neck. It's pushin' all my buttons, you know? I'm thinkin', That would feel real good right now, after all I been through. Very refreshing.

So I say, "Wake up, Carol, you win, forget it with the twenty bucks, just lay a bag on me."

Just then the Chink food shows up, and the guy, you know the way those guys are, kinda lookin' at you like they don't know what you're saying, and I'm just like, Cool, cool, here's the money for the food, get lost, you know? I had no appetite. Guy's standin' in the door, Snowball's barkin' at 'im, she hates the Chinese people, don't ask me why. Carol's cleaning drops of blood off those black leather pants a hers she's so proud of. I'm thinkin', People are fuckin' weird, ya know?

Anyway, I finally gets rid of the coolie, I stick the wings and the fried rice in the fridge so the roaches can't get at it, although I once found a roach in an ice cube, don't ask me how that got there. And Carol says, "I don't got no more. We gotta go cop."

And you know how it is, Terry, when that monkey wakes up. He doesn't just wake up, he takes speed. Hoppin' up and down on my back like he's on a two-hundred-pound pogo stick. So I say, fine, let's take a walk. So I had this C-note stashed away—I know I owe you money, Terry, I know, but hey, man, will you be decent for once in your skinny-assed, cheapskate life? I don't even know why I bother talkin' to you. You know? Do you want to hear the story or not? All right, so where was I?

We go cop. And we get beat. You know how it is, whenever you're desperate, you get beat. It's like life, man. It's like fuckin' life. So that's a hundred bucks down the drain. Then I remember, I didn't do the methadone yet. So me and Carol hikes back to my place, I walks in the door, Snowball is completely confused, we grab the 'done and go back to the corner where my usual guy is, and we sell the shit and I buy four bags.

And we come back to my place and she says, "You owe me two bags." And I say, "Why?" And she says, "'Cause I took you to my cop spot." And I said, "I got beat at your cop spot, you bitch." And she starts yelling at me and shit, but, man, fuck me if I'm going to lay two bags on her for gettin' ripped off. Plus, she never paid me for hanging in the first place.

Suddenly she gets real sweet on me and says, "OK, just gimme one." So I do. And then I bang a bag and it's not as good as what she had, but it's OK, on account that my dealer knows I'm trying to get straight so he wants me to have a good taste. OK. No. There's none left. 'Cause I closed my eyes for two seconds, next thing I know, Carol's gone, my dope's gone, the front door's open and Snowball's out on the landing barking her furry brains out.

So I'm kinda high but I'm also pissed off, so I jump up and run to the door to get the dog back inside before she gets kidnapped or some shit like that, but I'm running so hard that when I run out my door, I keeps going and I goes right off the landing—CRASH-BOOM—down the stairs, all the way down by where the mailboxes are.

And Snowball's standing at the top of the stairs kinda lookin' at me, she's not barkin' anymore, she's just giving me this look like, Why'd you do that? Right? And I try to move, but I can't, so I figure something must be broken. And the assholes who live in my building are coming into the building, like checking their mail and stepping over me. No one's helping me up. And I'm yelling. Somebody must a called EMS, 'cause about forty-five minutes later these two black dudes show up and throw me into the back of this stinking van somebody must a died in there. Lots a people probably died in there come to think of it.

So they like take me to the ER. Kinda drop me off on account of I could walk on one leg. I guess if you've got uncontrollable bleeding from a head wound or some shit like that, then they put you on a stretcher. Me they just dumped. So I'm in the ER, and they're cutting my pants off and I'm still stoned so I'm trying to tell 'em to gimme my wallet but no one's listening to me, they're just like dressing me up in these blue pants I got on now and they're saying shit like, "Why did you break your leg? Why did you break your leg? Don't you know you're HIV-positive and you could've gotten a life-threatening infection?" Like I do it all the time. Like it's my fuckin' hobby.

And this doctor comes in, right outta a med school. Clean, you know the type, young, serious. Probably got an A average in dissection class. Plays a mean game a racquetball. Probably does seven hundred pushups every morning and smokes cigars while he's doin' 'em. And he looks at my chart and says, "Why did you break your leg, you're HIV-positive? You could get an infection and die." And I get a little animated you know. And then he says, "Calm down, I know how you feel."

I said, "Hey. You don't know how I feel." And he says, "Yes I do." Like he does. And I lose it. I start yelling and I try to get off the gurney, and somebody pushes me back down and I push them away and I threw this roll of bandages and this bed pan and, uh . . . Well they got these bouncers at St. Vincent's now . . . And they threw me out on the street, they wouldn't let me back in. And I'm standing there out in the snow, blue-green hospital pants, this walking cast thing. I don't have my wallet, I don't have anything. I'm just standin' there, and this little old lady saw me standing there and she lays a fiver on me. Says, "God bless you."

So I comes home. And all the food was cold and coagulated. So I gave it to Snowball, who's thinking, This is my lucky day. And I'm thinking, When's mine?

98

GATED

A man is addressing a child, so crouching down a bit. Very upbeat:

What's your name? . . . Jimmy? Hi, Jimmy. I'm Bill. And how old are you? . . . Seven!! That's pretty big! Are you all excited about looking for a new house with Mommy and Daddy? . . . You're not? Why? . . . Who's Jeremy? Is Jeremy your best friend? . . . He is? Well, when you move here you're going to make lots of new friends. *Better* friends. See that lady over there? Her name is Sandy and she's going to give you one of our special lollipops.

(Standing up straight.)

Nice kid. Chip? Cathi? Before we look at the model home, let's just go over some of the things we said on the phone. First of all, when you buy here at Cedar Woods Community Estates, the maintenance is paid for for the first year. That would cover upkeep of the grounds, the tennis courts, the swimming pool, the guards at the front gate and the K-9 patrols. And, of course, the school, which Jimmy will be able to enter next year . . . Uh, no. The school is just for residents. Local townspeople are not allowed within the perimeter of the complex at any time. And . . . yes, oh, I almost forgot, the medical center is also here, if Jimmy falls off the bike—which is about the worst thing that can happen here. I tell you, I've been living here for five years, and the place is so quiet: no traffic, no sirens at night, no screams, no gunshots.

Now, our only requirement is no pets. No dogs, no cats, no gerbils, no Vietnamese potbelly pigs . . . Fish? Of course you can have fish, as long as they're under four inches. We choose the color of your house. Don't want any paisley houses. No more than two children per family here. Big families are not conducive to the kind of environment Cedar Woods Estates wants to foster. You've got Jimmy, so you can have one more.

And you have to be employed. You guys are all set, we did a little checking. Chip, we heard about your promotion and everyone is so excited. As long as you maintain employment you'll have no problems. If you're not employed for whatever reason, you get put on a list and it's possible you'd . . . it's no big deal . . . you'd have to be unemployed for over a year for it to mean anything. And that's not going to happen.

You cannot receive any kind of welfare payments. You can get medicaid, social security, stuff like that. But we don't want anyone to live here who is on welfare, for obvious reasons. It's one of the rules that work very well for us.

Now this development is in the new section. Like I said, the old section is five years old. Everything here will be just like the original. Except that we will be installing security cameras every one hundred feet along all the streets. It's kind of an experiment. Some of the houses will have sensors right inside the walls. Only if you want them. See how it works.

I think security is really the biggest factor for most people. People want to live somewhere safe, where they can be happy. And that's what we provide. All our security guards are ex-LAPD, great bunch of guys. All licensed to carry automatic weapons, tasers and mace . . . No. No pepper spray. Mace. Real mace. It's the little things.

Not only are we looking for crime since there's no crime here, we don't want anyone unusual in the area either. Our guys see somebody walking around who doesn't belong here, they stop 'em, they question 'em, and they escort them off the premises.

This is not a racial thing, we have many black families (not that many). And some Asian families. Very nice, you'd be surprised. (Well actually just one.)

We have our own recycling center. We don't want anybody picking up cans, going door to door, or asking for anything. We don't allow solicitation of any kind. Stop 'em right at the gate. We do our own fundraising every Christmas. Linda, where'd we send the money last year? Oh right, the displaced Costa Rican coffee farmers. Great cause. Because we don't just see this as a bunch of buildings, we see this as a living opportunity.

Which brings me to my favorite thing, the civic association. Now if you own a home here you are automatically a member of the civic association. But if you pay a small dues every year, I dunno, it's something like twenty bucks, they just add it to your maintenance, then you can be a certified member. And I would recommend that. You get a newsletter, we have our annual meetings, rallies, those kinds of things. The ones at night with the bonfires are a lot of fun. And you get to put a little plaque by your front door so that all your neighbors know you're a certified member in good standing: you know, you've paid your maintenance, you're employed, no fish over four inches. You even get a pin, see? Nice huh? In fact, we require that you wear it. Jimmy, how would you like to have a pin? It'll match the uniform all the little guys get to wear. Arm bands and everything!

You know, you're gonna love it here, Jimmy. On Halloween, we all go door to door, and everybody gives nice treats—no fishhooks in the apples, no rat poison. On Christmas, Santa comes to visit and we all go Christmas caroling. We're thankful because everything here is the way it's supposed to be. So whaddya say, Chip? Cathi? Jimmy? Let's go see that model home.

99

WOOD

I want *wood*. I want to live near woods. Trees. And I want to burn
wood in a fireplace and sit in front of it. And have a rocking chair
made of real wood. Maybe a pipe made out of wood. And all
this wood will make me feel nostalgic for the olden days when
things were only made of wood. No plastic. No styrofoam. Just
wood. Wooden wheels rolling over the prairie. Log cabins. Made
of wood. And wool. A wool comforter and a good book. Falling
asleep over a good book in front of a roaring fire. Of wood.

When you get older you become nostalgic, just like when
you're young you keep thinking about the future and how great
it's going to be. Then you get there and it's not so great, so you
switch over to thinking about how great everything used to be.

It works like this: First you're little and you're very excited
about everything, and everything is very important, and you feel
somewhat safe; then you get older and you think you know everything and you take chances; then you get disappointed and realize
you're getting older and things don't feel safe at all; then you are
even older and cherish any day in which you don't have aches and
pains; then you die.

I think I understood how it all works when I was about three years old. It was the fifties. I was three in the fifties. It was Christmas, an old-fashioned Christmas. Eisenhower was president, everything was completely depressing, the war had been over only a few years, even the stock market crash hadn't been that long ago. People just getting over their last bout of polio . . .

And I'm three, and all of a sudden one day I toddle out to the living room, and for some reason my parents, who up to now have seemed pretty unremarkable, have chopped down a tree and dragged it into the house. Not just any tree but a cone-shaped, very green, nicely smelly tree. And I like this. I like having a tree in the house. This could start a trend, bring a tree into the house, then a bush, maybe a cow, a horse, who knows? I can dig it. And then, even cooler, they get all these colored lights and glass balls and shiny tinsel and throw it all over the tree. Cool. Very cool. A side of my parents I have not seen before. Colors. Shiny shit. So I'm happy. I think, maybe this isn't going to be so bad living with these people.

And they seemed to be into it, too, taking pictures of me in front of the tree, laughing, singing songs about stars and bells and angels, very cool imagery. And I'm blissed out—we get presents, nuts, oranges, chocolate. Happy people all around.

So every morning, first thing, I run out to the living room and, yup, it's still there, the tree. And I just sit there and groove to this tree. Develop a relationship with the tree. Even gave it a name—Larry—Larry the tree.

And then one day I come out to find my dad taking all the decorations off Larry. And I go, "Whoa! Like what are you doing to my friend?" And my mom is standing there and she says, "Larry has to go back to the forest. Christmas is over."

And then my dad, who has always been neurotically committed to being honest, especially when it causes other people pain, says, "Larry's not going back to the forest." And he pulls out this ax and starts chopping up the tree!

I'm in shock.

I say, "But what's going to happen to Larry?" And my mom says, "Well . . . " And I say, "So where's he going?" Dad says,

"Either it'll get burned up in a giant bonfire someplace," which of course stuns me to hear this about someone I've gotten very close to, "or . . ." (now check this out) ". . . it'll get ground into mulch and be made into paper." I ask, "What kind of paper?" And my dad says, "I don't know, toilet paper maybe." Toilet paper. My best friend in the whole world is getting ground into toilet paper!

I was traumatized. And to this day, every time I wipe my ass, I think of Christmas.

100

POEM

And the little ones run in the streets. They run playfully and joyfully through the empty streets. They run hopefully through the dark ruined streets. Come here, my little children. Come here, small tender ones. Into my arms. Into my teeth of streets. Run into the midnight traffic. Fall against the hot drops of water from your mother's tears. Laughing into my teeth. With balloons trailing, kites flying, dresses all crisp and white and unspoiled by the oily rain of the midnight traffic. Run into the night, hopeful little children. Run into the streets and streets and streets and streets and streets. Little babes. Little babes in toyland. In magic land. In gentle rolling green hills of azure blue skies and fluffy clouds and giggling phosphorescent soaring expectant wonder. Come here, little children. Open your eyes. Open your mouths. Open your arms. Run into the night. Hold it close to your tiny chests. Let it into your veins of tiny power. Let the night into your hearts. Let your laughter echo through the dark ruined streets. Let the night into your hearts. Let the night into your hearts. Let the night into your hearts.

BUILDING CHARACTER
MY METHOD FOR CREATING THE SOLOS

In 1980 I wrote and performed a piece called *Men Inside*. It wasn't "stand-up comedy" or a "showcase" or "performance art." It was a play for one person. I had no intention of ever making another like it. I couldn't imagine that this initial exercise would morph into a series of solos that I (and others) would perform in venues across the United States and the world. *Wake Up and Smell the Coffee* is the sixth in this series of full-length solos. When I created *Wake Up*, I put it together pretty much the same way I did when I made *Men Inside* twenty years before. What follows is a description of how I first came to make these solos and my method for making them.

Around 1978, having arrived in New York three years earlier, I met the actor David Warrilow, a charter member of the Mabou Mines theater company. He had the most perfect speaking voice, so I asked him for some actorly advice on how to improve mine. He told me to get a tape recorder, tape my voice and listen to the results. He said I could be my own teacher.

I bought a cheap plastic cassette recorder and taped some off-the-cuff ramblings. I wasn't working off any particular text or play, so I improvised as I spoke. For instance, I'd "do" a Southern-style voice. I didn't try for any specific dialect, I was just screwing around. I'd launch into a Sam Shepardesque monologue about fast cars and guns and liquor without thinking too much about what I was saying. The words flowed.

Later, when I listened to the tape, I realized I had been improvising a little monologue. I hadn't consciously planned to create a character but someone waiting inside me had spoken up.

I made more tapes. As these improvs mounted up, I decided to catalog the "people who live inside me." I sorted them out and came up with twelve distinct male archetypes, ranging from a threatening street punk ("Nice Shoes") to a redneck deer hunter ("Rodeo") to a little boy playing ("Superman!"). All of these characters were the product of free-form vocal improv. I wasn't looking "out there" for characters, I was looking "inside."

This gallery of characters, this set of monologues, became *Men Inside*. I performed it first in 1980 at Franklin Furnace, a small loft space. Lots of people (fifty?) showed up and dug it. Later (after touring and playing clubs for two years), I performed it in a more polished version, at Joe Papp's New York Shakespeare Festival.

By then, I had become an exile from the traditional theater (I had come to New York with a theater degree, planning to work Off-Broadway), making performance pieces and performing them in lofts and back rooms. Other pieces like *Careful Movement* (performed at St. Mark's Poetry Project) and *Garden* (Artists Space) featured a few actors spouting chunks of text, some taped voices and slides. I also wrote "plays" like *Sheer Heaven* (at The Kitchen, performed entirely in Spanish for English-speaking audiences) and *The New World* (featuring fourteen actors and music by Glenn Branca). I had a nightclub act (*The Ricky Paul Show*) in which I played an obnoxious comedian who sang off-key and hurled insults at the audience.

During the *Ricky* show, fights would break out with the audience, sometimes bottles got thrown. I went to Berlin and goose-stepped onstage. In New York, an enraged feminist tried to throw me down a flight of stairs because I made bad jokes about women's lib. I was always booed and hissed. Gigs were canceled because my stuff was thought to be in poor taste or too violent or *negative!* I didn't care. The energy was exciting. In my own awkward way, I was trying to make a new kind of anti-theater.

I hung out at places like CBGB's, Max's, The Mudd Club and Hurrah's. I embraced a "punk" aesthetic. I liked the energy. Aggressive and loud. Antagonistic to the status quo, it didn't take itself too seriously, it liked to laugh. There was a new attitude in the music that said awkward was good, grotesque was fascinating. Punk was rough, it didn't smooth everything into lovely shapes.

In punk music, the chords were basic. I wanted to do the same thing with performance—make stuff that was straightforward, not precious, not effete. (I became a fan of Richard Foreman's Ontological-Hysteric Theater. His work was super-energized, sexual, multilayered to the point of madness, awkward, funny, beautifully designed and way too loud for most people.)

As fun as it was, by 1981 I had reached a point when I had to fish or cut bait. The plays, subsidized with my paycheck from The Kitchen, were not getting reviewed and they were expensive. I couldn't afford to do them anymore (I paid the actors, paid for rehearsal space, made the posters and sets myself, etc.). And as much as I loved the punk club lifestyle (late nights in the demi-monde, the frenzy of the shows, harsh personalities, beer-stink dressing rooms replete with cracked mirrors), *Ricky* was a one-trick pony.

So when the opportunity came up for me to tour as a solo act with a group of other performers, including the original Rock Steady Crew and Fab Five Freddy (the first rap/break-dance/dee-jay gang to hit the Midwest), I grabbed it. I decided *Men Inside* was the best piece to do. While on tour, one venue billed me as a "comedian." Because the audience expected to laugh, they did.

I liked this. I liked the idea of acting-out a dozen obnoxious characters, pissing off the audience but drawing them in as well. I liked the energy level of solo, it felt limitless. I kept working on the characters, refining them, giving them more dimension, finding the comedic beats, the aggressive beats.

I decided to focus my attention on my solo work, treating the pieces as one-person plays. I wasn't always sure where I was going with the new material, but to paraphrase Wallace Shawn: "I find out what I want to write about by writing it."

I want to get theoretical here for a page or two and discuss acting and character and, ultimately, writing for the stage, at least as it applies to what I do.

Theater is character, everything else is window-dressing. It's not the terrific story that makes Shakespeare great, it's the characters. It's not the atmosphere that makes the Greek tragedies awesome, it's the characters. And the same is true with Ibsen, Chekhov, Williams. (The exceptions might be Beckett and Pinter. Maybe.)

What makes a character tick is fascinating because we are all characters in the way we see ourselves and the way we see others. "Character" is our way of conceptualizing who we are. Character is what we create every time we interact with another. In his book, *The Presentation of Self in Everyday Life*, Erving Goffman says we learn how to *act* to be the people we are. "Acting" in day-to-day life is more than behaving, it is imitating, it is constructing. When I am interacting with other people, I am consciously or unconsciously imitating the behavior of other people I've known. And to take it one step further, because I live in a world of mass media, I experience all sorts of people who are not only in my life but who I "know" from movies or TV.

A doctor models his behavior after other doctors. A truck driver behaves like a truck driver because he's shown that he can act a certain way. In fact, if you visited the doctor and he behaved like a truck driver (gruff, for example), you'd wonder what sort of doctor he was. We tell each other who we are through our behavior. Not only do we hone our behavior according to the role we are playing in society, we spend a lot of time fine-tuning our act, especially in dynamic social situations, like trying to get laid or doing business. This information about how I *should* behave is not innate, it comes from outside myself.

I consider this when playing a part. For example, I am given the role of a soldier (Buchner's *Woyzeck*). I have no "sense memory" of being a soldier. I *do* have the memory of being in fist fights or being hurt or being scared. And, of course, when I act, I access those feelings. But I also have a memory of soldiers and how soldiers behave in the dozens of war movies I've seen, not to mention TV. So, in fact, I'm recalling a memory of an actor playing a soldier. And that's as real as anything else in life as far as my subconscious is concerned. The point isn't to replicate life onstage but, as Picasso said, "create a lie that tells the truth." And truth is what everybody agrees truth is.

We all have little theaters in our respective heads. The whole world is replicated in our minds. The way we imagine ourselves and other people is a cornerstone to the way we act in our daily lives. We make representations of people mentally and play out imaginary scenes with these imaginary people. From these mental exercises we feel we can predict how someone (say, our mother or father) will behave, and we act accordingly. The interesting thing is that the mother in my head has just as much to do with the real person as she does with the way I think about her. People are conceptual.

The goal of the theater artist is to take the imaginary "mother" and put her onstage in such a way that when other people come to see the play, they see a mother they recognize. If an audience doesn't *recognize* what they see, then the play doesn't work. The audience sees things laid-out in front of them and they compare the mechanisms of behavior (the acting, the behaving, the plot) to the way they think about them, as opposed to the way they "really" are, which is unknowable.

Theater is powerful because it works in exact concordance with the way our heads work (not the way reality works). To quote Samuel Johnson (via Harold Bloom in *Shakespeare: The Invention of the Human*): "Imitations produce pain or pleasure not because they are mistaken for realities but because they bring realities to mind." The truthfulness of the theater is determined by the audience. Theater is consensus. And that consensus is a function of characters who speak and act the way characters in our collective head speak and act. In other words: archetypes. Success can only be measured by the ratio of what I (the artist) see, versus what the audience thinks they see. Marcel Duchamp, a great lover of science, suggested this ratio. He said the closer to one-to-one this ratio becomes, the greater the artist. But of course, no one can measure such a ratio.

People don't remember what happened in life, they remember what they *think* happened. People don't see things, they see what they *think* they see. And they don't know people, they know what they *think* they know. To tangle with all that thinking, well, that's what art is all about. Effective art agitates the certainty that what you know is the truth. Art turns things upside-down and inside-out.

So enough theory. Here's how I make a solo. I start with a tape recorder and an empty room. I work in a space where I'm completely isolated and no one can overhear me. And I make sure there's enough room to bounce around. When I'm alone, I can let go and fantasize without self-consciousness. I can improvise freely, become the character and let him loose. Self-consciousness ruins creativity. I turn on the tape recorder, I note the date and the piece I'm working on. Then I start.

Once I get a chunk of improv down, I review the tape and try to find parts I like the sound of. I transcribe these. I keep collections of these transcriptions and revisit them later. Then I select pieces from the transcription that I like, sample them and commit them to memory. I then use these segments as a launch pad for another improv. Then I start the process all over again. The final edited piece of monologue is maybe three minutes long, after hours of improvs.

Good things happen when I do it this way. First of all, when I'm speaking I'm looser with language than when I write. There isn't as much editorializing going on. Secondly, the arc of the story of the finished monologue (and every monologue has a beginning, middle and an end) is not as predictable. This is the way people talk. They wander, they get interrupted, they think of ancillary ideas as they speak, they listen to the other person and react.

In my daily life, I overhear all kinds of conversations: people discussing or gossiping about their friends, lunatics shouting out at passersby, people swearing at each other from their cars, people sitting at a meal, lovers arguing on a subway platform, me yelling at my own children. When I hear something interesting, I note it, and I might use it later as a starting point for an improv.

When I begin the improv with a fragment of overheard speech, I repeat it like a mantra, using the phrase to invoke an attitude. For example, take the phrase: "Fuck you!" The improv might go something like:

> "Fuck you." "Fuck *you!*" "No, man, fuck *you!*" "You say-ing, 'Fuck you!' to me? Well fuck you!" "Come here and say that." "No, you come here." "I'll come there if you come here." "What, you're telling me what to do now? You think you're better than me?" "As a matter of fact I do, shithead." "Who you calling a 'shithead'? Fuck you!" Etc.

In "Upgrade" from *Wake Up,* I riff on the kind of officious check-in counterperson. The key word here is "sir."

> Here you go, sir, you're all set. You have a seat on this flight, it's leaving in ten minutes so you better hurry up! Yes, sir, that's right, it's a coach seat. Yes, I know you had a fully-paid-for-first-class ticket, sir, but this seat is coach. Well, let me see what I can do, OK? *(Types into keyboard)* All right, I'm looking at a first-class seat on a 3:30 A.M. departure with a six-hour layover in St. Louis. How's that sound?
>
> Yes, 3:30 in the morning, sir, that's correct. I under-stand that, sir. Yes, I can see that you have a gold card. All the people behind you have gold cards, sir. Well, sir, sir, sir, why don't we do this: Step aside for a sec here, let me get everyone on board, get them seated, let the flight leave and then we can see what we can do, OK? *(Signals to next person)* Next in line?

The trick with these improvs is not to aim for anything in par-ticular. Not to try to make it funny or poignant. I just want to become the person behind the counter and get into the situation and see what happens from there. The most important goal is to play and cut loose, to let the character speak for himself. This is not the time to worry about final performance, how inarticulate or articulate the character sounds.

Here is a fragment of the verbatim transcript of the first improv I did for *Wake Up*'s "Harmonious":

> What do we learn from this story? [I've just finished telling a story about a farmer who has a pig with one leg. The story was not included in the final piece.] That we are either in harmony or we are in dis-equilibrium and alienation. So let us make a list in our minds: what are the things that make us happy, what are the things that make us sad. Happy? Buying a new car. Sad: doing our taxes. Happy: swimming in our swimming pool. Sad: paying the doctor's bills. Happy: being on vacation. Sad: having to go to work. If we look at these things and we understand what they are telling us, we find a deep spiritual principle coming into play. And that is this: alienation is simply a lack of money. If we have money we don't have these problems. So our first goal is to make sure that we understand that money is the thing we must have above all.

The final script goes like this:

> The second thing you must understand is that we exist in two states. We are either in sync with the universe or we are out of sync with the universe. When we are in sync with the universe, we call this being *harmonious*. When we are out of sync with the universe, we call this being *alienated*.
>
> We are either in sync or out of sync, harmonious or alienated. How do we know which state we are in? *(Pause, smiles, shrugs shoulders)* We just know!
>
> So let us now clear our minds and still our centers. And let us contemplate these two states of being—harmony and alienation:
>
> I am warm, I am happy, I am harmonious.
>
> I am cold, I am angry, I am alienated.

I am swimming in my heated swimming pool. I am harmonious.

I am doing my taxes. I am alienated.

I am buying a brand-new Lexus with all-leather interior. I am harmonious.

I am working three jobs to pay for health insurance. I am alienated.

I am flying first class to St. Barth's. I am harmonious.

I am going to jail for food stamp fraud. I am alienated.

If we carefully meditate upon these two states of being, we find a deep and abiding spiritual principle becomes obvious: Alienation is simply a lack of *money*.

And, of course, the corollary: Money brings deep and abiding harmony.

When we have money, our days are full of sunshine, the air is fresh and clean. We love everyone we meet. And everyone loves us.

When we lack money, we become empty and angry. We listen to overly loud music. And we are frequently constipated.

And so each and every one of us is on a path and must answer the eternal question: "How do I get more money?"

This is the path that I am on. That is why you are here tonight.

I move from the original to the final version through transcription, memorization, repeated rehearsals, discussions with my director, live "workshop" performances and performances as part of the run, as well as touring. Every time I perform the piece, I look to see if its logic, tone, humor and rhythm are what I want them to be. Coincidentally, the more consistent and clear the piece becomes, the easier it is to memorize and perform.

Another way into the character during the improv phase is to find a physical aspect of the character and work with that. The way a junkie lights a cigarette for instance, nodding into the flame as he tries to puff. That can get me started. The way someone holds a beer bottle or a coffee cup. The way an old man might shuffle across a room (*Wake Up*'s "The Meeting"). At one point in Danny Hoch's great solo piece *Jails, Hospitals and Hip-Hop*, he sweeps a floor with a push broom. We see the anger with every swipe.

Finally, and most powerfully, would be to assume a vocal stance. Not outward mimicry, because mimicry is hollow, but letting the vocal posture shape the improv from within. Try reciting "The Gettysburg Address" in a Minnie Mouse voice and you'll get the idea. The medium is the message.

Taking a piece of the character, a way of speaking or a posture, or a vocal intonation sets me on the path. From this beginning, the world of the character can be discovered and a storyline develop. (To see where all this might lead, check out "Our Gang" or "Stag Party," two earlier monologues from *Drinking in America* and *Sex, Drugs, Rock & Roll*.)

Harking back to the way we perform in everyday life, behavior in front of an audience is always performance, no matter who the audience is: a teacher addressing a class, a preacher preaching, a trainer running a gym class or a lunatic yelling at passersby on the street. So I collect these natural situations for performance and use them to launch an improv. (I was influenced here by the late great Brother Theodore, whose whack comedic rants were in the guise of a sermon.) This is one place when in film actors cross over into the truly theatrical. Check out Burt Lancaster in *Elmer Gantry* or Alec Baldwin in *Glengarry Glen Ross*. Public figures make great performances; public speeches are an easy way to work with themes. In my first show, I played a preacher giving a sermon in "Looking Out for Number One." He was enormously fun to play. The new age guru in "Harmonious" does the same thing.

This guru, like many characters I play, says the opposite of what you expect. This is a writing device, akin to playing devil's advocate, which I use in a lot of what I do. I can't think of anything more boring than telling the audience what "I really think" because, in fact, I'm not sure myself. Playing against the grain of expectation is one way of doing this.

And I want the character to make a point. There's usually some angle I want to get at with each monologue within a show.

For example, I may want to show how even the biggest jerk has *his* side of the story. Like in "Breakthrough" (*Wake Up*):

> Well, I took the boys to the ball game. Oh yeah, it was fun. They're so great. Acting up, throwin' Cracker Jacks at each other. Yelling, screaming. And I'm like, "Hey! Hey! Hey! Quiet the fuck DOWN! RIGHT! NOW!" I'm so good with those guys, you know? Oh! Oh! And this busybody behind me is like, "Stop yelling at your kids, I'm trying to hear the game." And I'm dealing with boundary issues today, like we've been working on, so I'm like, "Are these *your* kids? Or are these *my* kids?" Right? "You don't hear me telling you to stick a sack over your wife's head 'cause she's so fuckin' ugly." And from this, the guy gets an attitude. You know? All indignant. Gets in my face. Now I'm in a fight. How did this happen? And I can walk away, I can walk away. But I have my needs today. And I've learned to respect my needs. And my need was to punch him in the face, so I did.

I want the character to feel like a living being to the audience. Ninety-nine percent of this is intuition and can't be taught. Scientific accuracy won't make a more compelling character onstage. (Although research might make a more grounded actor.) For me, being somewhere safe when I improvise helps me find this intuition. I want the character to be energetic, to be worth watching. One way of looking at this is to imagine performing in front of an audience that doesn't speak the character's language. Would these people, who don't understand a word, still find what's happening onstage worth watching? With that in mind, I try to create characters who are active: standing, moving, engaged. I stay away from mime because I find mime (and costumes) distracting for an audience. I want the essence of the character, not the hat. I don't want the audience judging me on how well I mime driving a car.

Characters in my shows vary in how broadly I play them. A broadly played character, played for laughs and very emphatic, is a "sketch" character, the sort of thing you might see on *Saturday Night Live*. But characters can also be so intense they frighten the audience (because they are so believable). Or they can be so grounded, the audience forgets that they are watching an actor. I make use of all these approaches when acting, because they are all part of the world of pretending to be someone else. The only question I can't answer is: "What is good acting?"

Another monologue I do is called a rant. It's a direct, emphatic, not quite logical address to the audience with some sort of theme. Here, the character I'm playing is me. But, of course, once I'm onstage, there's no such thing as "me," there's only character. I started doing stuff like this back when I did *The Ricky Paul Show*. I would go ballistic and rant about women, life in the city, injustice, etc. Later I played with the rant as Barry in the play *Talk Radio*. In the "rant" mode, I discover voices of characters who live within me, not so much as archetypes, but as purified attitude. Usually this attitude is anger.

For me, characters are not static, set creations, they are more like quantum particle clouds of behavior, attitudes, statements. One character merges into the next. Characters are contrivances, synthesized from my mind, my imagination. There is no outside objective reality with which to compare them. Ultimately, a "good" character is the one who possesses the most force. So I will borrow and steal and experiment until I cobble together a character who has the most "truth." It's like each character is a small universe and must work according to his own laws of physics. I experiment, like Frankenstein, until I get the character who sits up and lives.

As I rewrite and polish, rehearse and perform, I am honing facets of the piece: rhythm, humor, character, pace, verbal imagery, even theme. Once I know I'll be keeping a monologue in a piece, I try to take it to another level. The words must be organized in almost a rhythm, the music of the words. The way words run along on top of one another is, for me, part of the pleasure of performing. Finding the right combination takes time and rehearsal.

Live performance, trial and error, get the humor and pace right. Humor is a matter of taste. What makes me laugh isn't necessarily going to make you laugh. Laughter is perhaps the hardest element to control. And laughter works differently in a theater than in other art forms, because there are always some people who "get it" and they trigger other people. And there are those who "don't" and act as a brake. Again, consensus rules.

I keep polishing with Jo in rehearsal. This is a matter of continuing to look at the basic character I'm playing and asking fundamental questions that the initial improvs may have missed. For instance, "What was this character doing ten minutes ago?" "What is the character wearing, carrying?" "How old is this character, how does that affect his voice, posture?" "Are we outdoors? Is it warm? Cold?" And so on. These are almost standard acting class questions, but they work to jog my imagination, helping me find a new way to approach the material. Finally, there is just a question of right-ness: what feels right and what feels wrong. This happens in rehearsal with the traditional use of blocking and gesture.

So that's it. I don't think anyone can learn how to make another person's "art," but, hopefully, if you're someone who writes or performs or makes theater in any way, maybe all this is helpful by simply revealing how I get from A to B to C.

Ultimately, there's no way to really tell you how I actually find any particular arrangement of words, postures, themes, voices. It feels right or it doesn't. But I do look for the "right" arrangement, the configuration that best says what I have to say. And I do discard pieces if they don't feel right. Making art is about singing the song one's meant to sing. Or another way of looking at it is this: I put onstage what I would most like to see if I were sitting in the audience.

—Eric Bogosian
New York City

A version of this essay was published in *Wake Up and Smell the Coffee*, 2002.

A HISTORY

Productions, Recordings and Publications

This list reflects material from this volume only. Unless otherwise noted, all productions were directed by Jo Bonney.

PRODUCTIONS

Solos/Plays

Men Inside
Franklin Furnace, New York City, 1981; The New York Shakespeare Festival/Public Theater, New York City, 1982

Voices of America
Corps de Garde, Groningen, Holland, 1982

Men in Dark Times
The Kitchen, New York City, 1982

Advocate
Artists Space, New York City, 1982

funHouse
The New York Shakespeare Festival, Actor's Playhouse, New York City, 1983; Matrix Theater, Los Angeles, 1985

Drinking in America
Institute for Contemporary Art, Boston; Performance Space 122, New York City; The Institute for Contemporary Art, London; The American Place Theater, New York City, 1985–1986 (Wynn Handman, director)

Talk Radio
The New York Shakespeare Festival, New York City, 1987 (Frederick Zollo, director); Longacre Theatre, New York City, 2007 (Robert Falls, director)

Sex, Drugs, Rock & Roll
Orpheum Theater, New York City, 1991

Notes from Underground
Museum of Modern Art, New York City, 1993; Performance Space 122, New York City, 1994; Performance Space 122, New York City, 2003 (with Jonathan Ames; Eric Bogosian, director)

Pounding Nails in the Floor with My Forehead
Mark Taper Forum, Los Angeles, 1993; Minetta Lane Theater, New York City, 1994

31 Ejaculations
Not performed live; posted online via slate.com, 1996

Wake Up and Smell the Coffee
Jane Street Theater, New York City, 2001

This Is Now!
Merkin Concert Hall, New York City, 2006 (with Elliott Sharp; no director)

Orphans

These monologues were performed sporadically as part of shows before they officially opened in New York City.

RECORDINGS

Video

Though Jo Bonney directed all but one of the solos, there have been various films and videos of the performances. The film versions always followed the stage productions, directed by Jo Bonney. I am indebted to the directors for transforming the ephemeral into artifact.

funHouse
Filmed live at the Matrix Theater, Los Angeles, 1986 (Lewis MacAdams, director)

Drinking in America
Alive from Off-Center, PBS, 1986 (Howard Silver, director)

American Vanity
1989 (Robert Longo, director; bootleg only)

Sex, Drugs, Rock & Roll
Filmed live at the Wilber Theater, Boston, 1991 (John McNaughton, director; Avenue Pictures)

Confessions of a Porn Star
1996 (Rob Klug, director; bootleg only)

Wake Up and Smell the Coffee
Filmed live at the Jane Street Theater, New York City, 2001 (Michael Rauch, director; Docurama)

Audio

Live in London
Recorded live at the ICA London by the BBC, 1980 (Neutral Records)

Blood on the Canvas
Recorded and mixed with Frank Zappa, Hollywood, 1986 (Bootleg only)

Sex, Drugs, Rock & Roll
Recorded in 1991 (SBK Records)

Pounding Nails in the Floor with My Forehead
Recorded live at the Knitting Factory, New York City, 1994 (Blackbird Records)

PUBLICATIONS

"Men Inside," "Voices of America," "funHouse" and "Drinking in America" were originally published in *Drinking in America*, Vintage, New York, 1987; later published in *The Essential Bogosian*, TCG, New York, 1994.

"Talk Radio" was originally published as *Talk Radio*, Vintage, New York, 1988; later published in *The Essential Bogosian*, TCG, New York, 1994; and *Talk Radio*, TCG, New York, 2007.

"Sex, Drugs, Rock & Roll" was originally published as *Sex, Drugs, Rock & Roll*, HarperCollins, New York, 1991; later published by TCG, New York, 1996.

"Notes from Underground" was originally published as *Notes from Underground*, Hyperion Books, New York, 1993; later published as *Notes from Underground/Scenes from the New World*, TCG, New York, 1997.

"Pounding Nails in the Floor with My Forehead" was originally published as *Pounding Nails in the Floor with My Forehead*, TCG, New York, 2004.

"31 Ejaculations" was previously published in *Wake Up and Smell the Coffee*, TCG, New York, 2002.

"Wake Up and Smell the Coffee" was originally published as *Wake Up and Smell the Coffee*, TCG, New York, 2002.

A selection of "Orphans," was previously published in *The Essential Bogosian*, TCG, New York, 1994.

Visit the monologues at 100monologues.com

One of America's premier performers and most innovative and provocative artists, **ERIC BOGOSIAN**'s plays and solo work include *subUrbia* (Lincoln Center Theater, 1994; adapted to film by director Richard Linklater, 1996); *Sex, Drugs, Rock & Roll*; *Pounding Nails in the Floor with My Forehead*; *Griller*; *Humpty Dumpty*; *1+1* and *Skunkweed* (published as *Sex Plays*, TCG, 2013); *Wake Up and Smell the Coffee*; *Drinking in America* and *Notes from Underground*. He has received three Obie Awards and a Drama Desk Award.

His celebrated work, *Talk Radio*, which he wrote and in which he starred, premiered at The New York Shakespeare Festival in 1987, was adapted to film by director Oliver Stone in 1988, and premiered on Broadway in 2007, in a production starring Liev Schreiber. *Talk Radio* was a Pulitzer Prize finalist, and in 1988 Bogosian was awarded the Berlin Film Festival's Silver Bear for his work on the film.

Bogosian has starred in a wide variety of film, TV and stage roles. Most recently, he created the character Captain Danny Ross on the long-running series *Law & Order: Criminal Intent*, and starred on Broadway with Laura Linney in Donald Margulies's *Time Stands Still*.

He is the author of three novels: *Mall*, *Wasted Beauty* and *Perforated Heart*. The film adaptation of *Mall* is in post-production. In 2015 Little, Brown will publish *Nemesis*, Bogosian's nonfiction account of "Operation Nemesis," the assassination team that avenged the Armenian genocide in 1921.

He is married to director Jo Bonney and lives in New York City.